Napoleon on Elba

Portrait of Neil Campbell, 1818, by C. Carbonnier (courtesy of Neal Auction Company).

Sir Neil Campbell

Napoleon on Elba

Diary of an Eyewitness to Exile

Edited by Jonathan North

RAVENHALL BOOKS

Napoleon on Elba: Diary of an Eyewitness to Exile

First published 2004 by Ravenhall Books, an imprint of Linden Publishing Limited

British Library Cataloguing in Publication Data

Campbell, Neil
Napoleon on Elba: diary of an eyewitness to exile
1. Napoleon, I, Emperor of the French, 1769-1821 – Elba and the Hundred Days, 1814-1815 2.
Napoleon, I, Emperor of the French, 1769-1821 – Contemporaries 3. Campbell, Neil
4. Great Britain. Army – Officers – Diaries
I. Title
944'.05'092

ISBN 1 905043 00 7

Ravenhall Books
Linden Publishing Limited
PO Box 357
Welwyn Garden City
AL6 6WJ
United Kingdom

www.ravenhallbooks.com

While every effort has been made to trace the copyright holders, in some cases this has not been successful and should anyone get in touch about permissions we will be happy to amend further editions.

Publishing History
Neil Campbell's diary was first published in 1869 as *Napoleon at Fontainebleau and Elba, Being a Journal of Occurrences in 1814–1815 with Notes of Conversations* (John Murray, London) after being transcribed from Campbell's manuscript by Archibald Neil Campbell MacLachlan. This edition presents the diary complete and unabridged and those portions which were in French have now been translated. The text has been reset, some of the more archaic language modernised and new supplementary footnotes added to assist the reader.

Printed and bound in Great Britain
by Creative Print and Design (Wales), Ebbw Vale.

CONTENTS

Conversation, of September 16, of Three Hours with Napoleon – Arrival of Polish Lady and Child at Elba – Habits of Napoleon – Goes to Florence, and is Presented to the Grand Duke

INTRODUCTION

Neil Campbell of Duntroon was born on May 1, 1776, the second of three sons of Neil Campbell of Duntroon Castle and Jean Campbell of Blandfield. His was a military family and his entire life was to be dominated by the seemingly incessant war with France – whether the Republic born from the bloody Revolution or the Empire created by Napoleon – which was waged across the globe. Those wars, coupled with the family's martial traditions, meant that all three of the Campbells' sons were destined for a military career. His elder brother, James Campbell, was shot and killed fighting the forces of the French Revolution in Holland on October 2, 1799 but, by then, Neil had already entered the British Army.

Unfortunately for the young soldier his first mission was to take part in an expedition to the West Indies, then something of a graveyard for Europeans. In 1798 he was in Jamaica, serving as an ensign in the 67th Foot, a regiment which included a good number of former Irish rebels. By 1800 Campbell had purchased a lieutenancy in the 57th Regiment and, shortly afterwards, purchased the rank of captain in the 95th Rifles.

As the Peace of Amiens brought some respite to an exhausted Europe Campbell spent his time in training, coming under the wing of the capable Sir John Moore and being promoted to the rank of Major in the 43rd, then based at Shorncliff.

But the shadow of war was soon cast over these happy times and Major Campbell was transferred to the 54th Regiment and assigned to an expedition destined for Jamaica. He was soon in action. In February 1809 he participated in the attack on Martinique, which saw the French colony fall to the British. Almost a year later he participated in the capture of Guadeloupe which marked the end of Napoleon's colonial territories.

The surrender of Guadeloupe meant that the expeditionary force could return home for Britain needed soldiers. In 1808 Napoleon had sought to impose his rule on Portugal and, at the same time, expel the Bourbon's from Spain and replace them with a member of his own family (the unfortunate Joseph Bonaparte). Napoleon's plans went awry and the French were soon caught up in a brutal popular revolt. Britain seized the opportunity to despatch assistance to her new-found Iberian allies. An expeditionary force was sent to Portugal and, shortly afterwards, Sir John Moore marched into Spain. Chased out and killed at Corunna British hopes were invested in the talented Arthur Wellesley who assumed command of British forces in the Peninsula in April 1809.

For the energetic Campbell, the Peninsular War was the theatre to which he most ardently desire to be assigned. He returned to Britain in 1810 and was given a Portuguese Regiment (the 16th) to command in April 1811.

Portugal, and the struggle against the invading French, fully absorbed Campbell. He was present at Almeida and Fuentes d'Onoro in 1811 but spent much of the rest of the year sick with fevers. Even so, at the close of 1811, he was hoping to see more action in the coming year writing that 'the next campaign will give us opportunities to show off the Boys, not a Spanish undisciplined collection of peasantry, but three veteran regiments …'. His Boys were soon in the thick of the fighting, participating in the awful siege of Ciudad Rodrigo and assisting at that of Badajoz, before bursting into Spain in June 1812 (just as Napoleon was invading Russia). Campbell was present at the battle of Salamanca, which effectively opened the gates of Madrid to the British, and his gallant regiment pressed on towards Burgos and another siege. It was a difficult autumn. The French garrison showed themselves determined and energetic and digging trenches as the weather turned decidedly worse sapped the strength and morale of the besiegers. Campbell found the 'service very severe' but Lord Wellington (Arthur Wellesley, who had been rewarded with a number of titles) mentioned him in despatches, praising his brave conduct on September 21, 1812.

However, the very real fatigue of the campaign had taken its toll and Campbell had to return to England in January 1813 to recuperate. He had little respite. In February 1813 he was appointed Colonel on the staff of General Cathcart. Cathcart was ambassador to the Russian court at St Petersburg and was currently serving as an Allied liaison officer with the Russian armies. These had just chased Napoleon out of Russia and the new post afforded Campbell numerous opportunities for further adventures. Campbell was to serve with the eccentric Colonel Robert Wilson and the strange Colonel Hudson Lowe. In something of a coincidence, Hudson

Lowe was selected as Governor on St Helena when Napoleon was sent to that island for his second dose of exile in 1815.

Campbell sailed from Harwich on March 13, 1813 and spent some time at the Swedish court before sailing for Colberg in Prussia in April 1813. These were momentous times. Prussia had only recently joined forces with Russia in an attempt to eject Napoleon from Germany. The two Continental allies, backed by British gold, quickly cemented a sturdy alliance and began operations directed at driving Napoleon's exhausted or inexperienced troops westwards. Campbell soon joined up with Cathcart and rode with Imperial headquarters. He was introduced to the dashing Czar Alexander and his awkward brother – the Grand Duke Constantine – as well as to the King of Prussia. He was also present at some of the ferocious battles, grand affairs compared to the battles in the Peninsula.

Campbell was a sharp observer, thrilled by his position on a splendid staff and quite hypnotised by the power and fury of the 1813 campaign. He extolled his allies in letters home:

> The Russians have the finest materials of men I have ever seen, but ignorant officers, a great want of arrangement, and much of the Eastern loose mode in regard to baggage and followers. The Prussians are perfect in every way.

In June 1813 there was a brief armistice whilst the allies worked hard to bring Austria, so many times defeated by Napoleon, into the coalition. They succeeded and war began again in August. Campbell was present at the siege of Danzig and so impressed his Russian friends that he was awarded the Order of St George (4th class) and became a Knight of the Imperial Order of St Anne. But Campbell was restless for movement and was only released from the monotony in the trenches when the city capitulated in November. The Scottish colonel dashed off to join the main Allied army as it lumbered towards the frontiers of France having soundly defeated Napoleon at Leipzig.

On the first day of 1814 Campbell crossed the Rhine and he served with the 'brave and intelligent' Count Pahlen. But the French fought well on their own soil and their stubbornness almost cost Campbell his life on March 25, 1814. At Vitry he took part in a Russian attack on a French square but disaster struck:

> I called out to the French to cease firing or they would all be massacred. Some squadrons of Russian cavalry arriving to support those with whom I had

executed the first charge, and seeing me in the melée, as if giving orders to the French, considered me to be one of their opponents. One of the hussars of the front rank, who are armed with lances, struck his weapon through my back; and when I was upon the ground, another cut me with his sabre across the head, although I cried out lustily "Angliski Polkovnik" (English colonel). A Russian officer succeeded, by the use of better language, in preventing the infliction of a third wound.

The Czar had Campbell treated with his own surgeons, Crichton and Wylie, Scotsmen like their unlucky patient, but Campbell was out of action for some time. To compound this sorry state of affairs Campbell's baggage, with all his clothes, correspondence and papers, went missing at the same time. Campbell, as his diary relates, reached Paris on April 9 and here he received word of perhaps his most challenging assignment to date.

He had been selected as a distinguished officer to accompany the defeated Emperor Napoleon as he was sent into exile on the small Mediterranean island of Elba. Dr Crichton was concerned that his patient wasn't ready for such an arduous and exacting role but, for Campbell, it was too good an opportunity to miss.

The diary, which runs from April 1814 to February 1815 – when Napoleon escaped and headed off along the long road to Waterloo –, records, word for word, Campbell's sojourn with the former master of Europe. It has an immediacy which a memoir or a series of recollections would lack. Here we have fascination turning to loathing, excitement turning to escapism, trust turning to intrigue. It is a superb insight into life with Napoleon's miniature court on Elba but it is an even better insight into the mind and personality of the imperial adventurer caged on the Mediterranean rock.

Initially Campbell's presence was welcomed by Napoleon as the Emperor of Elba became accustomed to his new home and needed the backing of the Allied powers to impose some semblance of respect from feuding Mediterranean rivals. Campbell was treated as a comrade in arms, amicably given Napoleon's time and attention. But, sooner or later, Campbell, an amateur playing at a convoluted game of intrigue and secrecy, was, inevitably, in the way.

The relationship between Napoleon and the Scottish Colonel deteriorated, Campbell scribbling down his frustration and lambasting the gang of adventurers who served, or came to visit, Napoleon.

And then there is the gradual build up of tension as Napoleon's plans to capitalise on the unpopularity of the Bourbons, newly restored to the French throne, begin to take shape. Campbell is kept at a distance but this augments his concern. When the drama unfolds Campbell's suspicions are no substitute for readiness and the audacious moves of Napoleon catch Campbell, and the rest of Europe, with their guard very much down.

After Elba, life was more troublesome for Campbell. Viscount Castelreagh defended Campbell and absolved him from blame – as well he might as he had appointed Campbell and issued him his orders. In a debate at the House of Commons on April 7, 1815, he spoke eloquently on Campbell and his rather vague duties:

> Our Government never undertook a police establishment at Elba. Colonel Campbell was certainly there, for the purpose of occasionally communicating with our Government upon such matters as might pass under his observation ... it would have been out of Colonel Campbell's power to have attempted anything further.

Other matters intervened to sideline these grave debates. Napoleon, having carried out 'his unfortunate evasion' from Elba, and restored himself to the throne of France, was marching on Belgium in an attempt to win back some of his empire and divert a divided French nation with a dose of glory. Neil Campbell left London to join his regiment – the 54th – on the Continent. He dined with Wellington on June 15 but the meal was interrupted by news that the French had crossed the border and attacked Charleroi. For want of finding a suitable horse Campbell missed Wellington's first battle at Quatre Bras but was ready in time to rejoin the staff for Waterloo on June 18. He witnessed the battle and was amongst the first of the British to cross the French border on June 20, taking part in the storming of Cambrai (for which he received the Waterloo medal). Before long the British officer was in Paris and Napoleon was on his way to his second exile on isolated St Helena.

Campbell's war was over and, suffering from his 1814 wound, which had punctured a lung, he was invalided out of the Army in early 1816. He lived the life of a retired soldier, visiting Europe, tending to his estate's affairs. But, by 1825 he was restless again. He hoped to be sent to India or to the East Indies but, by a quirk of fate, the governership of Sierra Leone in Africa fell vacant. Perhaps ominously, the previous governor, General

Turner, had died of fever. Campbell worked hard at his new post, perhaps too hard. He had fallen seriously ill on August 5, 1827, wracked by fevers, and he died on the morning of August 14.

Campbell had succumbed to the 'baneful climate' of Africa. A melancholy end to a life of adventure, zeal and intrepid conduct. Perhaps the equal, in restlessness at least, to the life of the man the Scotsman had watched so intently as he, a former ruler of Europe, strutted across his island prison.

Jonathan North, 2004

CHAPTER I

Arrival in Paris – Appointed British Commissioner – Instructions from Lord Castlereagh – Goes to Fontainebleau – First Interview with Napoleon – Treaty of Fontainebleau – Various Anecdotes

Having received two wounds upon the afternoon of March 25, 1814, at Fêre Champenoise, near Vitry, I was prevented from accompanying the Allied Armies on their march to Paris, and did not arrive in the French capital until April 9. Even then, being still unable to undertake any duty, or to mix in society, I had no knowledge of the important arrangements in progress regarding the future destiny of Napoleon, except through the channel of the daily newspapers.

I was therefore quite unprepared for a message from Lord Castlereagh,[1] which I received on the 14th, making me the offer to accompany, in a day or two, the *ci-devant* Emperor from Fontainebleau to the island of Elba, an offer which I willingly accepted. For, although still very unfit for travelling and that it was entirely optional with myself either to accept or to decline this duty, it yet presented so many points of interest, that I resolved at all risks to undertake it.

Upon the 15th, I received a second message to wait on Lord Castlereagh the following morning at nine o'clock, provided with my own means of conveyance, as it was intended that my instructions should then be communicated to me, and that I should proceed directly from his Lordship's house to Fontainebleau, in company with his secretary, Mr. Planta.

These arrangements were put into execution. Lord Castlereagh delivered to me a paper of written instructions, and informed me that an Austrian,

---

1 Robert Stewart, 1769-1822, was an almost exact contemporary of Napoleon. Statesman and diplomat he was appointed foreign secretary by Lord Liverpool and later represented Britain at the Congress of Vienna which sat to decide the fate of post-Napoleonic Europe. Castelreagh slit his throat with a penknife and died on August 12, 1822.

Russian, and Prussian officer,[2] already at Fontainebleau, would proceed with me to fulfil the duty explained in that paper; that the period of my stay at Elba would depend on Bonaparte's wishes and my own management; that the mission would afford me many interesting and useful opportunities for the observation of his character and proceedings, feelings and position in his new residence.

His lordship's formal letter ran as follows:

Paris, April 16, 1814.
Sir,
I have to acquaint you that you have been selected, on the part of the British Government, to attend the late Chief of the French Government to the island of Elba.

You will be accompanied by an Austrian, a Prussian, and Russian officer of rank; you will act in entire concert with them in the execution of this mission, and conduct yourself, as far as circumstances will permit, with every proper respect and attention to Napoleon, to whose secure asylum in that island it is the wish of his Royal Highness the Prince Regent to afford every facility and protection.

Should you experience any interruption, either during your progress, or after your arrival, from any of His Majesty's officers by sea or land, you will explain to them the nature of the service with which you are entrusted, and that you are authorised by me to signify to them the Prince Regent's commands, that they do respect and conform to such orders as you may have occasion to issue in furtherance of this service.

You will acquaint Napoleon, in suitable terms of attention, that you are directed to reside in the island till further orders, if he should consider that the presence of a British officer can be of use in protecting the island and his person against insult or attack.

You will correspond with me in the execution of this service, and you will address yourself for assistance, so far as circumstances may require it, to any of His Majesty's servants, civil or military, in the Mediterranean.

You will exercise your own discretion as to the mode of communicating with His Majesty's Government.

I have the honour to be, Sir, your most obedient humble servant,

(Signed) CASTLEREAGH

Mr. Planta and myself arrived at Fontainebleau after dark on the evening of the 16th, crossing some picquets of the French Guards in bivouac, and

---

2   The Prussian Commissioner, according to his own account, arrived on the evening of April 16 and moved into the palace on the 17th.

Count Pavel Schuvalov

(courtesy of Alexander Mikaberidze).

Lord Castlereagh.

drove up to the iron railings in front of the palace. An officer, who was called by the sentinel, immediately came out from the guard, and led us into the palace. After a short interview with General Count Bertrand,[3] the *Grand Maréchal de la Cour*, he offered us apartments in the palace, stating that General Koller[4] and Count Waldburg-Truchsess, the Austrian and Prussian Commissioners, had already accepted a similar offer; but that the Russian Commissioner, General Schuvalov,[5] had preferred to take up his residence in the town.

Upon our expressing acceptance of this proposal, an under-chamberlain and servants with lights attended us to the suite of rooms prepared, and in about an hour afterwards presented us with a very good supper, informing us, at the same time, that the Commissioners would be expected to breakfast next morning, in company with Count Bertrand and a few of the principal officers of the Emperor's staff and household. We were further told that the usual hours at the palace were 10 a.m. for *déjeuner à la fourchette*, and 6 p.m. for dinner.

---

3 General Henri Bertrand, 1773-1844, was an engineer officer and was made Grand Marshal of the Palace in 1813. He later accompanied Napoleon to St Helena. He was married to an Englishwoman, Fanny Bertrand.

4 General Franz Koller, 1767-1826, was on Field Marshal Schwartzenburg's staff.

5 Count Pavel Schuvalov was the Czar's aide-de-camp.

General Henri Bertrand

Count Antoine Drouot.

(courtesy of Anne Brown Military Collection).

In the short conversation held by Mr. Planta and myself, on our first arrival, with Count Bertrand (who was very civil, but wore at the same time an appearance of great dejection), he expressed himself in most melancholy terms respecting the island of Elba; that it was very small, very barren, part of it extremely unwholesome from the exhalations of the salt-ponds, and that there was very little wood or good water to be had; that 'the Emperor' (which title appeared to be repeated with studied formality) was very anxious to quit Fontainebleau upon his journey, and to travel as much incognito as possible, but wished to change the place of embarkation from St. Tropez to Piombino, as being the nearest point of Tuscany to Elba. The reasons alleged for the anxiety to substitute Piombino for St. Tropez appeared very puerile when connected with changes of such vast importance as those of Napoleon's transfer from the Empire of France to the petty sovereignty of Elba! These reasons were that the French officer who commanded in Elba might refuse to receive us, and that while waiting off the island, until that difficulty should be removed, the vessel might be driven off by a tempest, etc. He further expressed a hope that I would go to the island of Elba, and even remain there until affairs were settled, for fear of a landing by pirates. He appeared greatly soothed when I told him that the instructions of Lord Castlereagh prescribed to me to prolong my stay, if considered necessary by Napoleon for his security.

On the following morning (April 17), the other Commissioners and myself assembled at breakfast, in company with generals Bertrand, Drouot,[6] Lefèbvre-Desnouettes,[7] and Flahault,[8] three or four other generals of the Guards, and some junior aides-de-camp. As soon as the meal was finished, Count Flahault informed us individually, that the Emperor was then in the chapel, attending Mass, and that immediately afterwards he wished to have separate interviews with each of us. General Koller passed out of the gallery, and saw him at his devotions. He described him as appearing in the most perturbed and distressed state of mind – sometimes rubbing his forehead with his hands, then stuffing part of his fingers into his mouth, and gnawing the ends of them in the most agitated and excited manner.

We were presently conducted to an antechamber, and called into Napoleon's room by an aide-de-camp, successively, in the following order:

First, the Russian Commissioner, who remained for about five minutes, and had some ordinary question, put to him respecting the Emperor Alexander.[9]

Next the Austrian Commissioner, whose interview was of the same nature and duration.

Thirdly, myself, who had the honour of remaining for a quarter of an hour.

Fourthly, the Prussian Commissioner, whom Napoleon only detained for about one minute, putting to him some very indifferent question, and then dismissing him with a cold bow.[10]

It was a strange feeling that came over me, when the aide-de-camp, after announcing my name, retired shutting the door, and I found myself suddenly closeted with that extraordinary man, whose name had been for so many years the touchstone of my professional and national feelings,

---

6   Count Antoine Drouot, 1774-1831, was an artilleryman born in Nancy. He was prmoted to general, and acted as Napoleon's aide-de-camp, in 1813.
7   General Charles Lefèbvre-Desnouettes, 1774-1822, a dashing cavalryman captured by the British in 1808. He lived in Cheltenham before escaping back to France in May 1812. The General did not accompany Napoleon to Elba but left for Nevers. He was wounded in 1815 and later emigrated to America upon the second return of the Bourbons. In 1822 he drowned when the ship bringing him back to Europe was wrecked.
8   Count Charles de Flahault, 1785-1870, was a General of Division and one of Napoleon's aides-de-camp.
9   Czar Alexander I of Russia.
10 Count Friedrich Waldburg-Truchsess, 1776-1844, noted that he was received coldly. He was asked how many Prussian troops there were on the road to Elba. Upon replying that there were none he was told that there was no need for him to bother coming along. Napoleon then complained to the Austrian Commissioner that there would be a Prussian present; the Austrian replied that each Allied country was represented. Napoleon snubbed this reply sarcastically by saying 'why didn't you send me one from Darmstadt or Baden then?'.

and whose appearance had been presented to my imagination in every form that exaggeration and caricature could render impressive. I saw before me a short active looking man, who was rapidly pacing the length of his apartment, like some wild animal in his cell. He was dressed in an old green uniform with gold epaulets, blue pantaloons, and red topboots, unshaven, uncombed, with the fallen particles of snuff scattered profusely upon his upper lip and breast.

Upon his becoming aware of my presence, he turned quickly towards me, and saluted me with a courteous smile, evidently endeavouring to conceal his anxiety and agitation by an assumed placidity of manner. He first asked me several questions about my wounds – which were plainly observable from the bandages upon my head, and my arm being carried in a sling – the circumstances under which they were received, the period and occasions of my service in the army, the particulars of my Russian orders and British military decorations, upon what claims and to what rank they had been accorded, what part of Great Britain I was from. On my replying from Scotland, he inquired whether I, like himself, was an admirer of Ossian's poems, adding here, 'I like them much, for there is something very martial about them.' 'Yes, Sire,' I answered, 'it has been said in England that your Majesty admired them greatly.'

While speaking of my professional occupations, he was led to remark upon the war in the Peninsula, and to contrast the characters of the Spanish and Portuguese people, saying of the former, 'They are a people of strong character. You have acted your part well there.'

He referred to the defences of Ciudad Rodrigo, Badajoz, and St. Sebastian, to the campaign in Egypt also, inquiring whether I was personally acquainted with Lord Hutchinson.[11] He spoke of the attack upon Bergen-op-zoom as an affair which did honour to the general (Sir Thomas Graham) who directed it, as well as to the British troops; but that we were quite misled as to the strength of the French garrison, and that they were prepared for the assault, having been made aware of our intentions.[12]

He asked whether the great road which he had begun from Bordeaux to Bayonne was finished, and then went on to inquire anxiously as to the

11 General Hutchinson succeeded to the command of the British army in Egypt, upon the death of Sir Ralph Abercromby at the battle of Alexandria, March 21, 1801, and was raised to the peerage as Baron Hutchinson. In August 1825 he became second Earl of Donoughmore.
12 The British had broken into this French-occupied fortress in March 1814 but the attackers were chased out by a counter-attack and lost heavily.

reports of an affair[13] which had occurred since the occupation of Paris between the armies of Lord Wellington and Marshal Soult.[14] He passed high encomiums upon the former, inquired as to his age, habits, etc. When I described his Lordship's great activity, he observed, 'He is a man of energy in war. To carry on war successfully, one must possess the like quality.'

His conversation turned almost entirely upon military subjects, and events connected with the British army, on which he seemed to reflect with the deepest interest; but he did not once touch upon the operations of the other allied armies.

He paid many compliments to the British nation for their union and national feelings, in which, he considered, they so much excelled the French. 'Yours is the greatest of all nations', he said, 'I esteem it more than any other. I have been your greatest enemy – frankly such; but I am so no longer. I have wished likewise to raise the French nation, but my plans have not succeeded. It is all destiny.'

Here he stopped short, seeming greatly affected, and tears were in his eyes.

After a pause, he asked whether Lord Castlereagh intended to remain long in Paris, as he supposed it would be necessary for him to return soon to England to meet the Parliament, and then proceeded to inquire as to the powers vested in me by his Lordship's instructions. He expressed satisfaction at hearing that I was to accompany him to Elba, if he so desired, and to remain in the island so long as my services might be required. He was anxious, he said, that a British man-of-war might escort, as a protection against Algerian pirates,[15] the corvette ordered by the French Government for his use; and inquired particularly what powers I would exert towards procuring such an escort, or in obtaining a passage for him, should he prefer embarking in a British man-of-war, or in case the French vessel might not be ready at the place appointed.

'Have you not the power of obtaining for me an English man-of-war, to accompany the corvette? For I do not know when the latter will arrive, and perhaps I may even prefer to embark in an English vessel.'

---

13 The battle of Toulouse, fought April 10, 1814.
14 Marshal Jean de Dieu Soult, 1769-1851, commanded the French armies in the South. These had been driven out of Spain by the Duke of Wellington.
15 At that time Barbary pirates, or corsairs, were a serious problem in the Mediterranean. Most sailed from Algiers and were commonly known as Algerines.

I stated the outline of my official instructions with regard to affording him facilities and protection *after* his arrival in the island of Elba; but as these did not provide precisely for the contingencies in question, he himself, and afterwards the Duke of Vicenza,[16] requested me to solicit from Lord Castlereagh exact directions, conveyed in such terms as would secure their being complied with by any British admiral or captains of His Majesty's navy, should it be found necessary to apply for their assistance.

He concluded by saying, 'Very well, I am at your disposal. I am your subject. I depend entirely upon you.'

And then, having been with him fully a quarter of an hour, he made me a bow of *congé*, free from any assumption of hauteur; and my first interview with Napoleon was ended!

I wrote in the afternoon of the same day to Lord Castlereagh for further instructions, and received in due course the following reply:

Paris: April 18, 1814.

Sir,

I have the honour to acknowledge the receipt of your letter. My instructions furnish you with authority to call upon His Majesty's officers, by sea and land, to give all due facility and assistance to the execution of the service with which you are entrusted.

I cannot foresee that any enemy can molest the French corvette, on board of which it is proposed that Napoleon should proceed to his destination.

If, however, he should continue to desire it, you are authorised to call upon any of His Majesty's cruisers, (so far as the public service may not be thereby prejudiced) to see him safe to the island of Elba. You will not, however, suffer this arrangement to be made a cause of delay.

There can be no objection (if the accommodation on board of the English ship-of-war is preferable) to Napoleon being received and conducted to his destination.

I have the honour to be, Sir, your obedient humble servant,

(Signed) CASTLEREAGH

Immediately on receipt of the above, I made known its contents verbally to General Count Bertrand.

---

16 General Caulaincourt.

Soon afterwards, we, the Allied Commissioners, assembled together, and agreed to communicate frankly to each other any circumstance worth knowing, of which we might individually become apprised. It was then that I was first made aware of the exact particulars of the treaty between Napoleon and the Allied Powers, signed at Paris upon April 11, of which each of the other Commissioners possessed a copy.

The reason of my ignorance appeared to be, that the treaty had not as yet been signed by Lord Castlereagh on the part of England, on account of certain objections;[17] and I therefore, as British Commissioner, had received no official intimation of its existence.

This treaty, composed of twenty-one Articles, had been signed by Prince Metternich[18] and Count Stadion on the part of Austria; Count Rasomovsky and Count Nesselrode on the part of Russia; Baron Hardenberg on the part of Prussia; and Marshal Ney and General Caulaincourt, Duke of Vicenza, on the part of Napoleon.

---

17 Viscount Castlereagh to Earl Bathurst:
'On the night of my arrival (April 10, 1814), the four Ministers had a conference with the Prince of Benevento on the subject of the proposed convention, to which I stated my objections, desiring at the same time, to be understood as not urging them then, at the hazard of the internal tranquillity of France, nor the impeachment of what was due, in good faith to the assurance given, under the exigency of the moment, by Russia.
  The Prince of Benevento admitted the weight of many of the objections, but declared that he did consider it on the part of the Provisional Government as an object of the first importance to avoid anything that might assume the character of a civil war, even for the shortest time. That he also found some such measure essential to make the army pass over in a temper to be made use of. Upon these declarations, and the Count de Nesselrode's, that the Emperor his master had felt it necessary, in the absence of the Allies, to act for the best in their name as well as his own, I withdrew my further opposition to the principle of the measure, suggesting only some alterations in the details. I desired, however, to decline, on the part of my Government, being more than acceding party to the treaty, and declared that the act of accession on the part of Great Britain should not go beyond the territorial arrangements proposed in the treaty. My objections to our being unnecessarily mixed up in its forms, especially in the recognition of Napoleon's title under present circumstances, were considered as perfectly reasonable, and I now enclose the Protocol and Note, which will explain the extent to which I have taken upon me to give assurance on the part of my court.
  At my suggestion, the recognition of the Imperial titles in the family were limited to their respective lives, for which there was a precedent in the case of the King of Poland, when he became Elector of Saxony.
(Enclosure – Protocol)
'Lord Castlereagh, Minister of His Britannic Majesty, declared that England could not become a party to the treaty, but engaged to notify, as soon as possible, the accession of his court to so much of that treaty as concerns the free possession and the peaceable enjoyment, in full sovereignty, of the island of Elba, and of the Duchies of Parma, Placentia, and Guastalla.'
18 Prince Clemens von Metternich, 1773-1859, was Austria's greatest diplomat and the mastermind behind the Congress of Vienna.

TREATY OF FONTAINEBLEAU
Articles of the Treaty between
the Allied Powers and His Majesty the Emperor Napoleon

ART. 1. His Majesty the Emperor Napoleon renounces for himself, his successors, and descendants, as well as for all the members of his family, all right of sovereignty and dominion, as well to the French Empire, and the kingdom of Italy, as over every other country.

ART. 2. Their Majesties the Emperor Napoleon and Marie Louise[19] shall retain their titles and rank, to be enjoyed during their lives. The mother, brothers, sisters, nephews, and nieces of the Emperor shall also retain, wherever they may reside, the titles of princes of his family.

ART. 3. The island of Elba adopted by His Majesty the Emperor Napoleon as the place of his residence, shall form during his life a separate principality, which shall be possessed by him in full sovereignty and property; there shall be besides granted in full property, to the Emperor Napoleon, an annual revenue of 2,000,000 francs, in rent-charge, in the great book of France, of which 1,000,000 shall be in reversion to the Empress.

ART. 4. The duchies of Parma, Placentia, and Guastalla shall be granted in full property and sovereignty to Her Majesty the Empress Marie Louise. They shall pass to her son, and to the descendants in the right line. The prince, her son, shall from henceforth take the title of Prince of Parma, Placentia, and Guastalla.

ART. 5. All the Powers engage to employ their good offices to cause to be respected by the Barbary Powers the flag and territory of the island of Elba, for which purpose the relations with the Barbary Powers shall be assimilated to those of France.

ART. 6. There shall be reserved in the territories hereby renounced to His Majesty the Emperor Napoleon for himself and his family, domains or rent-charges in the great book of France, producing a revenue, clear of all deductions and charges, of 2,500,000 francs. These domains and rents shall belong, in full property, and to be disposed of as they shall think fit, to the princes and princesses of his family, and shall he divided among them in such a manner that the revenue of each shall be in the following proportion; viz:

---

19 Napoleon's second wife, whom he married in 1810, was the daughter of the Emperor Francis I of Austria. She had gone back to Vienna with the King of Rome, her three-year-old son, and would never see Napoleon again. Indeed she fell in love with General Neipperg and lived with him whilst Napoleon was on St Helena.

To Madame Mère[20]	300,000 Francs
To King Joseph and his Queen	500,000 Francs
To King Louis (he refused his portion)	200,000 Francs
To Queen Hortense and her child	400,000 Francs
The King Jerome and his Queen	500,000 Francs
The Princess Eliza (Bacchiochi)	300,000 Francs
The Princess Pauline (Borghese)	300,000 Francs

The princes and princesses of the house of the Emperor Napoleon shall besides retain their property, moveable and immovable, of whatever nature it may be, which they shall possess by individual and public right, and the rents of which they shall enjoy (also as individuals).

ART. 7. The annual pension of the Empress Josephine[21] shall be reduced to 1,000,000 francs in domains or in inscriptions in the great book of France; she shall continue to enjoy in full her property moveable and immovable, with power to dispose of it conformable to the French laws.

ART. 8. There shall be granted to Prince Eugène,[22] Viceroy of Italy, a suitable establishment out of France.

ART. 9. The property which the Emperor Napoleon possesses in France, either as extraordinary domains or as private domains, attached to the crown, the funds placed by the Emperor, either in the great book of France, in the Bank of France, in the *actions des Forêts*, or in any other manner, and which His Majesty abandons to the crown, shall be received as a capital, which shall not exceed two millions, to be expended in gratifications, in favour of such persons whose names shall be contained in a list to be signed by the Emperor Napoleon, and which shall be transmitted to the French Government.

ART. 10. All the crown diamonds shall remain in France.

ART. 11. His Majesty the Emperor Napoleon shall return to the Treasury, and to the other public chests, all the sums and effects that shall have been taken out by his orders, with the exception of what has been appropriated from the civil list.

ART. 12. The debts of the household of His Majesty the Emperor Napoleon, such as they were on the day of the signature of the present treaty, shall be immediately discharged out of the arrears due by the public Treasury to the civil list, according to a

20 Napoleon's mother, Letitzia Bonaparte.
21 Josephine de Beauharnais, 1763-1814, was Napoleon's first wife. He divorced her in 1809. She died whilst Napoleon was on Elba.
22 Eugène de Beauharnais was Josephine's son through her first marriage and consequently Napoleon's son in law. He became Viceroy of Italy in 1806 and performed the role creditably until 1814. He subsequently retired to Bavaria.

list which shall be signed by a commissioner for that purpose.

ART. 13. The obligations of the Mount Napoleon of Milan towards all the creditors, whether Frenchmen or foreigners, shall be exactly fulfilled, unless there shall be any change made in this respect.

ART. 14. There shall be given all the necessary passports for the free passage of His Majesty the Emperor Napoleon, or of the Empress, the princes and princesses, and all the persons of their suites who wish to accompany them, or to establish themselves out of France, as well as for the passage of all the equipages, horses, and effects belonging to them. The Allied Powers shall in consequence furnish officers and men for escorts.

ART. 15. The French Imperial Guards shall furnish a detachment of from 1,200 to 1,500 men of all arms to serve as an escort to the Emperor Napoleon to St. Tropez, the place of his embarkation.

ART. 16. There shall be furnished a corvette and the necessary transport vessels to convey to the place of his destination His Majesty the Emperor Napoleon and his household; and the corvette shall belong in full property to His Majesty the Emperor.

ART. 17. The Emperor Napoleon shall be allowed to take with him, and retain as his guard, 400 men, volunteers, as well officers as NCOs and soldiers.

ART. 18. No Frenchmen who shall have followed the Emperor Napoleon or his family shall be held to have forfeited their rights as such by not returning to France within three years; at least, they shall not be comprised in the exceptions which the French Government reserves to itself to grant after the expiration of that term.

ART. 19. The Polish troops of all arms, in the service of France, shall be at liberty to return home, and shall retain their arms and baggage, as a testimony of their honourable services. The officers and soldiers shall retain their decorations, which have been granted to them, and the pensions annexed to those decorations.

ART. 20. The High Allied Powers guarantee the execution of all the articles of the present treaty, and engage to obtain that it shall be adopted and guaranteed by France.

ART. 21. The present act shall be ratified, and the ratifications exchanged at Paris within two days, or sooner if possible.

Done at Paris, April 11, 1814.

(Signed) The Prince de METTERNICH
J. F. Comte de STADION
André Comte de RASOMOVSKY
Charles Robert Comte de NESSELRODE
Charles August Baron de HARDENBERG
Marshal NEY
CAULAINCOURT

It appeared that all the arrangements in regard to Napoleon's journey to, and future residence in, Elba had been made between General Koller and Count Bertrand at Fontainebleau, and that the former carried on a correspondence with Prince Metternich, the Austrian Minister, then at Paris, in reference to the necessary details.

During our meeting, Count Bertrand was announced. He was the bearer of a protest from Napoleon against the removal of the guns and stores from the island of Elba, as directed by the Minister of War in the following orders, copies of which had arrived from Paris:

Paris: April 18, 1814.

To the Chief Commandant of the island of Elba

I address to you an order, in conformity with which you will make over to Napoleon Bonaparte, late Emperor of the French, the island of Elba, from the moment when he disembarks in that island. This arrangement is in accordance with the wishes of the Allied Powers, and nothing must oppose its execution. The troops which are in the island, and all the stores belonging to France, must be removed, and a formal act must be drawn up declaring the transfer of the island to Napoleon.

(Signed) Commissioner of the War Department,

General Comte DUPONT[23]

In addition to the formal note of objection, General Bertrand made several verbal observations on the part of Napoleon, stating that the Emperor would not voluntarily quit Fontainebleau, unless the demand contained in the above note was complied with; that he placed reliance upon the Emperor Alexander and the other potentates for granting his request, as the honourable execution of the treaty made with him depended upon them, and not upon the Minister of War or the Provisional Government; that the Commissioners of the Allied Sovereigns were the only persons who ought to be empowered to decide upon all the points which regarded his settlement in the island.

This communication was at once transmitted to the Allied Sovereigns and their ministers at Paris by the Commissioners. General Koller, upon whom the

---

23 General Dupont had been one of Napoleon's Generals but was disgraced by the Emperor after Dupont surrendered to the Spanish at Baylen. 'If they (the French Cabinet) had been gifted with far greater practical sagacity and acquaintance with men than they possessed, they would have been shattered by the unpopularity of General Dupont as Minister of War; an appointment the most unfortunate that could have been made, for it continually reminded the army of the disaster of Baylen.' Alison, *History of Europe*, vol x. ch. lxxvii.

responsibility of the travelling arrangements chiefly rested, complained that fresh difficulties seemed to be continually suggesting themselves to Napoleon regarding his journey, and that every possible excuse was urged that could delay his departure, which it was considered so important should not be postponed beyond the 20th, the day on which he had faithfully promised to set off.

With the exception of this last obstacle, all seemed to have been surmounted. The line of route originally planned by Prince Metternich, via Auxerre, and on which the allied troops destined for the escort of Napoleon had been already stationed, had been just changed, at his request, for the road by Briare and Moulins. The requisite authority from the French Government to the post-masters of the various stations along the route, to have relays of horses in readiness, had arrived, and an inspector had been appointed to precede us with orders. But this new objection raised by Napoleon seemed to render the projected start upon the 20th again uncertain. However, General Koller assured Count Bertrand that the Emperor's request would without doubt be complied with by the authorities in Paris, and that even if the answer had not arrived by the 20th, he hoped Napoleon would not alter his intention of leaving Fontainebleau that day.

Count Bertrand promised to make this representation, and we anxiously awaited the result.

During my stay at Fontainebleau, Napoleon did not leave the palace. He was constantly occupied in seeing officers who came from the army, from Paris, and from Rambouillet, where the Empress was then staying, and in making arrangements for his departure. He sent off a number of wagons with baggage, besides the regular convoy that had previously been despatched with the escort; but the chest containing the treasure of the army, amounting to four millions of livres (£200,000), he kept with himself. He gave away books, manuscripts, swords, pistols, decorations, coins, etc., to different officers present at Fontainebleau, and directed others to be transmitted to various favourites. He was in the habit of receiving regularly the *Moniteur,* all the daily journals, and hearing everything that went on at Paris; and he felt very bitterly the sarcasms that continually appeared in the newspapers about himself. He seemed very jealous of the great influence that the Emperor Alexander had, by his unvarying courtesy, obtained over the minds of the Parisians.

After hearing of the visit of the Czar to the Empress Josephine, he observed to a person in his room:

'The Emperor Alexander has paid a visit to my former wife. Bah! He first breakfasted with Ney, and after that, visited her at Malmaison. What can he hope to gain from this? He has also given the order of St. Andrew to La Harpe, that Jacobin. He pays court to the king. He flatters both the Parisians and the Jacobins.'

He spoke also of the Emperor Alexander's visit to Marie Louise at Rambouillet, and said it was insulting these women in their sorrow to appear before them as a conqueror. 'It is Greek-like.'

Josephine has always been a great favourite with the Parisians. La Harpe, a Swiss by birth, was formerly tutor to Alexander, and a great leader amongst the Jacobins.

After the formation of the Provisional Government, a person was asked by Napoleon what he thought of his situation, and whether he considered there were any additional measures to be taken. When he replied in the negative, Napoleon inquired what he would do in a similar situation. 'Blow my own brains out,' was the reply. Napoleon reflected for a moment. 'Yes, I can do that; but those who wish me well would not be benefited, and it would give pleasure to those who wish me ill.'

In a conversation with General Koller at Fontainebleau, Napoleon remarked that he had need of more courage to live than to die; that he knew the world expected him to make away with himself; that he had put himself in the way of losing his life often enough, particularly at Arcis,[24] where he had four horses killed or wounded under him.

This, however, does not agree with another statement I heard; for the groom, who used to follow him with led horses, told me that he only had one horse wounded there.

During the negotiations for his asylum, Napoleon desired the Duke of Vicenza to announce to the Allied Sovereigns, that if proper arrangements were not made for his security, he should wish to go to England. And afterwards, with reference to this point, he said to one of his staff: 'It is a great nation. I am sure that I should be in security, and treated with generosity;' adding however, presently, in his usual quick and abrupt manner, 'But in my island I shall be as if in a street of London.'

One day, while we were at dinner, the subject of punishment by impaling, as practised in the East, was mentioned. A French officer, present

---

24 The battle of Arcis-sur-Aube, between Napoleon and the Allies, continued for two days, March 20 and 21, 1814. Sir Neil Campbell had himself been engaged in the action, serving with the corps of the Russian general, Count Pahlen.

at table, said that he would not like to inhabit such a country. General Drouot observed: My word! I am not so sure of never seeing it, and Algiers also, may be!' alluding, I suppose, to the party being possibly captured by Algerian pirates!

M. Fourreau, physician to Napoleon, (under whose medical charge I had passed for my wounds, now that I was out of reach of Drs. Wylie and Crichton) told me that Caulaincourt, Ney, and Macdonald[25] were sent from Fontainebleau to negotiate with Alexander and the Provisional Government; that during the first interviews (of which they had five in one day), Alexander told them that the Allies would not make any peace with Bonaparte himself, but they might do what they could in regard to his son, or any other member of his family. After the fifth interview, Alexander changed his language, and said that Napoleon and his army were not in a situation to oppose the Allies if he refused any such terms as they chose to insist on. He then informed them of the capitulation entered into with Marmont.[26] They were obliged to confess that they were not upon such an equality as they had supposed.

In coming out, they met Marmont. Macdonald took him by the arm, and said 'Miserable man! It is you who have prevented the Napoleon dynasty from reigning.' Marmont asked him, 'How so? That he had acted for the best for his country.' Macdonald then told him that Alexander would have granted everything they asked for the Empress and her son, had he not deserted from the army. That alone prevented them from obtaining the terms they wished. Marmont's answer was (with a sudden outburst of remorse) that he would not for one of his limbs that he had taken these steps. 'One of your limbs!' said Macdonald. 'All your blood cannot change it now.' And then he went on to reproach Marmont for his desertion – he who owed everything to Napoleon!

---

25 Viscount Castlereagh to Earl Bathurst.
    'Paris: April 13, 1814.
    Your Lordship has been already informed, by Lord Cathcart, of the Act of Abdication which was passed by Bonaparte on the 4th inst, and of the assurance given him by the Emperor of Russia and the Provisional Government of a pecuniary provision of six millions, with a safe asylum in the island of Elba. The Act in question was deposited in the hands of Monsieur de Caulaincourt and the Marshals Ney and Macdonald, to be given up upon the due execution of engagements on the part of the Allies, with respect to the proposed arrangement. These persons were also authorised to agree to an armistice, and to settle such a line of demarcation as might be satisfactory to the Allies, and in the mean time prevent an unnecessary effusion of blood.'

26 Auguste Marmont, 1774-1852, was an artilleryman and was created a Marshal in 1809 for services against the Austrians. He surrendered his corps on April 3 as the Allies pushed towards Paris. Ironically, he was later made tutor to Napoleon's son.

Macdonald related this before all the officers in the waiting-room at Fontainebleau, upon his return from Paris.

The aide-de-camp of General Koller, the Austrian Commissioner, told me that he had accompanied the Emperor of Austria and Prince Metternich from Paris to Rambouillet, when they first went there to visit Marie Louise.[27] The former never called her 'Empress' in speaking of her, but always 'Ma fille', or 'La Princesse'. The aide-de-camp had been sent to Paris from Fontainebleau as the bearer of Napoleon's proposition that he should not proceed to St. Tropez, but go by way of Italy to Piombino.

He was directed to accompany the Emperor and Metternich to Rambouillet, with the understanding that he should receive the answer after their interview with Marie Louise. Upon their arrival there, the Emperor was received by an antiquated, stiff, full-dressed lady, who came out from the Empress's apartment through two others, and saluted him with great etiquette. She was proceeding with a speech, when the Emperor brushed past her, saying in German, 'Who the devil are you? Let me see my daughter.' Marie Louise met him at the door. She kissed his hand, and screamed. He threw his arms round her neck, and then led her to the couch; on which the door was shut. In about half an hour, the Emperor inquired for the aide-de-camp, and told him to inform General Koller that Napoleon's proposition for going by land to Piombino could not be granted, and that if any change as to the arrangements should take place, a courier would be despatched that same night to Fontainebleau.

In visiting the apartments of the palace at Fontainebleau, we were shown a room where Josephine had begged Napoleon to spare the life of the Duc d'Enghien.[28] After several ineffectual entreaties, she threw herself at his feet, and, clasping his leg, declared that she would not quit her hold until he had

---

27 Viscount Castlereagh to Earl Bathurst.
  'Paris: April 13, 1814.
  To the arrangements in favour of the Empress, I felt not only no objection, but considered it due to the distinguished sacrifice of domestic feelings which the Emperor of Austria was making in the cause of Europe.
  [Enclosure – Protocol.]
  The Plenipotentiaries of His Majesty the Emperor Napoleon having demanded that Her Majesty the Empress Marie Louise should be allowed, in full property, an annual revenue of two millions for herself and heirs, to be paid out of the funds placed by the Emperor either in the great book, in the Bank of France, in the *actions des Forêts* or in any other manner, all which funds His Majesty gives up to the crown, the Plenipotentiaries of the Allied Courts declared, that as the Provisional Government of France had refused taking, of itself, a determination to this effect, their courts had engaged to employ their good offices with the new sovereign of France, to grant to Her Majesty the Empress Marie Louise such allowance.'
28 A royalist assassinated, on Napoleon's orders, in 1804.

granted her request. He tore from her, exclaiming, 'The devil! Go, madam, to your own affairs; do not meddle with mine.' We saw also the suite occupied by the Pope, consisting of several large apartments in the upper story.

The concierge who conducted us had been with Napoleon in Egypt as a storekeeper. I asked him whether it was true that the Mameluke always lay at Napoleon's door. He said, 'Yes, on a mattress, and armed with a dagger.'

Napoleon experienced much heartlessness and ingratitude during his short stay at Fontainebleau. Among other instances was that of his favourite Roustam, the Mameluke just mentioned. This man, upon whom benefits of all sorts had been showered by his indulgent master, had arranged to accompany him to Elba, with the promise of receiving 8,000 francs a year as wages, with lodging, lights, and firing. Napoleon gave him leave to go up to Paris, in order that he might make arrangements for his wife and children to accompany him, and he then received 25,000 francs, by way of arrears. He never returned, but merely sent word that he had determined to remain in Paris. The same night Napoleon's own valet de chambre[29] went off, without any notice, taking with him 5,000 francs.

Savary, the Minister of Police, had received the sum of 70,000 francs out of Napoleon's private purse, when he was last in Paris, for the purposes of bribery and espionage in the case of any extraordinary tumult. After his abdication, Napoleon sent to desire his presence, in order that he might return the money. Savary not only refused to obey the summons, but protested that, so far from having in his hands any funds, public or private, he was, on he contrary, rather in arrear.

On the 18th, the Duke of Bassano[30] called to see Napoleon about the time of his dinner, and was invited to partake.

'Well, Bassano,' said Napoleon, 'they say in Paris that it is entirely my fault that peace was not made; that I would never make it, that I wished for a war to the death. Others blame you, that you upheld me in this determination, that you were not willing to give me sound advice. Ah! How shall we settle it between us? Eh! Is it not my own fault?'

The Duke of Bassano bowed, as if to acquiesce in that which seemed to please him, that he always acted *for himself,* without any advice.

'Yes, yes, it is so, it is I myself!' Napoleon added quickly.

---

29 Constant. He afterwards published his Memoirs, wherein he unblushingly related some of his own rogueries.
30 Maret.

CHAPTER II

The eventful morning of April 20th dawned, and at an early hour all were
astir in the palace. Although everything was in readiness for the journey,
we felt quite uncertain as to whether Napoleon would really start. The
courier had not yet arrived from Paris with the answer respecting the guns
and stores at Elba. It was therefore a relief when at nine o'clock General
Bertrand announced formally to the Commissioners that the Emperor
would set off in the course of the morning.

After interviews with the Duke of Bassano and other officers, Napoleon
sent for the Commissioners.

General Koller, the Austrian, was first called forward, and remained in
close conversation for more than half an hour.

Napoleon spoke warmly of his separation from the Empress Marie
Louise and the King of Rome, who he felt sure were desirous themselves
of joining him, and also complained bitterly of the order from the French
Minister of War to the Commandant at Elba, for withdrawing the guns
and stores from the island, thus proposing to leave him without means of
security or defence. He said he did not wish for a kingdom; he had not
asked for Corsica for that reason. He wanted no power beyond that of
securing his own person against the States of Barbary, and against pirates.
If he had this assurance, 'I shall live there like a justice of the peace'. But
he would not remain, unless the island were properly protected.

He had nothing to do, he said, with the Provisional Government. His
treaty was with the Allied Sovereigns, and to them he looked for its
fulfilment. He was not even now destitute of means of continuing the war,[31]
but it was not his wish to do so with certain ruin to France, and in view of

31

the many factions among the people. His troops were as much attached to him as ever, and they would be convinced that every effort which was possible without dishonour had been made. They were not numerous, but they would support him for a considerable time.

General Koller endeavoured to persuade him that the treaty would be fulfilled with honour. 'Well,' replied Napoleon, 'but there is no answer yet; and what could be said if I refused to depart?' 'Your Majesty alone,' General Koller said, 'can decide on that point; but I hope you will follow your former intentions, and the expectations of your departure entertained at Paris. The answer will no doubt overtake us on the road, and I am persuaded it will be favourable.'

If, continued Napoleon, this treatment did not change, and if an asylum were not afforded him in the manner agreed upon, and understood by the treaty, he would seek refuge in England. 'Eh, do you think they will receive me?' 'Yes, Sire,' replied the Austrian; 'for as you have never made war in that country, reconciliation will become the more easy.'

During this conversation, a knock was heard at the door.

Napoleon: 'Who is there?'

ADC: 'The aide-de-camp in waiting.'[32]

Napoleon: 'Come in! What do you want?'

ADC: 'Sire, the Grand Marshal has desired me to announce to your Majesty that it is already eleven o'clock.'

Napoleon: 'Bah! This is something new! Since when have I become subordinate to the watch of the Grand Marshal? Maybe I shall not leave at all.'

He felt himself Emperor and military chief to the last with all those about him, and he also appeared more and more averse to depart as the time approached.

After this Napoleon still pursued the conversation.

---

31 Viscount Castlereagh to Earl Bathurst.
'Paris: April 13, 1814.
A convention had been discussed, and would have, in fact, been signed in the course of the day by the Russian Minister, had not the approach of the Allied Ministers been announced. The motives for accelerating the immediate conclusion of this act were the inconvenience, if not danger, of Napoleon's remaining at Fontainebleau, surrounded by troops who still, in a considerable degree, remained faithful to him, the apprehension of intrigues in the army and in the capital, and the importance attached by a considerable portion of the officers to some arrangements favourable to their chiefs, in satisfaction of their personal honour; before they left him.'
32 The aide-de-camp in question was Colonel de Bussy.

He spoke with regard of the Emperor of Austria, and with esteem of England, but with bitterness of the Emperor of Russia, particularly in reference to his visit to the Empress Josephine, and for taking with him the King of Prussia.

He alluded to his own projects, and the various unsuccessful negotiations for peace. General Koller, wishing to explain that the Allies had on their side made every effort to come to terms, pointed out the very favourable opportunity at Prague. Napoleon answered, 'I have been wrong, maybe, in my plans. I have done harm in war. But it is all like a dream.'

In this, as in previous interviews which Napoleon had held with General Koller, he expatiated largely on the danger in which Austria was placed by the enormous power of the Czar, and the false politics of Metternich, in assisting to lower the influence of France, which should be the natural ally of Austria, and act as a counterpoise to the increasing weight of Russia. General Koller replied, that 'present evils were more to be considered than distant apprehensions'. Napoleon appeared much struck by the frankness of the answer, and said, 'I esteem you for the frankness of your remarks. If you speak and act in respect of your sovereign with as much, you are a subject above price. I have not been so fortunate.'

He again referred to the separation from his wife and child, and the tears actually ran down his cheeks. The conduct pursued in regard to them, he insisted, was cruel and faithless. The British Minister disapproved of it, etc.

He continued to talk in this wild and excited style, being at times greatly affected.

After General Koller had withdrawn, Napoleon called me forward, and was as courteous as on my previous interview with him, alluding likewise to much the same subjects as before – my wounds, the military operations in which I had been engaged, etc.

He praised the discipline and administration of the British army, as being superior to those of the French; remarked on our system of fighting in two ranks; said that corporal punishment was necessary, but should be applied as seldom as possible.

Then he went on, 'I have been a very great enemy to your nation. I have been frankly such, but I am so no longer. I esteem you more than all the other nations. They separate me from the Empress in order to leave me in the island of Elba without defence. If they act with trickery towards me, I will ask for an asylum in England. Do you think they will receive me?'

'Sire,' I replied, 'I presume that the sovereign and the nation will ever act in the ease of their engagements with fidelity and with generosity.'

'Yes,' said Napoleon, 'I feel sure they will not refuse me.'

After pacing up and down the room for some time, he at length added, 'Very well, we are going to leave today.'

During a short conversation with the Russian Commissioner (although he paid very little attention either to him or to the Prussian, scarcely speaking to either of them, and being very cold and distant in his manner), Napoleon asked if he had yet received a reply to the question, as to whether he should proceed as far as Elba; and being answered in the negative, said, 'It is of no importance, provided that the Englishman accompanies me.'

The Russian and Prussian officers had, so far, instructions only to proceed to the place of embarkation, but had written for further orders.

The Duke of Bassano, four or five generals, his aide-de-camp, and fifteen or twenty other officers, were in the antechamber. Upon coming out to the first room, there were only Generals Belliard and Ornano; when he arrived there, the aide-de-camp suddenly shut the door, so that I presume Napoleon was taking a particular leave of them. The door then opened. The aide-de-camp called out, 'L'Empereur!' He passed us all with a salute and a smile to the head of the stairs, descended into the court, and proceeded towards his carriage, which was drawn up between two ranks of his Old Guards, then assembled the officers and non-commissioned officers, and sending for us to be present, he addressed them in the following speech (as nearly as I could recollect the words, in conjunction with the other Commissioners):

'Officers, non-commissioned officers, and soldiers of the Old Guard! I bid you farewell. For twenty years I have found you ever brave and faithful, marching in the path of glory. All Europe was united against us. The enemy, by stealing three marches upon me, had entered Paris. I was advancing in order to drive them out. They would not have remained there three days. I thank you for the noble spirit you have evinced in that same place under these circumstances. But a portion of the army, not sharing your sentiments, abandoned me and passed over to the camp of the enemy. From that moment the prompt deliverance of the capital became impossible. I could with the three parts of the army which remained faithful, and aided by the sympathy and the efforts of the great majority of the population, have fallen back upon the Loire, or upon my strongholds, and have sustained the war during several years. But a foreign and civil war had torn the soil of our beautiful country, and at the cost of all these sacrifices and all these ravages, could we hope to

The departure of Napoleon for Elba on April 20, 1814 (engraving by L. Beyer). Campbell has his arm in a sling (courtesy of Anne Brown Military Collection).

vanquish united Europe, supported by the influence which the city of Paris exercised, and which a faction had succeeded in mastering?

Under these circumstances I have only considered the interests of the country and the repose of France. I have made the sacrifice of all my rights, and am ready to make that of my person, for the aim of all my life has been the happiness and the glory of France.

As for you, soldiers, be always faithful in the path of duty and honour. Serve with fidelity your new sovereign. The sweetest occupation of my life will henceforth be to make known to posterity all that you have done great, and my only consolation will be to learn all that France will do for the glory of her name.

You are all my children. I cannot embrace you all but I will do so in the person of your General. (Here he embraced General Petit, and kissed him on either cheek.) I will embrace these eagles, which have served us as guides in so many glorious days.' (Here General Petit presented to him the standard, which he embraced for half a minute.)

On quitting his hold, he lifted up his left hand, and added, 'Farewell! Preserve me in your memories!'

He then turned round, entered his carriage which had been drawn up close by, and was carried off at a gallop. Some of the officers and men wept, some remained silent with grief, while others called out 'Vive L'Empereur!'

The order of march was as follows:

A dozen cavalry.

Carriage with General Drouot and superior officers.

Carriage with Napoleon and General Bertrand.

Fifty or sixty cavalry, followed by the four carriages of the Commissioners, and by eight of Napoleon's carriages, which were occupied by officers of his staff and household, and by servants.

The cavalry was of the Guard, and relieved every two post-stations.

The horses (sixty) for the carriages were ready, outside the town or village where the station happened to be.

We arrived at Briare, 69 miles from Fontainebleau, in the evening of the same day, and rested there for the night in a large hotel (where all was duly prepared for us), in order that some changes might take place in the arrangement of the baggage. Napoleon supped with General Bertrand; while General Drouot and Lefèbvre-Desnouettes, and all the officers who had travelled with us, joined our company.

On the morning of the 21st, two hours before our departure from Briare, Napoleon sent for me. He kept me in conversation, on indifferent subjects, until the servant had prepared the table, when he told him to lay another cover, saying to me, with a polite smile of invitation, 'You will remain to breakfast with me?'. There was also a place reserved for General Bertrand. He asked me who commanded in the Mediterranean. I replied that I did not know, but that I believed Sir Sidney Smith was one of the admirals.[33] He seemed to be moved by this, but quickly laughed it off; and when General Bertrand sat down, he said to him, smiling, 'What do you think? Sidney Smith is admiral in the Mediterranean.' He then related that while on the coast of Syria, Sir Sidney Smith threw several thousand shots from his ships to the shore, without killing a single man. It was, Napoleon said, his great resource, for he paid so much to every man for collecting and bringing to him the spent balls. 'He sent me challenges, like a second Marlborough; but I sent them back again. I put in my order of the day that the English naval commander was mad.' Here he laughed heartily. 'He wanted to treat me altogether as an equal.'[34]

---

33 Sir Sidney Smith, 1764-1840, was an eccentric seaman Napoleon had encountered when invading Syria from Egypt in 1799.

34 'Napoleon said that Sir Sidney was a madman, and, if his story be true, Sir Sidney challenged him to single combat; to which he made answer, "that be would not come forth to a duel unless the English could fetch Marlborough from his grave, but that in the meantime any one of his grenadiers would willingly give the challenger such satisfaction as he was entitled to demand."' – Lockhart's *Life of Napoleon*, vol. i. p. 150.

After breakfast, an officer named Laplace, son of a senator, was introduced from Rambouillet. He proceeded to comment on the means that were still at Napoleon's disposal – the attachment of the army, the excesses of the Allies, etc. As to the latter, he did not believe that they had any idea of quitting France, in spite of all their professions.

He then endeavoured to excuse the Senate; for, situated as they were, what could they do? But Napoleon interrupted him hastily, and inveighed bitterly against them. They were dishonoured; there was not the like act recorded in history. They were not obliged to assemble, because there were 200,000 bayonets over them. They could no longer act. Their sitting was illegal. What had they to expect, too, looking only to their own interests? Ten of those very men had actually voted for the death of Louis XVI. As to the military resources he had left, even after the enemy had possession of Paris, what could have opposed them? He knew the cautious operations of Prince Schwartzenberg would never have allowed him to remain between Paris and the French army, but he would have retired to Montmartre. He (Napoleon) would have attacked the Allies, and although the action would not be a victory, yet he would destroy so many of his enemy, as to prevent them from remaining so advanced. He knew well what the Russians and Austrians were capable of, notwithstanding their superiority of numbers. He would amuse them for two hours, and then advance with his thirty battalions of guards and eighty pieces of cannon upon one point, himself at the head, and he knew nothing could oppose them. After this he would increase his force by means of the population of the country, marching either upon the Loire or the fortresses. All this he could easily have done; but, he added, plaintively, it was not his wish to ruin his beloved France by a civil war. Although it was but a faction which declared against him, he preferred the steps he had taken, to continuing a contest for his rights, with certain misery to his country, when his yielding could afford comparative tranquillity.

I remained during all this time, as when I was preparing to leave the room, he told me to stop. At length he said, 'We are about to go!' It appeared to me be had no great opinion of M. Laplace's sincerity.

The night of the 21st we slept at Nevers. In coming into the town, I heard a non-commissioned officer call out to the other soldiers, 'Shout Vive L'Empereur!'

Having met at Nevers with Lieutenant-Colonel Pelley, who had been prisoner at Moulins, and was proceeding to Paris, I availed myself of the opportunity to send a despatch to Lord Castlereagh, with the particulars of our journey.

An escort of French cavalry, relieved at short distances, had accompanied us hitherto. The inhabitants saluted Napoleon with the usual shout of 'Vive L'Empereur!' mixed with cries of 'Vive la Mort!' In some places they allowed him to pass without any compliment, although incited thereto by the soldiers of the guard, who are cantoned upon this route. I am told that they prevent the inhabitants from wearing the white cockade, and from other demonstrations of the satisfaction they feel at the change of sovereignty.

About 7 o'clock, on the morning of the 22nd, we proceeded towards Lyons till we reached Roanne, a distance of 120 miles, where we determined to rest. Our three last stages had been performed without any escort, but from thence we were to be attended by Austrian detachments.

In the course of this day Napoleon hinted to me his wish that I should proceed in advance, in order to arrange for a British man-of-war to convey him to Elba, and also begged that I would write immediately to Admiral Emerian at Toulon, to expedite the French corvette. He then sent off express to Auxerre, to order his heavy baggage with the escort of 600 guards and horses to go by land to Piombino, in order to diminish the distance of the sea voyage, or, if that was not feasible, to proceed at once to Lyons and drop down the Rhone.

At night the Austrian officer who had been sent to Paris with the note containing Napoleon's protest against the removal of the guns and stores from the island of Elba, overtook us with the decision of the Allied Sovereigns, acquiescing in his demand.

Madame Mère and Cardinal Fesch were in the neighbourhood of Roanne, at a chateau belonging to the latter, about a mile off the road, but we could not learn that they had any communication with Napoleon.

At the moment of quitting Roanne, on the morning of the 23rd, Napoleon (as I expected from his hint on the previous day) requested me to proceed, if possible, without a halt to Aix, and from there to transmit through Marshal Masséna an application to the admiral commanding off Toulon for a British ship-of-war.[35] The reason alleged for preferring this to a French vessel was, to avoid any unpleasant observations which might be

35 André Masséna, 1758-1817, began his career as a cabinboy. His major success came onland however and he was one of the best of Napoleon's Marshals and was awarded the title of Prince of Essling. During Napoleon's exile Masséna was military governor of much of southern France and had his headquarters at Marseilles.

made by the crew of the latter. It was my wish to obtain this demand in writing, but as Napoleon immediately stepped into his carriage, I had no opportunity of doing so.

In the course of this journey, while in advance of the cortege, at a short distance from Valence, I met Augereau, and told him that Napoleon was coming on. He appeared to be disconcerted, thinking that Napoleon was to pursue the other road by Grenoble. He abused Napoleon's ambition and waste of blood for personal vanity. He did not show himself at last, as he ought to have done, and as many expected. 'He is a coward! I always have thought him such. He ought to have marched full upon a battery, and put an end to himself.'

Augereau showed me that he had taken off all his orders, and simply wore the red ribbon of the Legion of Honour. He said that if Napoleon gave him an opportunity, he would tell him his mind.

Hearing at Aix that a British ship was at Marseilles, I proceeded there, arriving on the 25th, and found HM frigate *Undaunted*, commanded by Captain Usher, who immediately complied with my application that he should proceed to Frejus Bay, either to convoy or to carry Napoleon to Elba. On his way (as I afterwards heard) he fell in with Admiral Sir R. King, who approved of the step he had taken, and gave him a written order to execute the service.

I then returned to Aix, and from thence went on to Frejus, which I reached at 7 a.m. on the 27th. At 10 a.m. Napoleon and his suite arrived. They had rested for some hours at the residence of the Princess Pauline, which was near the town. She had been there for some weeks past, and proposed soon to follow her brother to the island of Elba.

After I parted from them at Roanne, the Commissioners informed me they had met Augereau. It was on the road between Lyons and Valence. When his carriage approached, Napoleon and he both stopped, alighted, and embraced. Napoleon pulled off his hat, but Augereau only touched the forage-cap which he wore, and scarcely returned the embrace. They walked aside, and conversed for about ten minutes. The dialogue seemed to become more earnest as it drew to a conclusion. Napoleon embraced and saluted before parting, but Augereau returned the compliment in a cold and formal manner.

The enmity of the inhabitants against Napoleon increased in violence as he travelled southwards. This feeling was not confined to the lower orders only. All classes and ages, and both sexes, united in cries of hatred and insult.

At Orgon Napoleon faced the hostility of the population.

At Orange the women and boys climbed upon the carriage, and it was with difficulty that the Commissioners and attendants forced them off, there being at that point of the journey no escort. They called out the most opprobrious epithets, and with shouts of derision and excited gestures exclaimed, 'We will do no harm to the monster, but we only want to show him how much we love him.' Meanwhile Napoleon sat within the carriage with General Bertrand, apparently very much frightened, without attempting to stir from the corner. Several large stones were thrown at the carriage, but happily without effect. As soon as the carriages were able to force their way through the crowd of assailants, the post-boys set off at full speed, and when they had got to a safe distance from the town, Napoleon quitted his carriage, mounted one of the horses, and, dressed in a plain great coat, wearing too a Russian cloak and a common round hat with a white cockade, rode on in advance of the carriages, accompanied only by a courier. He related that when he arrived at the first post-house in his disguise, he held a conversation with the landlady, who enquired of him when Napoleon would pass, and abused him. When the rest of the party came up, and found Napoleon already there, General Bertrand requested that no sort of compliments might be paid which could possibly lead to the Emperor's being recognised at the inn. The Commissioners remarked that he threw the wine out of his glass, and that he neither swallowed his soup nor ate any meat. During the remainder of the journey he changed caps and coats with the Commissioners, assumed alternately the names of Colonel Campbell and Lord Burghersh, mixed with the members of his household in going in and out of the room, and his carriage did not, as heretofore, occupy the place of honour in the procession.

Upon every occasion he evinced, by the finesse to which he had recourse, much anxiety to save his life, whenever he considered it to be in danger.

At Avignon some carriages which preceded with officers of the household were stopped, and the eagles defaced. One of the servants was threatened with instant death if he did not call out 'Vive le Roi!' It was Sunday. The people had a fête to celebrate the accession of Louis XVIII; and as many of them were intoxicated, had Napoleon himself been there, he would certainly have been killed. He however passed quietly the following day, by going round the town, and changing horses outside.

At Orgon an effigy was prepared in uniform, representing Napoleon, smeared all over with blood, and placarded with the words, 'There, then, is the hateful tyrant! Sooner or later crime is punished.'

The place of embarkation had been changed from St. Tropez to Frejus, in consequence of the latter being easier to approach by land; and as they were both situated in the same bay, this deviation was considered admissible by the Commissioners.

Soon after Napoleon's arrival at Frejus, the following paper was put into my hands:

Note pour le Colonel Campbell, Commissaire de S. M. britannique, adressée par le Comte Bertrand. The Emperor Napoleon would wish to know which is the proper flag of the island of Elba, in order that it may be hoisted in the island. In testimony thereof, a *procès-verbal* shall be drawn up by Colonel Campbell and the other Commissioners. It shall be sent to the English cruising-ground at Leghorn,[36] and wherever else may be necessary.

The Princess Pauline, sister of the Emperor, is anxious to come to the island of Elba, but as she is indisposed she cannot leave Frejus for five or six days. HM would wish for an English frigate to come and fetch her, and convey her to the island.

The equipages of the Emperor and the battalion of escort ought to arrive at Lyons on the 30th. It is desirable that they should be directed by Mount Cenis upon Savona, where they will be embarked. If the English Admiral would be so far obliging as to charge a frigate with their transport, orders shall

---

36 Livorno, the Italian port.

General Cambronne.   The cockade as worn on Elba.

be sent to Lyons, in order that the equipages may arrange their route accordingly. They will arrive at Savona on the 19th of May. There is attached hereto a return of persons, horses, and carriages to be embarked.

If the frigate could attach to itself some despatch-boat or brig it would be a convenience.

The Emperor would wish, when we are off Leghorn, to despatch someone of his household to make some purchases, and be the bearer of a letter to the King of Naples. This latter request is of a very pressing character, seeing that the Emperor has nothing of any sort which can be suitable for his use in the island of Elba, and that the King of Naples will be able to send him many articles. General Koller can, if he so pleases, commission an Austrian officer to accompany the person who may be sent by the Emperor.

The Emperor would wish to expedite the departure of General Drouot, in company with Colonel Clam[37] and an English officer, to take possession of the island of Elba.

For that there will be required a despatch-boat, in order that they may arrive twenty-four hours before us, so that the Emperor will be able to disembark subsequently to the island having been taken possession of in his name.

The Guard of the Emperor not being expected to arrive for some time in the island of Elba, it is possible that the Emperor may require, in the early period of his residence there, a body of one hundred English marines for its protection. The Emperor wishes to know whether in case of necessity he can depend upon that.

(Signed) Le Comte BERTRAND. Frejus: April 27, 1814.

---

37 Karl Clam-Martinic, born in 1792, accompanied Koller.

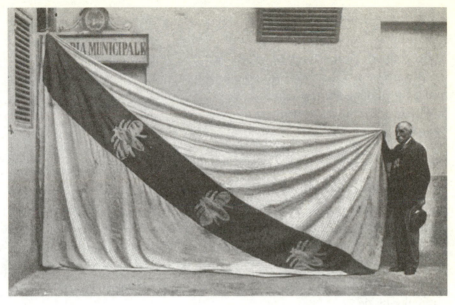

Napoleon's flag on Elba.

State of the troops, horses and vehicles of which the column, commanded by General Cambronne,[38] destined to embark at Savona to Elba is composed:

	Men	Horses	Vehicles
Wagons			8
Carriages			8
Horses		18	
Draft horses		24	
Mules		5	
Staff	35		
Cavalry	80	80	
Infantry	600		
Total	715	127	16

---

38 Pierre Jacques Etienne Cambronne, 1770-1842, was born in Nantes and was promoted to general in 1813. He was wounded four times at the battle of Craonne on March 6, 1814. He served Napoleon faithfully, was captured at Waterloo and was arrested by the Bourbons after his return to France.

In consequence of Napoleon's request, as above stated, the other Commissioners and myself held a meeting, and drew up the two following documents: the one being a letter addressed to the commandant at Elba, enclosing Count Dupont's order with reference to the guns and stores; the other accrediting Count Clam as the bearer of our despatch, and authorising him to proceed with it immediately to the island.

At first I felt some reluctance in affixing my signature to these documents, inasmuch as they were founded upon a treaty which had never been *formally* exhibited to me and as to which I had received two instructions from Lord Castlereagh.[39] But as my refusal would have prevented the embarkation of Napoleon, and put a stop to the whole of the proceedings connected with it, I considered it my duty not to offer any further objection. This course appeared to me consistent with the spirit of my instructions, and there was likewise no possibility of evading the difficulty by delay.

---

39 As a fact, it was not till this very day, April 27, that Lord Castlereagh gave a qualified accession to certain portions of the Treaty of Fontainebleau.
[Enclosure.]
'Whereas their Imperial and Royal Majesties, the Emperor of Austria, King of Hungary and Bohemia, the Emperor of all the Russias, and the King of Prussia, have entered into a treaty, concluded at Paris on the 11th of April of the present year, for the purpose of granting, for such respective periods in the said treaty are mentioned, to the person and family of Napoleon Bonaparte, the possession in sovereignty of the island of Elba and the duchies of Parma, Placentia and Guastalla, for other purposes which treaty has been communicated to the Prince Regent of the United Kingdom of Great Britain and Ireland, by the Ministers of their Imperial and Royal Majesties the Emperor of Austria, King of Hungary and Bohemia, the Emperor of all the Russias, and the King of Prussia, who, in the name of their respective sovereigns have jointly invited the Prince Regent to accede to the same, in the name and on the behalf of His Majesty.
His Royal Highness the Prince Regent, having full knowledge of the contents of the said treaty, accedes to the same in the name and on the behalf of His Majesty, as far as respects the stipulations relative to the possession in sovereignty of the island of Elba and also of the duchies of Parma, Placentia, and Guastalla. But His Royal Highness is not to be considered, by this act of accession, to have become a party, in the name of His Majesty, to any of the other provisions and stipulations contained therein.
Given under my hand and seal, at Paris, this 27th day of April, in the year of our Lord 1814. By command of His Royal Highness the Prince Regent, acting in the name and on the behalf of His Majesty.

(Signed) CASTLEREAGH

(I.)

We, the undersigned, Commissioners of the Allied powers charged with accompanying His Majesty the Emperor Napoleon during his voyage, are authorised by Monsieur le Comte de Clam, Chamberlain to his Imperial Majesty, the Emperor of Austria, Aide-de-Camp of Prince Schwartzenberg, Chevalier of the Imperial Order of Russia and the Military Order of the King of Bavaria, Max-Joseph, to send at once to Commander of the aforementioned isle of Elba the Ministry of War's order that the isle be handed over to the Emperor Napoleon and that he should enjoy full sovereignty and property, including all munitions and military equipment which might be found there. General Count Drouot has been named as commissioner by Napoleon to assist in this process.

Frejus. April 27, 1814.

(II.)

We, the undersigned, Commissioners of the Allied powers have the honour to acquaint General Francois, Commander of the isle of Elba, with the orders drawn up by the Ministry of War that all munitions and military equipment which might be found there, should be handed over to the person designated by the Emperor Napoleon, in consequence thereof no equipment shall be evacuated. In a treaty between the Allied powers and the Emperor Napoleon it has been stipulated that he should enjoy full sovereignty over the isle in his lifetime and he shall enjoy the prerogatives due to him in that capacity. General of Division Count Drouot, Commissioner on the part of Napoleon, shall arrive in Elba to take care of the hand over and he shall be accompanied by Count Clam, Chamberlain to his Imperial Majesty, the Emperor of Austria, and Thomas Hastings, Lieutenant of the Royal Navy's *Undaunted* to assist him as he takes possession of the isle.

Frejus, April 27,1814.

Baron de KOLLER,
Lieutenant-General in the service of Austria
Count SCHUVALOV,
General in the Armies of his Imperial Majesty Czar of all the Russias
Count WALBOURG-TRUCHESS,
Colonel-General in the armies of His Majesty the King of Prussia
NEIL CAMPBELL,
Colonel in the service of his Britannic Majesty

CHAPTER III

The *Undaunted* anchored off Frejus at midday on the 27th. Captain Usher came on shore to be presented to Napoleon, and the baggage was sent off at once for embarkation. Soon afterwards the French frigate *Dryade*, in company with a corvette and a transport, arrived in the bay. The officer commanding stated that his orders were to embark the Emperor in the corvette, the frigate forming the escort. This displeased Napoleon extremely, as he considered it should have been optional with him to choose in which of the vessels he should make his voyage, and he was by this incident confirmed in his resolve to embark on board the English frigate. Such a plan of course greatly offended the French officers, who tried, though in vain, to persuade him to decide in favour of the corvette.

In contrast with the treatment he had received from the Provisional Government of France, he spoke in grateful terms of the liberal disposition evinced towards him by the Ministers of HRH the Prince Regent, although he had always been the avowed enemy of the British nation.

At sunset, on April 28, Napoleon and his suite left the inn at Frejus in carriages, which conveyed them to the beach, distant about an English mile. Here a small wharf had been prepared, at the extremity of which was the barge of the *Undaunted*. He embarked with Captain Usher and General Bertrand, and on his arrival on board the frigate was received with a royal salute of twenty one guns.

Some little difficulty had arisen with regard to this salute, as instead of Napoleon proceeding on board in the forenoon, as had been intended, he was prevented by a temporary indisposition from leaving the inn until

46

much later. It was represented to him that it was not customary to salute after sunset, in the hope that he would dispense with the compliment; but this he decidedly objected to, and desired General Drouot to say to me he would postpone the embarkation till the following morning, as, on account of the impression it would make on the inhabitants, he particularly wished to be received with a royal salute. As it was very important that there should be no unnecessary delay in Napoleon's reaching his new sovereignty, I urged Captain Usher strongly to waive on this occasion the usual etiquette; and in consequence Napoleon was persuaded to embark on the day originally fixed, and was, as related above, received with the honours he so much valued.

The Russian and Prussian Commissioners accompanied the rest of the party on board the *Undaunted*, but they took leave of Napoleon, and quitted the ship before she weighed anchor, as their instructions did not allow of their proceeding farther.

Napoleon had the whole of the after-cabin to himself, and his two generals slept in the half of the captain's, which was screened off. In the other half he breakfasted at ten, and dined at six, in company with General Koller, Count Clam, Generals Bertrand and Drouot, Captain Usher, and myself. Throughout the voyage Napoleon conducted himself with the greatest condescension and cordiality towards us all. He remarked himself that he had never felt in better health, and officers of his suite observed that they had never seen him appear more at his ease. It seemed to me that one great source of his happiness and satisfaction arose from the security of his person; for it was evident, during his stay at Fontainebleau and the following journey, that he entertained great apprehensions of attacks upon his life, and he certainly exhibited more timidity than one would have expected from a man of his calibre.

Although at Fontainebleau he expressed his desire to pass the remainder of his life in retirement at Elba, studying the arts and sciences, he inadvertently gave frequent proofs in his subsequent conversations on board the *Undaunted* of the active restlessness of his disposition, and indicated his expectation of opportunities arising, which would once again afford scope for the exercise of his ambition.

He evidently persuaded himself that the greatest portion of the population in France remained favourable to him, although this feeling did not extend to the coast. He explained this by observing, that France in former times had always made treaties of commerce with Great Britain, which were extremely discouraging to her internal industry, though beneficial to Marseilles, Bordeaux, Nantes, etc., whose chief interest lay in peace with that nation. But as his system went to encourage the manufactures of France, Lyons, Tarare (a manufacturing town between Lyons and Roanne), and all others similarly situated, were attached to him, and had given proofs to that effect on his journey. Such demonstrations, however, had not been perceived by the Commissioners!

General Bertrand has likewise told me that he considers a great part of France still for Napoleon; that Augereau's troops were so, and the Marshal's life was in danger for the part he took against his old master; that Napoleon had often been told Augereau would betray him; that, near Lyons and other towns, many inhabitants informed them as they passed along, it was for fear of the Austrians they carried the white cockade. At Valence the French soldiers held up the tri-coloured cockade clandestinely in their hands, shaking their heads at the same time, and even shedding tears.

Addressing himself particularly to me one morning at breakfast, General Koller, Count Clam, Captain Usher, and General Bertrand being likewise present, Napoleon said:

That England had, ever since the time of Cromwell, set up her extraordinary pretensions of domination on the sea. I here remarked that, since the French Revolution, she had found it necessary, in order to preserve her very existence.

That her finance was now on such a footing, that she could not exist excepting by having sale without limits for all her manufactures.

That, if she had not this extraordinary commerce with all the world, she would still be a respectable nation, in power and riches, from her ordinary means, population, and institutions, but she would be greatly diminished.

That, after the Peace of Amiens, Lord Sidmouth[40] wished to renew the former treaty of commerce, which had been made by Vergennes[41] after the American War; but he [Napoleon] was anxious to encourage the

---

40 Prime Minister, as Mr. Addington, from March 1801 to May 1804. Created Viscount Sidmouth, January 1805. The Peace of Amiens only lasted from March 1802 to April 1803.
41 He was Prime Minister under Louis XVI, from November 1781 to February 1787 when he died. The Peace between France and Great Britain, called the Peace of Versailles, was signed February 20, 1783. In consequence of the censure passed upon it, the Shelburne Ministry was dissolved on February 26, 1783.

interior industry of France, and therefore expressed his readiness to make a treaty, though not like the former (which was known by the portfolios of Versailles to be injurious to France), but upon terms of reciprocity. Thus, if France receives so many millions of English imports, England must take away an equal quantity of French productions. Lord Sidmouth said, I cannot make a treaty on these terms; this is totally new. Very well, replies Napoleon, I cannot force you to a treaty of commerce any more than you can force me; but we must remain as we are. Then, says Lord Sidmouth, there will be war; for, unless the people of England have the advantages of their commerce upon the terms they have been accustomed to, they will force me to declare war. As you please, rejoins Napoleon. It is my duty to study the just interests of France, and I shall not form a treaty of commerce on other principles than those I have stated. England under Mr. Fox (1806) was certainly not prepared for the steps which he took in retaliation for her blockading an entire line of coast from the Elbe to Brest.[42] It was that which forced him to the continental system.

Then England made pretences about Malta, but all the world knew that was not the cause of quarrel. He was sincere in the desire for peace; as a proof of which he sent his expedition to St. Domingo.[43] I told him our Ministers thought him not sincere, both from his refusing the treaty of commerce, and likewise sending consuls to Ireland in company with engineers, for the purpose of examining the harbours.[44] He laughed at my remark, and said, 'Oh! That was not necessary, for every harbour in England and Ireland was known.' General Bertrand added, that every ambassador or minister to another country was a spy.

Napoleon observed that Spain was the natural friend of France and the enemy of Great Britain; that it was for their mutual interest to ally

---

42 'The British, who, by Mr. Fox's order, declared the coast from the Elbe to Brest in blockade.' – Alison, *History of Europe*, vol. x. ch. lxxvi.

43 This refers to Napoleon's expedition to Haiti. An expedition, commanded by General Leclerc, was sent to reimpose slavery on the rebellious island and landed in February 1802. The French force was eventually defeated and most of the participants succumbed to Yellow fever.

44 Under pretence of establishing French consuls for the protection of commerce, he [Napoleon] sent persons, chiefly of the military profession, who carried orders to make exact plans of all the harbours and coasts of the United Kingdom. These gentlemen endeavoured to execute their commission with all possible privacy, but the discovery of their occupation was soon made; they were sent back to France without ceremony, and this treacherous measure of their Government was openly denounced as a violation of every rule of international law, and a plain symptom of warlike preparation.' – Lockhart's *Life of Napoleon*, vol. i. pp. 264-5.

themselves in support of their commerce and foreign possessions, which were equally offensive to England; that it was a shame to Spain to allow us to hold Gibraltar: it needed only to bombard it from the land night and day during a year, and it must be worn out. (Here he asked, whether we still held Ceuta.) He did not invade Spain in order to put one of his own family on the throne, but to revolutionise her; to make her a kingdom *en règle*, to abolish the Inquisition, feudal rights, and the inordinate privileges of certain classes.

He spoke also of our attacking Spain without a declaration of war, and without cause. I told him we knew for a certainty that the Spanish Government intended to make common cause with him, as soon as the treasure amassed in America for a long time should arrive. He replied that he did not want it: all he needed was five millions a month to Frenchify it ('pour la francifier:' he used this term repeatedly).

The Treaty of Utrecht, he said, directs that the boarding of vessels shall be done out of gunshot. America behaved with spirit in the matter of search. I asked here whether America showed hostility to Great Britain upon principles of right, or whether the President engaged in war in order to force the people to form a navy and army, so that the protection of his trade was a mere excuse. To this question he made no direct reply, but only laughed while saying, 'Ah! You always treat the Americans as if they were still your subjects.' He thought their state correspondence with us was very well written, and contained much sound reasoning. I told him I was not sufficiently master of the general question to judge of that; but as to the original ground of quarrel – the boarding of their men–of–war – that was only the aggression of a single officer, which was disavowed by our Government, and for which they offered to make any proper atonement.[45] As to their style of writing, we found in it great imperfection. Whether it was a State-paper, a naval or military despatch, although the words themselves were the same, the language appeared

---

45 '*The Chesapeake*, American frigate, was cruising off Virginia (June 23rd, 1807), and was known to have some English deserters on board, when she was hailed by the *Leopard* of 74 guns, Captain Humphries, who made a formal requisition for the men. The American captain denied he had them, and refused to admit the right of search upon which Captain Humphries fired a broadside, which killed and wounded several on board the *Chesapeake* whereupon she struck, and the deserters were found on board, taken to Halifax, and one executed. The President, upon this, issued a proclamation, ordering all British ships-of-war to leave the harbours of the United States; but the English Government disavowed the act, recalled Captain Humphries, and offered to make reparation, as the right of search, when applied to vessels of war, extended only to a requisition, but could not be carried into effect by actual force.' – Alison, *History of Europe* vol. x. ch. lxxvi.

totally different in meaning from our own.

Napoleon went on to say, that the Americans acknowledged the justice of his principles of commerce. Formerly they had brought some millions of cotton and tobacco, and taken away the payment in specie from France. Then went light to England, and from thence conveyed British manufactures. But afterwards he would not admit their tobacco and cotton, unless they took away an equal value of French productions. They yielded to his system as being just. But now England has no power which can oppose her system, and she may pursue it without limits. She may impose upon France any treaty she pleases.

'The Bourbons, poor devils!' Here he seemed to check himself, but presently added: 'They are like great nobles, content as long as they enjoy their estates and their mansions. But if the people of France become dissatisfied with that, and find that they have not such encouragement for their manufactures in the interior as they ought to have, they will be driven out in six months.'

Here he again checked himself, as if seeming aware of his own indiscretion, and soon afterwards rose from table, breakfast being finished. He evidently possesses no command over himself while in conversation.

Upon April 29 we communicated with HM brig *Merope*, Captain Roberts, which remained in company all day. This officer came on board and dined with Napoleon; and I took the opportunity of writing by him to Admiral Sir Edward Pellew, then at Genoa, enclosing likewise a letter for Lord William Bentinck, and sending to each copies of Lord Castlereagh's instructions with regard to my present mission.

At table one day Napoleon showed us his snuffbox, on which is a portrait of the Empress, with a date set in diamonds. This led him to produce another, on which was the figure of a naked infant, representing the King of Rome. He did not seem at all affected in referring to the Empress, but of the other he spoke with some feeling, and mentioned that the child did not wish to quit Paris when the family were going to Orleans; that he held by his hands on to the table, and they were obliged to tear him away by force. Napoleon called him 'The poor devil!'

When off Calvi in Corsica, May 1, we passed HMS *Berwick*, having on board Commodore Brisbane and General Montresor, in command of a force destined for that island, the frigates *Aigle* and *Alcmène*, with six sail of transports bound for Ajaccio. The captains of the two frigates, Sir I. Louis and Captain Coghlan, came on board, and dined with Napoleon. He was extremely anxious to know the state of affairs in Corsica, whether there were any armed parties in the interior, whether the Deputation sent to Genoa, requesting the presence of a naval and military force, came only from Bastia, or also from the whole island.

Napoleon was informed that General Count Berthier commanded at Ajaccio; that British troops and colours were at St. Florenzo, Calvi, and other places, in compliance with the wish of the inhabitants; that this occupation had taken place before the arrival of the officer from Paris, with the news of Louis XVIII having been declared by the Provisional Government; and that General Berthier[46] and his troops had taken the oath of allegiance. General Bertrand requested that I would ask one of the English officers to take charge of an open letter to General Berthier at Ajaccio, and another addressed to an individual in Corsica, adding the assurance that the Emperor refrained from all interference in public affairs, and that these letters were merely of a private nature. I told him that the letters should be delivered to General Montresor and Commodore Brisbane, who would no doubt take care that they reached their destination.

The abdication of Napoleon appeared to be unknown to these officers; I therefore acquainted them with the exact state of affairs; and as one of the frigates was returning to Genoa, I again wrote to the Admiral and to Lord William Bentinck,[47] to inform them of several fresh demands which had been made to me by General Bertrand on the part of Napoleon, enclosing at the same time a letter to Lord Castlereagh, in which I begged for further instructions.

General Bertrand had constantly impressed upon me, that as the island of Elba does not afford the supplies necessary for Napoleon's table, and as he has only with him the baggage which accompanied him in the campaign, he was in want of many things, which would oblige him to have recourse to the Continent. Although Napoleon could himself have ordered them, yet, in order to show his confidence in the Commissioners, he had directed his intentions to be fully detailed in a note; it was to the same purport as that before given, and sent to Lord Castlereagh.

---

46 General Berthier, brother of the more famous Marshal, had been governor of the Ionian Islands but made his peace with the Bourbons.

47 Bentinck had been British minister in Sicily, the refuge of the Neapolitan Bourbons whilst Murat was on the throne of Naples.

Napoleon is perfectly conversant with all the details of naval affairs,[48] such as the cost and daily expense of a ship-of-war, the number of rounds for service on board, the difference between French and British battleships, the ropes in the case of the former being worked upon the upper-deck, so that more men were exposed.

He is extremely inquisitive as to all points respecting our navy, its establishment, discipline, etc., and General Bertrand daily puts similar questions to Captain Usher and myself, which are doubtless desired by Napoleon; for on other occasions it has been evident that the General himself has no curiosity or interest in anything connected with naval affairs.

One morning Napoleon described to Captain Usher, by my interpretation, the system for his marine conscripts, which he was persuaded would succeed. It was immaterial to him whether the youth was from a seaport or from the interior. He went into the navy at fourteen. For a certain number of years he remained in harbour, in order to practise getting under weigh and anchoring, which were considered the most difficult parts of a seaman's duty, then to run out on a voyage of four or five months, and home again. This was every preparation necessary for manning a fleet, which would next proceed out in squadrons to manoeuvre and fight the enemy. In this way he would have had, within three or four years, a fleet of 300 sail of the line. It was this system which made it requisite for him to possess himself of Holland, the Zuyder Zee being useful to his great plan for forming seamen. Not that he wanted the Dutch ships, which were only fit to carry horses. He found it necessary to send them artisans of all kinds for construction.

He spoke of the bad behaviour of several of his frigates, particularly the *Clorinde*, near Madagascar.[49] 'I did all I could to get the captain's head

---

48 'There are hundreds of letters from Napoleon on naval matters many of which relate to his projected invasion of England. In these he not only gives the minutest directions respecting the flotilla at Boulogne, but he issues the most positive orders to his fleets in all parts of the world, as to the conduct to be pursued under every possible circumstance. We confess ourselves incompetent to eliticise his plans of naval warfare; but on the very face of the thing it certainly argues great presumption on the part of one totally unacquainted with the sea to speak so authoritatively, and the frequent reverses which his fleets suffered go far to corroborate this first impression. At any rate, one would naturally take for granted that he spoke, if not by the advice, at least with the concurrence, of his Minister of Marine. There are, however, undeniable proofs that this was not the case.' – *Edinbourgh Review*, No. 258, October 1867, Art. I., 'The Napoleon Correspondence,' pp. 336-7.

49 The action between the *Clorinde*, of 44 guns, and the *Eurotas*, under Capt. Phillimore, of the same force, commenced February 25, 1814. The next day, when they were again nearing each other, two more British vessels, the *Dryad* and the *Achilles*, appeared, and the *Clorinde* then struck. Out of a crew of 360 men, she had 120 killed and wounded.

cut off; but they only condemned him to prison for three years.'

He praised Admiral Villeneuve's dispositions at Trafalgar, but said that the Admirals on the two flanks did not follow his signals, so as to close in rear of Nelson, when he pushed to the centre.[50]

He thought the policy of England was mistaken in making the attack on Copenhagen, for, in consequence of it, Denmark, from being a sincere friend to us, had become a decided enemy. I alluded to the secret article in the Treaty of Tilsit. He said, that although Denmark might be forced to declare war against England, she would not carry it on sincerely, and a few ships more or less could be no object to England.

The expedition against Antwerp,[51] under Lord Chatham, was on too great a scale to be rapid. It must be carried by a *coup de main* of 10,000 men with artillery, who would land at Williamstad, execute their object, and be off again before a large force could be assembled to oppose them. He wrote from Vienna to warn the authorities in France of that expedition being destined against Antwerp.

England could not hold Walcheren without 14,000 men, and half of these would be lost by disease annually. Even if she had got possession of Antwerp, he had such resources in its neighbourhood as to be able to attack it suddenly with great superiority of numbers, and then it must fall. France would be nothing without Antwerp, for while Brest, Toulon, and other ports were blockaded, a fleet could be equipped there with wood brought from Poland. He never would consent to give it up, having sworn at his coronation not to diminish France. He told me that the smugglers carried on an unceasing espionage, bringing him immediate information of any expedition being prepared, copies of our newspapers, and quantities of guineas. They took back the productions of the Continent. They were admitted only to Gravelines, and assembled under certain regulations. His system of espionage in England cost him five millions of livres (£250,000).

Besides what he had mentioned, the smugglers, Napoleon said, had offered to be of service to him in various ways. One of them, for instance,

---

50 The only other French Admiral was Rear-Admiral Dumanoir. Admiral Gravina commanded the Spanish fleet, and was mortally wounded, returning to Cadiz to die.

51 The Walcheren expedition, which proved so disastrous a failure, sailed from England July 28, 1809, and was composed of 40,000 troops with 35 ships of the line and 200 smaller vessels plincipally transports. The island was finally evacuated December 23, 1809.

proposed to carry off General Sarrazin,[52] but he did not want him, 'He is a madman, a man who was not worth the trouble, of whom I had no need.'

As much as to say, that such means would always be resorted to, if there was an object to serve of sufficient interest.

He had the Elbe sounded carefully by engineers, and found it was as favourable as the Scheldt for the erection of great naval establishments near Hamburg. It surprised him this was not known before. He would have built ships of the line there with wood from Poland.

He described to us, on a plan of Cherbourg, a basin cut out of the solid rock, with docks for twenty-five ships of the line, as executed under his orders. He drew with a pencil a line of fortifications erected for its protection against any expedition from England, which he always expected. The Empress Marie Louise visited Cherbourg last year, when he was at Dresden, upon the completion of the work. Had we landed there, he would have destroyed the mouth of the basin by which we entered by means of mines, so that not a man could have escaped after they had once got in with their fine ships.

He intended to form establishments for shipbuilding at Bouc, so that materials might come there directly by the Rhone. A canal was already cut to join the two. Toulon, in that case, would only be used as a shelter for his fleets. He had found great inconvenience in being obliged to complete the provisions and stores of his men–of–war after they went out of the inner harbours, as it gave information of his intentions to the British cruisers. They were then on the watch, and either blockaded or cut them out. To avoid a similar difficulty, he contrived so as to send the *Rivoli*[53] out in a few hours from her original station at Venice towards Corfu, where, however, she was taken. He fixed *chameaux* (camels) on either side, which prevented her from sinking in the water in proportion as her weight

---

52 He had escaped from Boulogne to England in 1810 in a small boat, leaving behind him his wife, who was an Englishwoman. Whereupon she wrote a letter, which was published by order of Napoleon, giving out that her husband had been deranged for seven years. Sarrazin replied by a series of letters addressed to the *Times*, proclaiming his own sanity and violently abusing Napoleon. 'General Sarrazin (an anecdote relates) was on duty when Napoleon and his newly-married wife arrived at Boulogne. After viewing the fortifications, they went upon the heights overlooking the sea. The Empress, telescope in hand, observing a vessel cruising at some distance, enquired what it was, and was told it was English. Seeing five others in the harbour, she asked why they did not go out and take it. Snatching the glass out of her hand, Napoleon said, 'Because – the wind is not fair!'

53 The *Rivoli*, an eighty-four-gun ship, had been built at Venice, and was captured, after a severe engagement, by the *Victorious*, seventy-four, Captain John Talbot, on March 21, 1812, off the point of Grao in Istria.

increased. With these she was floated out. They were then cut away, sail was made, and the voyage pursued.

He referred to a map of Toulon harbour, and went over the whole of the operations against Lord Hood and General O'Hara. At this time he commanded the artillery there with the rank of Major. All the other French officers were for a regular siege. He gave in a memoir for the purpose of showing how to drive off the fleet from the opposite side, and that the English would not hazard the total loss of their garrison. The event justified his belief.

He related an anecdote of one of the Representatives of the People, who ordered his battery to fire, which unmasked it too soon. The only time he was ever wounded was by an English gunner at Toulon, who ran a pike into his thigh. He was endeavouring to enter a battery by the embrasure. His people got round by the rear, and entered at the same moment. It was at this period also that, while Junot was in the act of writing, a cannon-ball struck and spattered the ground all about his party; on which he remarked that it was sand for the letter.

Captain Usher here asked him, whether it was true that he had charged at the head of a column across the bridge of Lodi. He said it was.

With reference to caricatures, I told Napoleon that no one in England was exempt from them, neither our Sovereign nor the Ministers. Napoleon remarked that there were plenty of him, at any rate in England, and that no doubt his present voyage would form a fertile subject for them. Captain Usher said it would immortalise the *Undaunted*. General Bertrand observed, that it was most unaccountable to him how *The Spirit of the Book* – a libel on the Princess of Wales – could have been published by the bookseller of the Prince, as expressly stated on the title-page.

Napoleon asked Captain Usher and myself whether we belonged to the Opposition. Captain Usher said, he did. I told him that I did not approve of all that Ministers had done in former times, but that latterly my opinion of their policy had become much more favourable. He inquired of me in what estimation Sir Francis Burdett was held. I replied that, in his private character, he was considered very amiable, but his influence over the minds of the people had been much diminished since he escaped clandestinely from the Tower.

Captain Usher told Napoleon that the Duchess of Bedford, who had been presented to him at Paris as Lady Georgiana Gordon, was now in the Mediterranean. He said he recollected her; she was a great dancer, and often danced with the Viceroy of Italy. Her mother was a large woman.

'Nap dreading his doleful doom, or his grand entry in the isle of Elba'. From an English caricature of
April 1814.

On the 2nd May we were becalmed off St. Florenzo. Napoleon seemed
very anxious to learn the news of the island, and frequently proposed to
send on shore. Seeing a fishing-boat, he said jocularly, 'Go and make that
fisherman come here!' Captain Usher said to me that he was surprised to
hear Napoleon propose to stop a fishing-boat, an interruption upon the
high seas so contrary to his system. I did not choose to communicate the
remark, but he desired me to translate it. On this being done, he laughed
and patted Captain Usher on the back, saying, 'Ah, capitaine!'. The Austrian
Commissioner said to me, aside, that he was so accustomed to *seize*, that he
could not yet abandon his old tricks.

Before sunset a small *tartane* was seen standing in for St. Florenzo, and
the master was brought on board. Napoleon asked him fifty questions in
rapid succession, speaking Italian, and then left him abruptly. These had all
reference to Corsica, and in answering them the man exulted in the present
change of affairs, the British flag flying everywhere, and so large a force of
English being at Genoa. On being informed who it was he had been
speaking to, the man stared hard at Napoleon; but when, as he was passing
along the deck, the latter put to him some further questions, he replied with
much less respect than before, on which Napoleon left him, and asked
Captain Usher to send him away. The *tartane* was on its way to Sardinia from
Genoa, where, the man told us, the King of Sardinia was, as well as Sir
Edward Pellew and Lord William Bentinck.

On the morning of May 3, a boat came off to the frigate from Capraja, an island between the northern point of Corsica and Elba, conveying a deputation of several of the inhabitants, one of whom represented himself as the president of a municipal council lately formed. They stated that, two weeks before, they had revolted against the French garrison and sent them to Corsica; that they had forwarded an address to Lord William Bentinck on April 24, requesting to be taken under British protection. Captain Usher sent an officer on shore, to remain with them, for the purpose of signing passports for their boats, until superior orders should be received.

The same afternoon we were off Porto Ferrajo in Elba, it being too calm for the frigate to enter the harbour. General Drouot with Count Clam and Lieutenant Hastings were sent on shore to take possession. I accompanied them. The inhabitants appeared to view us with great curiosity. We were conducted, in the first instance, to the house of General d'Alhesme, senior officer, who informed us that, two days before, an officer had arrived from Paris with orders dated April 18, for the embarkation of all stores, and notifying the appointment of the Provisional Government; in consequence of which the General and his troops had given in their adhesion to Louis XVIII, and raised the white flag. At the same time the General expressed his desire to do whatever should be agreeable to Napoleon.

In reading out quotations from his instructions in my presence, General Drouot stated to General d'Alhesme, on the part of Napoleon, that he should wish to receive the names of all officers, non-commissioned officers, and privates, who might be willing to enter his service. Napoleon said last night that the whole force in the island amounted to only about 250; but I am informed that there had been more than 2,000 troops in all, although by desertion, and the discharge of discontented foreigners, they are now reduced to 600 or 700. There are two small vessels of the French marine in the harbour, the crews of which have deserted and Napoleon intends, I believe, to retain them also.

General Drouot likewise desired a deputation of the principal inhabitants to come off in the course of the evening. They arrived about 8 p.m., consisting of all the civil and military authorities, and the frigate anchored at the same time.

For several weeks the inhabitants had been in a state of revolt, in consequence of which the troops occupied only the fortifications which surround the town of Porto Ferrajo. The General had discharged all foreign soldiers and landed them on the Continent, on account of their disaffection. The spirit of the inhabitants is very inimical to the late Government of France, and personally to Napoleon, so that he will certainly require the French troops for his protection until his Guards arrive from France. He has also so strongly urged Captain Usher and myself to land the marines, that we could not refuse – although, as I told him last night, I presume that will not be necessary, so long as the French troops remain in the island.

During the night, by Napoleon's request, the aide-de-camp of General Koller was sent off to Piombino, to notify his having taken possession of the island of Elba in virtue of a treaty concluded with the Allies, and also to invite a renewal of communications for purposes of commerce, news, etc. The Austrian officer was the bearer of a letter to this effect, addressed to the Commandant, and signed by the Commissioners. He however politely declined the proposal, until he had received the permission of the King of the Two Sicilies, to whom he had referred.

At daylight, May 4, Napoleon was on deck with the Captain of the port, and remained there for two hours, conversing with various officers, and making inquiries as to the anchorage, fortifications, etc.

At 8 a.m. he asked for a boat, and embarked, wearing his great coat and round hat. Count Bertrand, Captain Usher, Colonel Vincent the chief engineer, and myself accompanied him. When we were half-way across the harbour, he remarked that he was himself without a sword. Soon afterwards he asked whether the peasants of Tuscany were addicted to assassination. Evidently he is greatly afraid of falling in this way.

His purpose in crossing the harbour was to look at a house of imposing appearance near the beach. We remained there for nearly two hours, walking about and waiting for the keys.

Returning on board, he fixed upon the flag of Elba, and ordered two to be made immediately, in order that one may be hoisted upon the fortifications at 1 p.m., while he himself will disembark with another at 2 p.m. The flag is white, with a red stripe diagonally, and three bees on the stripe. It is as nearly as possible one of the flags of ancient Tuscany, and the bees formed part of his own arms as Emperor of France.

At 2 p.m. he landed, Count Bertrand, General Koller, Captain Usher, and myself being in the same boat with him. There were boats with officers upon either quarter, and others filled with musicians and inhabitants of the island. The yards of the frigate and of the two French corvettes were manned, and royal salutes fired. At the beach he was received by the prefect,

Napoleon arriving at Elba.

clergy, etc., and the keys were presented upon a plate amid acclamations of 'Vive L'Empereur!'. We next proceeded to the church in procession, and from thence to the town hall, where all the authorities and principal inhabitants were assembled, with each of whom he conversed. After this he mounted his horse, attended by about a dozen persons, and visited part of the fortified outworks. Dinner was at 7 p.m.

May 5.

From daylight to breakfast at 10 a.m. Napoleon was on foot, inspecting the castles, storehouses, and magazines.

At 2 p.m. he went into the interior on horseback, a distance of two leagues, and examined various countryhouses.

May 6.

At 7 a.m. he crossed the harbour in Captain Usher's boat, proceeded on horseback across the island to Rio, and examined the mines, then ascended a number of hills and mountain tops upon which there are ruins. After a *Te Deum* in a chapel, we had breakfast. On our return we re-embarked in Captain Usher's boat, but, instead of returning direct, Napoleon visited the watering place, the height opposite the citadel on which he proposes to establish a sea-battery, and a rock at the mouth of the harbour on which he also thinks of placing a tower.

In talking at dinner of his intention to take possession of a small island without inhabitants, which is about ten miles off the coast of Elba,

Napoleon said, 'All Europe will say that I have made a conquest already.' He laughed at this.

Already he has all his plans in agitation; such as to convey water from the mountains to the city, to prepare a country-house, a house in Porto Ferrajo for himself, and another for the Princess Pauline, a stable for 150 horses, a lazaretto for vessels to perform quarantine, a depot for the salt, and another for the nets belonging to the fishery of the tuna.

May 7.

From 5 to 10 a.m. Napoleon visited other parts of the town and fortifications on foot, then embarked in boats, and visited the different storehouses round the harbour.

In making the excursions into the country, yesterday and the day before, he was accompanied by a dozen officers. A captain of gendarmes and one of his *Fourriers de Palais* always rode in front; and, on two occasions, a sergeant's party of *gendarmes-à-pied* went on about an English mile before.

On taking our places in the boat, some of us, following Bertrand's example, kept off our hats; on which he told us to put them on, adding, 'We are here together as soldiers.'

The fishery of the tuna is carried on by the richest inhabitant of the island. This person, by his own industry, has, out of a state of extreme poverty, amassed a fortune. He employs a great proportion of the poor, and has much influence. The removal of the stores by Napoleon to a very inferior building, merely for the convenience of his horses, is likely to cause disgust; but this shows how little Napoleon permits reflection to check his desires.

May 8.

Before landing from the frigate, Napoleon requested that a party of fifty marines might accompany him to remain on shore. This intention was afterwards changed; and one officer of marines and two sergeants, to act as orderlies, together with a lieutenant of the navy, were sent.

One of the sergeants, selected by himself, sleeps outside the door of his bedchamber, upon a mattress, with his clothes on, and a sword at his side. A valet occupies another mattress at the same place. If he lies down during the day, the sergeant is called to remain in the antechamber.

May 9.

Napoleon has requested General Koller and myself this day to sign a passport for one of his valets, to proceed to Genoa in His Majesty's ship *Curaçoa*, Captain Tower, and from thence to the Viceroy of Italy. The motive alleged to us by Count Bertrand is to receive a quantity of furniture, his own private property, which is in the palace at Milan. I have considered it my duty to notify the circumstance to Lord William Bentinck, by General Koller, who goes in the same ship on his way to Paris, and I have requested him to wait upon his Lordship, in order to give every information in his power regarding Napoleon, and all occurrences since our departure.

The Commandant at Piombino has permitted every intercourse by order of the General in command of that province, and Napoleon has profited by it to send over to a palace of the Grand Duchess of Tuscany, to bring over furniture which he alleges to be his private property.

Napoleon visited Longono, and was received with vivas and acclamations. Many old women presented petitions; others fell on their knees across the road to ask charity; while others again laid hold of his hand to kiss it. He appeared to be displeased at their importunate manner. After quitting the town, a young lad fell on his knees at the side of the road – I am not certain whether to ask charity, or only to mark his respect. He took no notice of the lad, but turning away towards me, said: 'Ah! I know well these Italians. It is the education of the monks. One does not see this among the people of the North.'

On proceeding a little farther we met two well-dressed women, who saluted him with compliments. One of them, about twenty-five years of age, told him, with great ease and gaiety, that she had been invited to the ball at Longono two days before, but, as the Emperor did not come, as was expected, she remained at home.

In place of returning by the same road, he turned off by goat-paths to examine the coast, humming Italian music, which he does very often, and seemingly quite in spirits. He expressed to me his fondness of music. Soon afterwards he told me that it all reminded him of passing the St. Bernard, and of a young peasant with whom he entered into conversation. The man did not know who he was, and spoke of the happiness of those who possessed a good house, a number of cattle, sheep, etc. He made him enumerate his greatest desires, afterwards sent for him, and gave him enough to purchase all that he had described. 'That cost me 60,000 francs.'

After his return from Longono at 8 p.m., he made General d'Alhesme and myself remain to dinner. During the meal he entered upon the operations of the armies at the conclusion of the last campaign, and continued the conversation for half an hour until we got up from table. The actions against the Allies, he said, were always in his favour, whenever the

A view of Longono with its citadel.

numbers were in any equal proportion. In the affair against the Prussians near Château Thierry he had only 700 infantry en *tirailleurs* with 2,000 cavalry, and three battalions of his Guards, in reserve against double their number. The instant these old soldiers showed themselves, the affair was decided, and yet the Prussians were infinitely the best of all the Allies. He paid many compliments to Marshal Blücher: 'That old devil always attacked me with the same vigour. If he was beaten, the moment afterwards he showed himself ready as ever for the fight.'

He then described his last march from Arcis to Brienne; said that he knew Schwartzenberg would not stand to fight him, and he hoped to destroy half his army upon his retreat. He had already taken immense quantities of baggage and guns, when it was reported to him that the enemy's army had crossed the Aube to Vitry. This induced him to halt. He would not credit it, but General Gérard assured him that he saw 20,000 infantry. He was overjoyed at this news, and immediately returned by St. Dizier, where he attacked Witzenrode's cavalry, which he considered to be the advance of Schwartzenberg's army. He drove them before him a whole day – the 25th or 26th of March – like so many sheep, at a full gallop; took from 1,500 to 2,000 prisoners, and a quantity of light artillery. To his surprise, he could not perceive any army, and again halted. His best information led him to believe that, instead of retreating to Langres, they had returned to Troyes. He marched in that direction, when he ascertained, after a loss of three days, that the Allied Armies of Schwartzenberg and Blücher had marched upon Paris. He ordered forced marches, and went forwards himself on horseback, and accompanied by his suite in carriages, day and night. Never were he and all his friends more gay. He knew that all the workmen of Paris would fight for him; and what could the Allies do against such a force, with the National Guard beside them? Barricade all the streets with casks, and it would be impossible for the enemy to advance before he arrived to the support of his party. At 8 a.m., while a few miles from Paris, he met a column of stragglers, and they mutually stared at each other. 'Who is there?' he demanded. They stopped, and seemed stupefied. 'What, the Emperor?' They informed him that they had retreated through Paris. He was still, however, confident of success. The army were burning with desire to attack the enemy, and drive them out of the capital. He knew well the composition of the Allied Army as compared with his own, and that Schwartzenberg would never hazard a battle with Paris in his rear, but would take up a defensive position on the other side. He would have engaged the enemy at various points for two or three hours, and then have marched with his thirty battalions of Guards and eighty pieces of cannon upon one part of their line. Nothing could withstand that attack; and although his inferiority of numbers could not enable him to hope for a complete victory, he would yet kill so many of the enemy, with much less loss to himself, as to force him to abandon Paris and its neighbourhood. What he would afterwards do must depend upon various circumstances.

Who could have supposed that the Senate would have dishonoured themselves by assembling under the force of 200,000 of the enemy's bayonets? – a timidity unexampled in history! And then, that Marmont, a man who owed everything to him, who had been his aide-de-camp, and attached to him for twenty-one years, should have betrayed him! Still it was but a faction which ruled Paris under the influence of a foreign force. The rest of the nation was for him. The army, almost to a man, would continue to fight for him; but with so great an inferiority of numbers it would be the certain death of many of his friends, and a civil war to last for years. He preferred rather to sacrifice his rights, although the army wished to support him in them. It was not for the sake of a crown that he had continued the war, but for the glory of his country, for plans which he now saw no prospect of realising. He wished to have made France the first nation in the world, but now it was at an end. 'I have abdicated. Now I am a dead man.' He repeated this latter expression several times.

In remarking on his confidence in his own troops, particularly his Old Guards, and the inefficiency of the Allies, he referred to me to say candidly if it was not so. 'Tell me, Combell,[54] frankly; is it not true?' I told him it was; that when with the Allies, I never yet saw a considerable portion of his army, but everyone spoke of 'the Emperor and his Guards,' as if there was something in them more than human to be dreaded – that the inferiority which he conceived of Schwartzenberg's army was justly founded. There was no confidence in themselves or in their Allies. Each party thought he did too much, and his Allies too little; and they were half beaten before they closed with the French. However, in assenting to his character of the Allies, I requested him not to include Wellington's army; and I added, that the French officers of the army from Spain did us ample justice in this respect.

He sneered at Marmont's anxiety for his life. 'Never was anything so absurd as this capitulation!' He wished to protect his own person, and so he deserted, leaving the whole of his comrades open to the surprise of the enemy, for it was his corps which covered the whole front of the army. The night before his desertion he told Napoleon, 'I can answer for my division of the army:' and so he might, for the officers and soldiers were enraged when they found what had been done. 8,000 infantry, 3,000 cavalry, and 60 pieces of cannon! 'That's history!' he said to General d'Alhesme. He enlarged also on Marmont's conduct before Paris, saying, 'Who ever heard the like? – 200 pieces of artillery in the Champ de Mars, and only six on the heights of Montmartre!' General d'Alhesme asked whether Marmont had not fought with vigour there; but he gave no answer to this question.

This was nearly what passed at table. After accompanying him to another room, he resumed the story of his campaigns, enlarging upon the politics of France, the incapacity of the Bourbons, and the antipathy of the nation to them; and continued the conversation with great agitation of manner until midnight, having then been for three hours on his legs! He seemed to regret his abdication. Had he known that it was owing to the treachery of Augereau only that that part of his army fell back behind Lyons, he would

---

54 Sic in MS., apparently to show how Napoleon pronounced the name.

have united his own army to it, even after Marmont's capitulation. He animadverted strongly upon Augereau, having met him with all the kindness of a friend. The first idea of his treachery was after separating from him on the road between Valence and Lyons. General d'Alhesme expressed his surprise at Augereau's duplicity, and asked Napoleon whether he had seen the Marshal's proclamation. Napoleon said he had not – that the spirit of the troops was such that Augereau dared not remain among them for his arrival – that many old officers and soldiers came up to him weeping, and said that they were betrayed, and requested that he would put himself at their head. (If this were so, it could only be one or two in a very quiet way, for none of the Commissioners observed it, and Napoleon only changed horses at the spot.) He had a body of 30,000 fine troops there, many of them of the army of Spain, which ought to have held its ground against the Austrians.

He again spoke of Marmont's defection; that it was reported in the morning, but he did not believe it. He rode out, and soon afterwards met Berthier,[55] who confirmed the fact from undoubted sources.

He referred to the armistice between Lord Castlereagh and Talleyrand. He thought the Allies failed in their own policy by reducing France so much, for it would hurt the pride of every man in France. The French people might have been left much more without any risk, and without being on an equality with several other Powers. They had no longer any fleet or colonies. A peace could not restore either ships or St. Domingo. Poland no longer remained to them, nor Venice. These were aggrandisements to Russia and Austria. Spain, which was the natural enemy of Great Britain, even more so than France, was now incapable of doing anything as an ally. If to these sacrifices was added that of a disadvantageous treaty of commerce with England, the people of France would not continue tranquil under it – 'not for six months after the foreign Powers leave Paris.' He then remarked that already a month had passed, and the King of France had not yet come over to the people who had placed him on the throne. England, he said, did now as she pleased; the other Powers were nothing in comparison, 'For twenty years at least no Power can make war against England and she will do as she likes.' Holland would be entirely subservient to her. The armistice gave no information as to the ships at Antwerp, or in the Texel. 'The brave

55 Marshal Louis Alexandre Berthier, 1753–1815, was Napoleon's capable chief of staff.

Verhuell[56] still holds out.' He enumerated the ships he had in each of these ports, and besides them, in three or four years, he would have had three hundred sail of the line. 'What a change for France!' He continued in this strain; upon which I said, 'But we do not know why your Majesty has wished to annihilate us!' He laughed, and replied, 'If I had been Minister of England, I should have tried to make her the greatest Power in the world.'

May 10.

Napoleon rode nearly to the summit of the highest hill above Porto Ferrajo, from whence we could perceive the sea in four different quarters, and apparently not an English mile in a straight line to each, from the centre where we stood. After surveying the scene for some time, he turned round to me and smiled; then shaking his head, he observed, 'Eh! my island is very little.'

On the top of this hill is a small chapel, and a house where a hermit resided until his death. I remarked that it would require more than common devotion to induce persons to attend service there. 'Yes;' Napoleon said, 'here the priest can talk as much nonsense as he likes.'

This day, during dinner, General Drouot reported the arrival of some vessels, one of them having on board an aide-de-camp of the King of Naples, who had been sent to Marseilles in charge of Frenchmen on Murat[57] declaring war, and was now returning to Naples. Although General Drouot twice repeated the fact of the Neapolitan vessel having arrived, Napoleon would take no notice, but kept on speaking of the British frigate. This shows that he wishes any communication he may hold with the King of Naples to be unknown.

The Austrian General Stahremberg, who has come from Leghorn to Piombino for the purpose of taking possession of that place, as well as of Lucca, on the part of the Grand Duke of Tuscany, informs me that Count

---

56 On the Russians, under Bulow, overrunning Holland in November 1813, Admiral Verhuell, Dutch by birth but a naturalised Frenchman, threw himself into the forts of the Texel, and only surrendered them by express order of Louis XVIII. He had previously shown his fidelity to Napoleon in 1805, by bringing the Dutch flotilla in safety from Dunkirk to Ambleteuse, near Boulogne, although exposed all the way to the attacks of the British cruisers under Sir Sidney Smith. When the throne of Holland was offered to Louis Napoleon, Verhuell formed one of the deputation, and was appointed Minister of Marine. In the 'Almanach de la Cour' of 1819, his name appears among the 'Grande-Croix' of the Legion of Honour Promotion du 11 juin 1806, M. le comte Verhuell, vice-amiral.

57 Marshal Murat, 1767-1815, was King of Naples and married to Napoleon's sister Caroline. Napoleon had created him king of the southern Italian kingdom in 1808 but Murat had changed sides in 1814 to save his crown. His position was not clear in 1814 as the Allies were considering restoring the Bourbon royal family of Naples.

Clam, the Austrian ADC who was sent to notify Napoleon's arrival at Elba, was charged with letters to the King of Naples and the Viceroy of Italy. He opened them both, and they ran in the same terms as follows: 'The Emperor Napoleon has the honour to inform the King of Naples, and the Viceroy of Italy, that he has arrived in the island of Elba. It would give him pleasure to hear from them.'

I cannot account for General Koller's having concealed the fact of these letters having been sent, as we were in hourly communication, and it was reciprocally arranged, among the four Commissioners at Fontainebleau, that every occurrence and conversation should be equally made known to each of us.

While General Koller was here, Napoleon never lost an opportunity of endeavouring to point out that Austria had mistaken her own policy in joining against France in a coalition, which would strengthen Russia, and compromise the safety of Austria.

May 11.

At breakfast Napoleon told Bertrand that he had a few thousand livres at Venice. 'It remains to be seen whether my good father-in-law will give them up.'

In talking of sieges I remarked that a regular fortification did not seem so difficult of escalade if it had not a wet ditch, or some other physical obstacle. If the attacking party was in sufficient force to make various attacks, and the defending party not very strong in proportion to the extent of the works, probably one or two of the attacks would succeed. The main breach appeared to me capable of being made the strongest point at all times, and therefore the difficulties might be considered to remain very much in their original state.

Napoleon replied: 'With enough guns, a good commander, and good troops, an escalade cannot fail to succeed.

If the attacking party keep up the fire with a great many small mortars upon the breach, all the defences and retrenchments on the other side ought to be so completely destroyed that no one could show himself. Your engineers showed ignorance of this at Badajoz, for the breaches had *complete* defences when you made your assault; this ought never to be.

If you place a great many mortars that throw shells,' (I think he said 60 mortars), 'it is impossible that they can keep on working, and the breach ought to be so complete, that the soldiers can mount easily to the assault.'

Napoleon entered into a long conversation with General Drouot, who was with Villeneuve in Sir Robert Calder's action, as to that Admiral's operations.[58] General Drouot said that he did not want either zeal or talents, but he was extremely nervous, and impressed with a great fear of the British navy; that, after the action, he was entreated by all his officers to pursue the British squadron and re-engage them, having a superiority of numbers.

May 12-14.

Napoleon has frequently spoken to me of the invasion of England, and stated that he never intended to make the attempt without a superiority of fleet to protect the flotilla.[59] This superiority would have been obtained for a few days by leading our fleet out to the West Indies, and suddenly returning. If they arrived three or four days before ours in the Channel, it would be sufficient. The flotilla would immediately push out accompanied by the fleet, and the landing would take place on some part of the English coast. As he should march immediately to London, he should prefer landing on the coast of Kent; but this must depend upon wind and weather. He would place himself at the disposal of the naval officers and pilots, so as to land the troops wherever they thought they could arrive with the greatest security and in least time. He had 100,000 men in all. Each of the flotilla had her own boats to land her men. Artillery and cavalry would have soon

---

58 At Portsmouth, Nelson at length found news of the combined fleet. Sir Robert Calder, who had been sent out to intercept their return, had fallen in with them on the 22nd of July [1805], sixty leagues west of Cape Finisterre. Their force consisted of twenty sail of the line, three fifty-gun ships, five frigates, and two brigs: his, of fifteen line-of-battle ships, two frigates, a cutter, and a lugger. After an action of four hours, he had captured an eighty-four and a seventy-four, and then thought it necessary to bring-to the squadron, for the purpose of securing their prizes. The hostile fleets remained in sight of each other till the 26th, when the enemy bore away.' – Southey's *Life of Nelson*, ch. ix p. 318.

59 *Edinburgh Review*, No. 258, October, 1867, Art. I. 'Napoleon Correspondence', p. 337. 'During the whole month of August, 1805, Napoleon remained at the camp of Boulogne, awaiting impatiently the arrival of Admiral Villeneuve from Spain and Ganteaume from Brest with their respective squadrons. The presence of the two Admirals in the Channel, with the combined fleets of Spain and France, would be sufficient, in the opinion of the Emperor, to protect the passage and landing in England of his invading army. But while Napoleon was waiting at Boulogne, Villeneuve, instead of joining Ganteaume at Brest, and from thence making sail with him for the Channel, had gone to Cadiz. When he left that port in October he was destined, as everybody knows, to encounter Nelson and suffer defeat at Trafalgar. Now let us see how events appear in the correspondence. We find there twelve letters for one single day, August 22, 1805, six of which are addressed to Decrès, the Minister of Marine, though he was at Boulogne at the time, within two miles of his master One of the letters is addressed to Ganteaume at Brest. It contains an order to appear in the Channel as soon as possible with Villeneuve and their combined forces, and ends thus: 'Come here for we shall revenge six centuries of insult and shame. My soldiers and sailors have never exposed themselves to so many risks'.

followed, and the whole would have arrived in London in three days. He armed the flotilla merely to deceive the English, and lead them to suppose that he intended them to fight their way across the Channel.

I told him that we expected to be treated with great severity in case of his succeeding, and many of us to be transported to France. I also asked him what he proposed to do after arriving in London. He replied that it was difficult to answer that question, for a people with spirit and energy like the English was not subdued even by taking possession of their capital. He would certainly have separated Ireland from Great Britain, and the occupation of the capital would have been a deathblow to our funds, credit, and commerce.

He asked me to tell him frankly whether we were not alarmed at his preparations for invasion. I told him that the Ministers, as well as the army and navy, viewed them far more seriously than other persons, but never expected that he would be able to subdue us. We knew how confident he and the French were, the more from their successes against the people on the Continent, and that a regular army had a great superiority over inexperienced militia and volunteers; but that the greater part of the people in England were of the opinion that nothing could overcome the latter, fighting for their homes and families. I also told him that he was not aware of the numerous casualties attending an expedition by sea. This he would not admit. He had made all his calculations, and reduced his landing to a perfect certainty. After that it was like any other operation. I told him that many thought he intended first to take Dover, and establish himself there as a sort of *tête-de-pont*. He said he had no such plan. To land soon and march at once to London was the only plan he had formed.

I told him that many were of opinion he never intended to attempt an invasion of England at all; that it was merely to intimidate our Ministers, to shake our credit, and prepare his army for other operations which were thereby masked. Others thought he was glad of the excuse to march against the Austrians, being convinced an invasion was impracticable. He denied this, and said he certainly intended to put his plans into execution, being only diverted from them by the Austrians.

May 15.

The feeling of the inhabitants had previously been very inimical to the late Government of France, and personally to Napoleon, so that he certainly required the French troops for his protection, until his Guards arrived from France. My present information induces me to believe that the spirit of dislike towards Napoleon has subsided. The *éclat* given to him on landing, by the salute of His Britannic Majesty's frigate, and other marks of attention and protection which he has evidently sought for all along, on purpose to make an impression on the minds of the people, have contributed materially to the change of feeling. The principal inhabitants have also been impressed with the opinion, that the possession of the island by Napoleon will afford them extraordinary resources and advantages; which opinion has extended itself to all classes, and they ascribe to his residence the communications which have already been opened with the mainland.

May 16.

I inquired of Count Bertrand the history of the Order of the Three Golden Fleeces – *l'Ordre des Trois Toisons d'Or*. He told me that it was never carried into effect – in consequence of the Emperor's last marriage – for fear of giving offence to Austria. The Duke of Burgundy had first instituted the Order, and his daughter married into the family of Austria, who kept it up. It was afterwards established in Spain after the War of Succession. Napoleon thought France had a prior right to either Austria or Spain, and therefore meant to institute it with an inscription commemorating his entry twice into Vienna and once into Madrid; from which he termed it 'Les *Trois* Toisons'. He intended to have established the Order in every regiment. No person could receive it unless he had been wounded three times in three different actions.

In the evening of this day a drawing-room salon was held at Napoleon's house. About fifty or sixty females assembled in their best dresses, and placed themselves on each side of the saloon in chairs, with the gentlemen standing behind them. When Napoleon entered they stood up. Accompanied by the chief of the National Guard and the *Prefet*, he went round the whole party, asking a question of each female after her name was announced if unmarried, as to her father; if married, how many children she had. After this farce was played off he spoke to two or three of the gentlemen who were nearest him at the end of the room, and at last walked off, apparently impressed with the ridiculous nature of the scene. The ladies were then handed off by their beaux. I recognised close to me a young girl, in company with her two sisters, whom I had seen at their house a few days before, having employed them to work embroidery upon a uniform coat.

The wives of the two French Generals were there, but those of several other French *employés* are reserved for a similar invitation some days

Napoleon's court on Elba, a French satirical print.

following. This has given great offence to the latter. They say that the inhabitants of Elba are very jealous of their receiving places in the new administration of the island, and that Napoleon is forgetful of his former friends. This neglect seems inconsistent, if he hopes to resume his influence in France.

A Council of State has been formed, consisting of the twelve principal inhabitants, Generals Bertrand and Drouot, and the *Intendant-General.*

There are six officers of the rank of captain and subaltern, as orderly officers (*officiers d'ordonnance*), two of whom are on duty daily. If Napoleon walks or rides abroad, they accompany him, and one always sleeps at his door, 'in case of despatches arriving during the night'.

Four chamberlains are named, consisting of the mayors of Porto Ferrajo and Rio, the commandant of the National Guard, and another principal inhabitant of the island.

All the soldiers composing the garrison of Elba, who are not Frenchmen, such as Tuscans, Italians, etc., have been discharged, and sent to Piombino. General Duval likewise sailed for Marseilles last week with the small remainder of the French garrison, excepting the gunners, who remain here until the arrival of the Guards, who reached Savona upon the 13th. From thence they are to be conveyed to Elba in transports sent out from Genoa this day by Sir E. Pellew. The military of the island will ultimately consist of the 600 volunteers of the French Guards, and 1,200 of a sort of militia, called the *Corps Franc*, which formerly existed. One half of this corps is to be on permanent duty, receiving daily pay; the other half will parade on Sunday only.

May 17.

HMS *Undaunted*, Captain Usher, sailed for Frejus today, to bring back the Princess Pauline.

Napoleon told me that, in his opinion, the Russian Army has never recovered from its losses at the battle of Borodino, where he killed an immense number of their best troops – 50,000 of them.

In speaking of some of his successes against the Allies in the last campaign, with very inferior forces, he told me smiling, with an air of triumph, 'I have commanded in eighty-five pitched battles, and more than six hundred combats.'

May 18.

Napoleon went upon a tour of the greatest part of the island, accompanied by two chamberlains, two officers of ordnance, one captain of gendarmes, the *intendant-général* and mayor, the president of the lawcourt and his secretary, General Bertrand, a lieutenant of the British Navy, the Austrian aide-de-camp, and myself. We visited, among other places, Marchiana di Marina, where there was a *Te Deum*.

May 19.

Visited Marchiana, Pogio, Campo, and a chapel of the Virgin on the summit of a hill. At each of these four places we had Divine Service. At dinner Napoleon said to me, 'You now go so often to church that you will become devout.'

During all these visits he was received with firing of musketry and cannon, triumphal arches with inscriptions, processions of priests bearing a canopy, and accompanied by young girls and children strewing flowers, who led him into the church. He breakfasted and dined with half a dozen select persons. In the evening there was a ball, which however he did not attend.

May 20.

To an island, Pia Nosa, which Napoleon took possession of as a dependency of Elba. He carried two horses with him, and rode out at two different times to examine every part of the island. We dined altogether on the grass under a sail, he at one extremity, seated at a small table with his hat on.

In returning he visited a small rock about a musket-shot from the harbour of Pia Nosa. He was informed that the *Sea-Horse* frigate, when she attacked this place, had mounted two guns upon the summit. He attempted to ascend it, but after getting up half-way, although assisted occasionally both by the lieutenant of the Navy and myself, was obliged to desist. Indefatigable as he is, his corpulency prevents him from walking much, and he is obliged to take the arm of some person on rough roads.

We left Pia Nosa at sunset, supped at Campo, and arrived at Porto Ferrajo after midnight.

May 21.

The valet, sent in the *Curaçoa* on the 9th, charged with a letter for the Viceroy of Italy, returned here some days ago. He told me that he did not think it consistent with his own personal safety to proceed further than Genoa, having been advised to change his dress, and not inform who he was. He had therefore gone on to Leghorn, and returned here, bringing back the letter for Beauharnais. I suspect that part of his mission was to obtain information with respect to furniture in a palace near Leghorn (public property), which had been placed at Napoleon's disposal, and which he had requested Captain Usher to allow one of his officers to convey here in the British frigate. With this demand Captain Usher and myself did not judge it advisable to comply.

I have reason to believe that a Neapolitan officer has been here privately; for a person in that uniform was seen to enter Napoleon's house about two weeks ago, and from my not being able to trace him, it appears that pains have been taken to conceal the circumstance.

I had already remarked the early anxiety which Napoleon evinced to place himself in communication with Murat and Beauharnais, and shall direct my attention to it.

In a conversation with General Bertrand, in which he vaunted the great qualities of Napoleon, he, without any hint on my part, said that Napoleon was not sanguinary, but acted solely from motives of patriotism; that the death of the Duc d'Enghien was not from personal enmity, but was necessary to secure his crown; and that similar steps had been taken by other sovereigns at all periods. I made no reply. General Bertrand then commented upon Napoleon's military genius; that nothing could withstand the rapidity of his movements and the justness of his combinations, by which he assembled his corps in the rear of his enemy without giving him time to oppose the unexpected attack; that the same manoeuvre took place at Jena and several other of his principal actions.

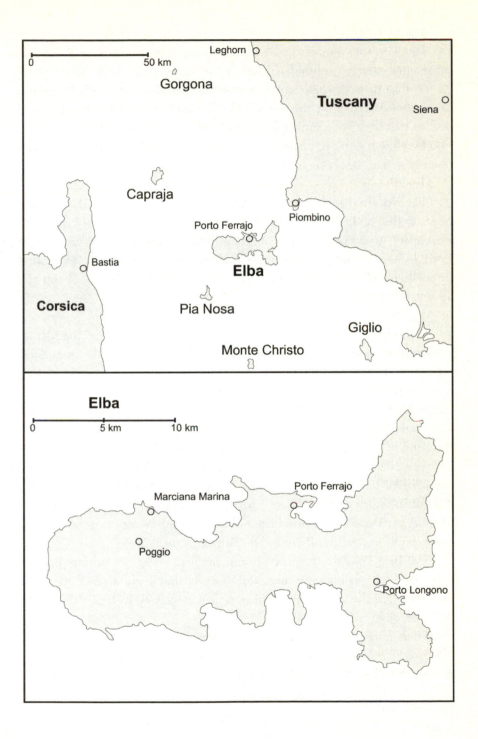

May 22.

Napoleon told me that he had taken Malta by a *coup de main*;[60] that the inhabitants were so intimidated 'by the name of those republicans, man-eaters', that they all took refuge within the fortifications, with cattle and every living animal in the island. This created so much confusion and dismay, that they were incapable of opposition.

He requested me to write to the consul at Algiers, to secure the respect due to his flag, agreeably to the treaty.

May 23.

I have received a letter from the Admiral, dated Genoa, May 19, in which he states that he had sent transports to Savona for the Guards of Napoleon. He expects to be off this place in a few days, on his voyage to Sicily, with Lord William Bentinck on board. I shall take that opportunity of waiting upon them, to give every information in my power, and to obtain the advantage of their counsel.

May 24.

Four officers of the 20th Dragoons, of whom two were in the former uniform of their regiment, were presented to Napoleon by me. After separating from them he remarked this difference, and I informed him that great changes had taken place in the British uniforms, which were generally ascribed to the Duke of Cumberland. He told me that at Tilsit he was surprised to find the minute attention which the Emperor Alexander and the King of Prussia gave to uniforms. They counted the number of buttons upon his coat, and knew more concerning the French uniforms than he did himself. 'All these changes cause much useless expense to the officers, and tire out the spirit of the soldiers. I have never troubled myself with that sort of thing. At Potsdam I found in the library at least twenty caps of different kinds, brought together there by the King of Prussia.'

HM brig *Swallow*, Captain James, arrived. After presenting him to Napoleon, I acquainted the latter with the fact that many of the ships of the fleet were already sent home. 'Ah! now it is necessary to lessen the public debt', he observed, laughing.

When I informed him that some regiments were about to be sent to America,[61] he inquired whether it was intended to conquer a part of the American States. I told him that perhaps our Ministers might consider it right

---

60 June 12, 1798, the island being then under the dominion of the Knights of the Order of St. John of Jerusalem.

61 Three regiments of Wellington's army, the 4th, 44th, and 85th, were embarked at Bordeaux on the 2nd of June [1814].'– Alison, *History of Europe*, vol. x. ch. lxxvi.

to add to our possessions in Canada. He observed that he thought it probable they would take possession of Louisiana, as a barrier against any encroachment which the Americans might make from that side upon the Spanish colonies, and in view of disturbances which might facilitate such possession.

May 25.

Arrived HMS *Undaunted*, Captain Usher. He states that, on his arrival at Frejus, he found that the Princess Pauline had some days before sailed for Naples, with a Rear-Admiral of the King of Naples' Navy. The *Curaçoa* was anchored at Nice, and Captain Tower had gone by land to Frejus for the same purpose (to convey the Princess to Elba), but he also was too late.

In passing the forts the frigate was hailed, to know whether the Princess Pauline was on board.

Captain Usher, Captain James, and myself went up to Napoleon's house, where we found him with a chessboard playing with General Bertrand. The two chamberlains were looking on apparently very sulky. Those two men were interrupted from attending to their private affairs, or being with their families, for 1,200 livres a year.

Napoleon only asked two or three formal questions of Captain Usher, when he invited him and me to walk with him, and passed through several apartments to the garden. As it was very dark and rainy, incidentally he would not have trusted himself there with everyone, he returned to the house, and went into his bedchamber.

He then inquired with great eagerness, What was the news? What was happening in France? What said the people at Frejus? Did he see any French troops, or troops of the Allies? One question was scarcely answered before it was succeeded by another.

Captain Usher stated that there had been riots at Nice between French and Austrian officers; that many persons at Frejus inquired anxiously for His Majesty; that some commercial arrangements were going on, in order to give France the advantage of the duties immediately; and that the manufacturers of France had made representations with regard to the encouragement wanting to them, which proved the justice of HM's statements on that subject, and the observations he had often made. He showed the strongest exultation at all this, and chuckled with joy.

Captain Usher informed him of the remark of the King of France, that he did not expect any war, but that if there was, goutified as he was, he would put himself at the head of his marshals. He laughed heartily. 'Ha! ha! The marshals and the army will find themselves well commanded.'

Napoleon inquired whether the Prince Regent was coming to Paris, and on being informed that it was understood to be his own desire, but that the consent of Parliament had not yet been obtained, he said, 'Oh! I do not think that he will come. The people of England will not be over-pleased at their sovereign having too much acquaintance with those other kings of Europe.' He inquired whether Lord Castlereagh was still in Paris, and whether the Parliament had yet assembled?

Captain Usher remarked that he thought the people of France had shown great ingratitude towards him. He said, 'Oh! they are a fickle people.'

Captain Usher informed him that Antwerp was occupied by a British garrison. 'Ah! you will find there 40 vessels, and 4,000 pieces of cannon.' I told him that it would be decided at the general treaty, what was to become of Antwerp. The possession would only be for the moment. He replied, smiling, 'Oh! They are yours. They are in your hands.'

Captain Usher said that, at the peace, France would only retain thirteen ships of the line and twenty frigates. Napoleon remarked that all the other Powers were increased, while France was now reduced beyond all proportion. 'But even that is not doing such a wrong to the nation as their dishonour in receiving a king from their enemies!'

When informed that there was a misunderstanding about the laurels worn in France by the Allies, and that they had been taken out by order of Alexander in presence of the King of France – he laughed with a contemptuous smile, and spat on the floor, adding that certainly that settled the question. 'But what do these laurels of the Austrians mean? They wore them always in Italy, at the very moment when I have beaten them, and driven them away in every direction.'

Captain Usher told him that the people at Frejus said, no one believed the frigate had carried him to Elba. I remarked that the officers of the Navy sent from Toulon said the same. He laughed, and inquired what they thought had become of us? Did they suppose we had carried him to England? Captain Usher told him that the people of Frejus said we had seduced him, for he preferred going in our frigate. He took this in good part. 'What! did they say I had now become an Englishman?'

On it being remarked that he had many adherents still in France, he said 'Oh! the Emperor is dead. I am no longer anything.' However, immediately afterwards he told us, that not one of his Guards had deserted him; that at Lyons hundreds of persons had gone out to meet them; and that the Austrians found it prudent to be under arms.

He was extremely inquisitive as to the force sent to America. When Captain Usher told him that 25,000 men were sent from Lord Wellington's army, and that the Americans had lost in him their best friend, he asked whether it was intended to subjugate them entirely, for such a force could not be meant only to oblige them to make peace. He again expressed his opinion, that our Ministers intended to take Louisiana and Florida.

Napoleon, as usual, blended his observations with something amusing. He asked, for instance, what the old King of England would now say to the new American war? Was he in such a state as to reflect upon it? If he was, no doubt he would exult at the humiliation of the Americans.

He asked whether there were any accounts from Corfu; and whether we had not sent an expedition against it?[62] He had certainly heard so, or supposed so, for he affected to ask the question with an assurance of our conviction that such an expedition had taken place.

The French frigate *Dryade* and the brig *Inconstant* arrived here today from Toulon. The former will return, but the brig remains, conformably to the treaty.

May 26.

This morning, at 6 a.m., Napoleon went quite unexpectedly on board of the French frigate *Dryade*, and the crew hailed him with cries of 'Vive L'Empereur!' This, I am told, placed the captain in a very awkward situation. It was not a visit to the captain personally, for he had anchored on the preceding afternoon, and then Napoleon declined seeing him, when he waited upon him, until the following morning at 10 a.m. So that it was certainly done to try the disposition of the Navy, and to keep up a recollection of him in France.

Napoleon also visited the British frigate *Undaunted*, and made a speech to the crew. He thanked them for the good-will with which they had performed their duties during the voyage, said that he felt himself under obligations to them for the period he had been on board, which he had passed so happily, and that he wished them every success and happiness. He sent them, in the course of the day, 1,000 bottles of wine and 1,000 dollars, and presented Captain Usher with a box containing his portrait set in diamonds. Napoleon speaks most gratefully to everyone of the facilities

---

62 'In 1807, General Berthier, with a French force of 17,000 men, arrived at Corfu, and drove out the Russians, or, as some say, occupied it under the connivance of Alexander; he was shortly after relieved by General Donzelot, who commanded until the arrival of the British in 1814, when Corfu surrendered to our arms on conditional terms.' – Montgomery Martin, *Hist. of British Colonies*, vol v. ch. iii.

which have been granted to him by the British Government; and to myself personally he constantly expresses the sense he entertains of the superior qualities which the British nation possesses over every other.

Five British transports arrived here this morning from Savona, with about 750 volunteers of Napoleon's Guards, his horses and baggage.

Today I informed General Bertrand that, in case either Napoleon himself or others might ascribe any underhand motive to my remaining here, I was ready to quit the island at once, should such be his wish; that I had only remained after the other Commissioners in order to procure for him those facilities which he had requested, through me, from the British Admiral.

After repeating my conversation to Napoleon, General Bertrand was directed to assure me that my remaining with him after the departure of the other Commissioners was indispensable for his protection and security, in obedience to Lord Castlereagh's instructions; that even after the arrival of his troops and baggage, there was another article of the treaty not fulfilled, although guaranteed by the Allied Sovereigns, and the execution of which depended entirely upon His Britannic Majesty's ships in the Mediterranean, i.e. the security of his flag against insult from the powers of Barbary; that it would be necessary for me to communicate with the Consul at Algiers and the Admiral, as soon as possible, for that object. I requested that he would address the application to me in writing, and stated that I would prolong my stay in the hope of receiving further instructions from Lord Castlereagh, not having heard from his lordship since I left Fontainebleau.

May 27.

Today I received the following note:

Note adresée au Colonel Campbell par le Comte Bertrand. Colonel Campbell is requested to be good enough to send to Algiers the flag of the island of Elba, informing the Consul of His Britannic Majesty that the Allied Powers have engaged among themselves to have that flag respected, and that it ought to be treated by the Barbary Powers upon an equality with that of France.

The presence of Colonel Campbell at Porto Ferrajo appears indispensable, seeing the great number of English ships of war, of transport, and of commerce, which come and anchor in the island.

On this occasion I can only reiterate to Colonel Campbell how much his person and his presence are agreeable to the Emperor Napoleon.

(Signed) Le Comte BERTRAND.

Porto-Ferrajo, May 27, 1814

I at once despatched a copy of the above to Lord Castlereagh, stating at the same time that I awaited his lordship's commands in regard to the prolongation of my stay.

Napoleon sometimes, in conversation with me, while remarking on public affairs, throws off all restraint, and expresses himself so openly as to leave no doubt of his expecting that circumstances may yet call him to the throne of France. He says that France is humiliated even beyond what, in his opinion, the interest of the Allies should have prescribed; that more might have been left to her with equal security towards her neighbours, and without the risk of exasperating the people; that the family of the Bourbons will be driven out in six months, on account of the disadvantageous treaty with Great Britain. In addition, the minds of the people are very unsettled. If a portion were for the Bourbons, it was only the emigrants, and persons of ancient titles and property; while the greater number of the population and the whole of the army are for himself. The Guards had received unequivocal proofs of this on the march, particularly at Lyons, where 2,000 of the inhabitants came out to welcome them. Napoleon certainly regrets that he gave up the contest, and has almost declared to me that, had he known the spirit and power of Augereau's army, and that its exertions were only paralysed by the defection of that Marshal, he would have joined it, and carried the war into Italy.

However, his ties of esteem towards all his marshals appear to have diminished. A few days ago he described to me their respective good and bad qualities. St. Cyr and Masséna ranked highest in his list. He regretted that he had not left his marshals unemployed (for they were tired of war), and sought for younger chiefs among his other generals and colonels: this, he said, was his ruin.

I have never seen a man in any situation of life with so much personal activity and restless perseverance. He appears to take so much pleasure in perpetual movement, and in seeing those who accompany him sink under fatigue, as has been the case on several occasions when I have accompanied him. I do not think it possible for him to sit down to study, on any pursuits of retirement, as proclaimed by him to be his intention, so long as his state of health permits corporeal exercise. After being yesterday on foot in the heat of the sun, from 5 a.m. to 3 p.m., visiting the frigates and transports, and even going down to the hold among the horses, he rode on horseback for three hours, as he told me afterwards, 'to tire himself out!' These details show, that if opportunities for warfare upon a great scale and for important objects do not present themselves, he is likely to avail himself of any others, in order to indulge this passion from mere recklessness. His thoughts seem to dwell perpetually upon the operations of war.

Napoleon appears very anxious to know the extent of the British forces reported to be lately sent against America. When informed by an officer of the Navy, that 25,000 men were sent from Spain, he said that this must be intended against Louisiana or Florida; that he had no doubt of a civil war in Spain, that her provinces in South America would separate from her, and that these would form a sort of barrier for Great Britain to prevent the encroachments of the United States.

Upon landing here, Napoleon's plan was to prepare a very large house in the town for his residence. He afterwards changed to a very small one, requiring much less labour, which he already inhabits. He has not made any such arrangements as evince any expectation of his being joined by Marie Louise, nor has he mentioned her name in any way.

The small island, called Pia Nosa, which Napoleon has taken possession of, is about fifteen English miles south of Elba, and has generally been considered a dependency of it. There are no inhabitants at present, but Napoleon means to place some upon it for the cultivation of grain, with a small garrison to protect them against pirates.

May 28.

Went to sea with Captain James, of HM brig *Swallow*, in hopes of seeing Lord William Bentinck and Admiral Sir Edward Pellew, as the latter had directed him to look out for him near Porto Ferrajo in the beginning of June, but unfortunately they passed on their way from Genoa to Sicily without being seen by us.

May 29-31.

Upon my return to Porto Ferrajo, I found at anchor the Neapolitan frigate, *Letitia*, which had arrived the day before with Napoleon's sister Pauline, wife of Prince Borghese, and three persons of her household. They had been forced to put into Villa Franca, near Nice, soon after their departure from Frejus, and had come direct from thence. After remaining for twenty-four hours at Elba, they sailed for Naples. They were at pains to state that the Neapolitan frigate had been sent by the Queen of Naples of her own accord for her sister. Napoleon went on board the frigate on her arrival, when he was received with cries of 'Vive L'Empereur!' and the yards were manned.

The Mulini Palace, Porto Ferrajo. Napoleon moved in on May 21, 1814.

The grand salon of the Mulini Palace.

June 1.

M. Ricci, who was formerly British vice-consul at the port of Longono, under an appointment from Mr. Davenport, consul-general at Naples, has lately returned here, and has applied for permission to resume his functions. He has produced unquestionable testimony favourable to his character, as well as proof of his having suffered oppression at the hands of the French Government in consequence of the appointment he formerly held, being thus reduced from affluence to poverty, with a numerous family. After very minute inquiries relative to these circumstances, I submitted his name to Lord Castlereagh for the appointment of consul in the island of Elba.

June 2.

A British merchant-vessel from Malta, bound to Leghorn, was captured by a privateer of Porto Ferrajo, and brought in there on April 14. As soon as the communications with Elba were opened after Napoleon's arrival, the Board of Health at Leghorn applied to the public authorities at Elba to send over the captured vessel to perform quarantine. A lazaretto had been established at Leghorn for many years, and it is one of the few places where persons or property arriving from ports infected with the plague can be purified. Instead of complying, the cargo was disembarked, and placed in a retired part of the fortifications close to the sea, under a guard. The governor of Leghorn, General Spannochi, who is also president of the Board of Health, accordingly put Elba into a quarantine of twenty-five days, which still continues; and this has been followed by Genoa, Marseilles, and Corsica, and probably by every other port of the Mediterranean.

After Corsica had put Elba in quarantine for ten days in deference to Leghorn (as is the custom with all minor places), Napoleon retaliated by laying the same upon Corsica, but withdrew it in a few days. His alleged motive was a fever which raged there, but of which no other person ever heard.

Napoleon, a few days after his arrival here, at the suggestion of some person devoid of reflection and information, selected a spot in the harbour of Porto Ferrajo, in an insulated position, and directed it to be immediately prepared for a public lazaretto, alleging that vessels would come there in preference to Leghorn to be purified by quarantine, as the locality was so favourable; that this would occasion a great assemblage of vessels, and consequently become a considerable source of revenue. He therefore ascribes the measures pursued by Leghorn as arising from jealousy of his projects, and from commercial intrigue. So General Bertrand and he himself told me. And he persists in refusing compliance with long-established practice, although it cuts off his communication with every other part of the world, except by clandestine means, to his own loss and inconvenience, as well as that of every other person in this island.

June 3.

At Napoleon's request I went to Leghorn in the *Swallow* brig, to convey an application from the *Intendant-Général* of Elba to the Board of Health. This I was enabled to do under the usual precautions, without landing. From their explanations and those of the British men-of-war stationed there, I ascertained, to my perfect conviction, that Napoleon's suspicions of commercial intrigue are without the slightest foundation; that it is against the interest of Leghorn to be deprived of open communication, for the supplies of every kind required by Elba are derived from thence. Leghorn too, being a mercantile town of considerable importance, the credit given by every other port in the world to the honour and probity of the Board of Health is in proportion to that consequence. And therefore Porto Ferrajo cannot vie with Leghorn until its commercial importance becomes superior, and the lazaretto shall be transferred there in accordance with the unanimous opinion of the mercantile world. I did not interfere in the question further than by affording the means of communication between the two parties, and ascertaining for my own information, from the best sources, the real state of the case, which I candidly submitted to Napoleon on my return.

Since that, General Bertrand has assured me that Napoleon never interfered in the matter, leaving it to the public authorities to act according to their judgment and experience. This, I trust, may be considered as a proof of his being inclined to concede.

June 4.

This being the anniversary of His Majesty's birthday, it was celebrated by the two captains of the British ships, *Curaçoa* and *Swallow*, in the harbour of Porto Ferrajo. A royal salute was fired, the yards were manned, and three cheers given. The royal standard was hoisted on the main, the flag of Louis XVIII on the fore, and that of Elba on the mizen. The French frigate *Dryade*, which was in harbour for the purpose of conveying General d'Alhesme and the remainder of the garrison to France, displayed the British ensign at the fore, and Napoleon's brig did the same during the whole of the day. In the evening a ball was given on board the *Curaçoa*, where Generals Bertrand, Drouot, and Cambronne, of Napoleon's household, as well as the principal inhabitants, attended. About nine at night, during the festivities, it was announced that Napoleon was approaching in his barge. He remained for an hour, and visited every part of the ship.

June 5-12.

Napoleon continues in the same state of perpetual movement, busy with constant schemes, none of which, however, tend to ameliorate the condition of his subjects. He has ordered several pieces of road to be improved for the conveyance of his carriage, without any other object, and new ones to be executed, limiting the period to a particular hour by which they were to be finished, and appropriating no funds for the payment of the peasants who have been hastily assembled on the requisition of the mayors.

He has even employed his own Guards, who came from France, on fatigue duties, such as destroying houses for the improvement of his own residence, and working upon the pavement of the streets. This has given great disgust.

He has demanded of the inhabitants to pay, in the course of this month, the contributions from September 1, 1813, to May 1, 1814. This has occasioned unusual outcry and supplications, but without avail. Such is the poverty of the inhabitants, that most of them will be obliged to sell their houses, furniture, and clothing, in order to raise money.

In riding lately near a village, I saw a collection of the inhabitants insulting the tax-gatherer with shouting and the sound of horns. He has been informed that he will be again sent back very soon to levy the contributions, and that 100 of the Guards are to accompany him, to live upon the inhabitants at free quarters until the required sum is paid.

Napoleon appears to become more unpopular on the island every day, for every act seems guided by avarice and a feeling of personal interest, with a total disregard to that of others. The inhabitants perceive that none of his schemes tend to ameliorate their situation, and that while the blessings of peace have restored to their neighbours commerce, a ready sale for the produce of their labours, exemption from contributions and from military service, they derive none of these advantages by Napoleon's arrival among them. The cries of 'Vive L'Empereur!' are no longer heard, notwithstanding the study to give popular effect to every movement, and the formation of a court from among the principal inhabitants. People exclaim against his oppression and injustice, so much so that if his restlessness is not tempered by more discretion, nothing but the military force of his Guards will prevent the inhabitants from rising against him.

I am likewise of the opinion that even the attachment of his Guards to him diminishes daily. They will soon tire of having expatriated themselves; and as all the officers were confident of his being called to the throne of France in a very few months, they perceive daily that there is less prospect of realising the expectations formed upon these grounds. One of the private soldiers some days ago said in my hearing, upon being asked how he liked the island of Elba, 'It's a good hole for a fox'; another said it was a desert; a third, who was destined to go to the uninhabited island of Pia Nosa with the first detachment, said to me that, rather than remain there according to Napoleon's scheme (marrying and cultivating a piece of ground), he would blow his brains out. This expedition, consisting of thirty men of the Guards and ten of the Free Corps, was sent from Elba upon the 9th instant, with several pieces of cannon, one mortar and ammunition, and with fascines to form fortifications in case of an attack from the Algerian pirates, which is to be apprehended.

M. Pons, a Frenchman, who formerly served in the army as a *chef de bataillon*, has for some years past held the management of the iron mines in Elba, the produce of which netted annually to Government about 350,000 livres. His appointment, his character, and talents justly entitled him to the first consideration in the island. He paid every tribute of respect to Napoleon upon his arrival, and having a wife and children, it was his intention to have remained in the administration of the mines until the state of France was more established. But he is so disgusted with Napoleon's proceedings, that he now intends to return at once.

Napoleon applied to M. Pons for payment of money derived from the mines previous to his arrival. This demand was evaded, then declined, and afterwards peremptorily refused. The conversation became so loud that it was heard in the adjoining rooms. At length M. Pons told him: 'Sire, this money is not at my disposal; it belongs to France, and three hundred thousand bayonets shall not force me to give it into other hands.'

The poor peasants employed at the mines work until midday, and, having small wages, are allowed patches of ground, which they cultivate for the rest of the day upon their own account. Napoleon wished to employ them upon the roads after their labour in the mines was finished. This M. Pons refused to allow, although repeatedly urged.

Napoleon gave orders to send a vessel with iron ore to the United States of America, but this has not been executed. What renders the proposition more absurd is, that it is not iron which is exported from Elba, but the ore

Pons de L'Hérault, the administrator of the
mines at Rio.

The Robinson Crusoe of Elba, a satire
on Napoleon.

precisely in its original state. There are no furnaces for extracting and fabricating the iron, on account of the want of fuel. The wages of all the superintendents of the mines, as well as of many other persons holding inferior appointments in the island, have been reduced one-fourth, without any regard to age or other circumstances.

As the whole of the island was in revolt against the Government of France previously to Napoleon's arrival, M. Pons removed his wife and family to Porto Ferrajo, within the fortifications. Upon their return lately to their residence at the mines, the workmen and others met them in procession, strewed the road with flowers, and accompanied M. Pons to his house, which had been carefully preserved during his absence. This was reported to Napoleon, who sneeringly took notice of it the first time he saw M. Pons, and told him, 'You have been received like a monarch'. The other replied, 'As a father, Sire'. About the same time Napoleon received M. Pons and his wife to dinner, as he has done lately a few of the principal inhabitants. Madame Pons being in mourning, he inquired for whom she wore that dress. Being told for a parent, he laughed and said, 'Those are fine things.'[63]

All these circumstances were related to me by M. Pons himself, or

---

63 Napoleon, however, must eventually have succeeded in attaching M. Pons to his interests, as the name will be found amongst those of the persons who accompanied him in his escape.

derived from other sources; and I have every reason to credit them. I notice them as tending to throw light upon the character and conduct of this extraordinary man in his new situation, which do not seem to have altered the least by a change of circumstances. The more he is brought upon a level with others, and the more the opportunities of observing him, the more unfavourably does he appear.

General Drouot, a man of talent and merit,[64] who commanded the artillery of the Guards, and accompanied Napoleon here, applied some time ago for leave to resign the situation of governor, to which he was appointed on his arrival, stating in his letter that he had followed him to his retreat merely from attachment, that his income was sufficient without the emoluments of governor, and that he was desirous of prosecuting his studies. This desire has been refused, on account of which and his disapproval of the way in which matters are carried on, it is his intention to make some pretext soon for going to France. Several of Napoleon's servants have already returned to France, disgusted with the island and with their treatment. M. Pellard, the principal valet, has also left this; but as it was on good terms, with the promise of returning again, he may perhaps have been sent on some mission to Paris, which he told me was his destination. M. Gatte, apothecary to Napoleon, who accompanied us from Fontainebleau to Elba, has lately disappeared. They give out that he went to Leghorn in quarantine to purchase medicines. I shall probably be able to ascertain this.

The organisation of the military force does not keep pace with Napoleon's wishes. Most of the Free Corps of the island have either sold or lost their arms, equipment, and clothing; and very few have come forward to serve since the first inspection, upon which occasion the new terms of service were made known to them. About thirty or forty officers of the French garrison, belonging to the 35th Regiment of Infantry and the 3rd Regiment of *Étrangers*, have remained here in consequence of offers of service from Napoleon. Since their comrades left, they have been informed that they must go to Italy, or the islands adjoining, to obtain recruits, otherwise that their pay will be stopped. Some of them, who are natives of Corsica, have already gone there. Of this I have given information to General Montresor.

---

64 It is related of Drouot that 'he always carried a bible with him. It was on his person in battle, and the reading of it constituted his chief delight. He made no secret of this among the staff of the Emperor, which showed more courage than to face a battery.'

Porto Ferrajo seen from the south.

June 13.

General Bertrand showed me, in one of the French journals, a paragraph, wherein it was stated that the rank of colonel on the Continent and in Elba has been conferred upon me. I am induced to believe that this may have been copied from the *London Gazette*, and that therefore my remaining here is the pleasure of the Prince Regent, although I have not received any orders to that effect. General Bertrand remarked at the same time, that the appointment would be very agreeable to Napoleon, who continues to show it by his civilities and marks of attention.

A view of Elba from the Tuscan coast.

CHAPTER III

STATISTICS RELATING TO THE ISLAND OF ELBA
I. STATE OF THE REVENUE

1. Administration of the mines.

The only mine which is in use in the island is one of iron at Rio, opposite the coast of Italy. This is managed by an administrator, who directs the whole establishment, a treasurer, two storekeepers, and four superintendents of the workmen.

This is the most valuable source of revenue in Elba, and it nets annually the sum of 500,000 francs.

The emoluments of the persons employed are as follows:

The administrator, 15,000 francs a year, and 6,000 francs for his table, on account of expenses from travellers.

The treasurer, 4,000 francs. The two storekeepers, 1,000 francs each.

The four superintendents, 900 francs each, a year.

The other expenses consist of the wages of the workmen, who dig out the iron, and transport it to the sea, for which there are employed 400 men, with 100 horses and oxen. These workmen receive daily 1 franc 20 centimes. They labour from daylight till midday. The rest of the day is at their own disposal, and they employ it in tilling small patches of ground appropriated to their vines and vegetables. Napoleon wished to curtail this time. There are likewise 40 invalids, either superannuated, or who have been disabled at the mines. These have wages and ground, equally as if in active employment.

Loadstone is found in some parts.

2. Tuna Fisheries.

There are two fisheries of the tuna, one in Porto Ferrajo, the other near Marchiana. These net annually 24,000 francs.

3. Salt Ponds.

The only salt ponds now in use are at Porto Ferrajo. These net annually 50,000 francs. Those at Longono have not been permitted for many years, in consequence of the bad air produced by them; but Napoleon has ordered them to be re-established.

4. Contributions directes.

This is a tax paid upon the productions of the soil by every inhabitant, chiefly upon wine and oil. It nets about 25,000 francs annually. The person who levies this duty receives two per cent upon the whole sum which he collects.

6. Droits d'Enregistrement et du Timbre.

This source of revenue yields annually about 30,000 francs, and consists of sums paid for all acts and transactions which are rendered valid by a public registrar.

6. Administration sanitaire. (Administration of Health.)

This administration is under the direction of the *intendant* of the island, formerly called *sous-préfet*. In each port there are two deputies, who collect from all vessels a fixed sum, according to their tonnage. This tax nets about 16,000 francs.

7. Productions.

The chief products are wine and fruits, which are cultivated in the valleys, and on the lower slopes of the hills, for the upper parts are incapable of cultivation, being rocky, with very little soil of a poor quality. The produce in wine is, at an average, about 150,000 barrels yearly, each barrel weighing about 120 lbs. Tuscan of liquid, but too delicate for foreign exportation.

II. ADMINISTRATION

Before the arrival of Napoleon, the island was considered an arrondissement or district, directed by a *sous-préfet,* who superintended the administration, and the execution of all laws. There was a council which regulated the contributions. The *sous-préfet*'s salary was 4,000 francs annually. Since the arrival of Napoleon, the *sous-préfet* assumes the title of *intendant-general*.

III. JURISDICTION

There is a tribunal composed of a president, a procureur imperial, and two judges. The salaries of the two former are 3,000 francs a year, and of the two latter 2,000 francs each.

IV. Military Force

The Imperial Guards, who volunteered to accompany Napoleon from France, consist of about 600 infantry, with officers in proportion.

There is also a battalion composed of inhabitants of Elba, formed into five companies of 80 men each, including officers, or 400 in all. Their pay is understood to be as follows:

Major	2,000 francs a year.
Captain	1,200 francs a year.
Lieutenant	1,000 francs a year.
Second-Lieutenant	900 francs a year.

There are several officers at Longono engaged in the formation of this battalion. They are chiefly Corsicans. Five of them left Longono on June 6, for Corsica, to procure recruits. Their names are, Salerni (Captain), Moltedo (Lieutenant), Gabrielli (Lieutenant), Caviglioli (Lieutenant), Restorien (Second-Lieutenant).

The corps is to be completed to 1,000 men.

CHAPTER III

ABSTRACT

Revenue:

Iron Mines	500,000
Tuna Fisheries	24,000
Direct Contributions	25,000
Registers	30,000
Administration of Health	15,000
Salt Ponds	50,000
Total revenue	644,000

To be deducted for Public Charges:

Salary of *Intendant-Général*	4,000
Salary of President, *Procureur*, etc.	10,000

Free battalion (without men):

Chief	2,000
5 Captains at 1,200 francs,	6,000
5 Lieutenants at 1,000 francs,	5,000
5 Second-Lieutenants at 900 francs,	4,500
Total	17,500

Total expenses	31,500

If the battalion is increased to 1,000 men:

Double the pay of officers	17,500
Pay of 1,500 men, (in round numbers, including the Guards,) with rations, but without clothing	1,095,000
Total	1,144,000

The pay of the Guards is 30 sous, or 1.5 franc a day, and, with bread, say in all, 2 francs.

In the preceding estimate, the pay of three Generals, and all the officers of the Guards, the chamberlains of the household, etc., are not included.

CHAPTER IV

FLORENCE – COUNT STAHREMBERG – ROME – INTERVIEWS WITH THE POPE –
RETURNS TO LEGHORN – DISCOVERY OF NAPOLEON'S SECRET AGENTS –
ESCORTS MADAM MÈRE AND SUITE TO ELBA

June 30.

Florence. Having obtained an opportunity of evading the quarantine, I thought it advisable to come to Leghorn, and then to this place, in order to establish an acquaintance with Mr. Grant, the late British Vice-consul, and Mr. Felton acting *pro tempore*, for the security at once of my correspondence and for information.

I have likewise made a short detour to the baths of Lucca, on account of increasing deafness and general derangement of health, caused by the wounds in my head and back. Of late I have had an immensity of correspondence in a public way, keeping my journal to assist my memory, writing my despatches, and taking copies of them, obtaining information from a variety of parties in Italy. I have no one to assist me, and when I write long, there is a wearisome feeling which becomes very unpleasant, from the muscles in my back not having yet acquired their tone. This tour to Florence and Rome will relieve my mind, and prove a very acceptable release from the sultry confinement of Elba, besides assisting me in my public duties, which luckily do not require my banishing myself entirely in that island.

After establishing Napoleon there, according to Lord Castlereagh's instructions, I have still considered it my duty to prolong my stay, in order to judge his intentions, and not to quit Elba until directed by His Majesty's Ministers. Besides, my remaining is in compliance with Napoleon's own request, communicated to me both verbally and by means of a formal note from Count Bertrand.

Various constructions, I find, have been attached by the agents of the different Governments in Italy to my continuing at Elba after the other Commissioners. The evident restlessness of Napoleon's disposition, his plans for sending out officers to various parts of Italy in order to recruit soldiers clandestinely, there being no British Minister in Italy, and indeed scarcely a public and recognised agent between Vienna and Sicily, all this made me anxious to compare my suspicions with what information I could obtain on the Continent.

My visit here has gained me important advantages, more particularly with respect to General Count Stahremberg, of the Austrian service, who commands all the military force of Tuscany, Lucca, Piombino, etc., and who is also civil governor of all the country except Tuscany. I have found him extremely frank and perfectly unreserved. He showed me the reports which are regularly transmitted to him from Elba, so that my absence is of less consequence. He has also promised to write me if there is any particular occurrence within his command, connected with Napoleon, after my return to Elba.

The Princess Eliza and her husband General Bacchiochi, in evacuating their possessions, carried off most of the plate and furniture from several of the palaces. These were already on the road to Bologna, whither the entire family had fled, when Count Stahremberg, on his first arrival, ordered the whole to be transported back to this place, in order that the articles might be examined, verified, and restored to the several palaces, as might be found most just, to await the coming of the Grand Duke Ferdinand. After several letters had been written by the Princess Eliza, she likewise called to her aid the well known Marquis Lucchesini,[65] formerly Minister of the King of Prussia, but finding all of no avail, she set off from Bologna to Vienna in order to see the Emperor of Austria. When within three posts she was prevented from proceeding on her journey, and it is said she is gone to Gratz in Styria to visit her brother. Marshal Bellegarde was much surprised and displeased when he was informed by the Austrian General commanding at Bologna that he had permitted her to go towards Vienna. His excuse was a letter from the Empress Marie Louise to the Princess Eliza, inviting her, which the latter showed. The discarded favourites of the Bacchiochi family, who are scattered over Italy, triumphed over the other party, and gave out that the princess had been sent for by the Emperor of Austria to treat for an indemnification. At the head of the Bacchiochi party

---

65 'It is said that the first idea of the Legion of Honour arose in the breast of Napoleon on witnessing one day, from a window at the Tuileries, the admiration with which the crowd before the Palace regarded the stars and crosses worn by the Marquis Lucchesini, ambassador of Prussia, as he descended from his carriage.' – Lockhart's *Life of Napoleon*, vol. i. ch. xvii.

is the Marquis Lucchesini, who returned to Lucca, the place of his nativity, after quitting Prussia several years ago, and attached himself upon the most intimate terms to the household of that family. His son, a favourite of the Princess Eliza, accompanied her to Bologna.

Napoleon carries on a constant correspondence with his sister Eliza, as well as with Naples. Count Meyer, the Austrian Minister at Naples, lately sent to Count Stahremberg a letter from the Queen of Naples, and one from her sister the Princess Pauline, addressed to Napoleon, which they had requested him to forward. They were opened by the Count, and then sent on to their destination. They contained nothing worthy of remark, but the Count is convinced they were sent merely to blind their other correspondence, carried on through more direct and clandestine channels. Two couriers have for some time past been stationed by Napoleon at Piombino. They receive his letter-bag separately from the other sent over in the packet-boat from Elba. These couriers carry his letters to Leghorn, where his agent transmits them to their various destinations. The Count has ordered that in future Napoleon's letters shall be received by the postmaster at Piombino only, and by him transmitted to the postmaster at Leghorn, *where no doubt they will receive that inspection which is made no secret of here!*

The reports from Elba since my departure state that Napoleon continues the same sort of life as before, engaged in perpetual exercise, and busy with projects of building, which, however, are not put into execution. Many artists have been flattered by expectations of employment, and have gone over from Italy to Elba, but are now starving in quarantine. It is said Napoleon wishes to change the name of Porto Ferrajo to Cosmopoli, City of the World; an equivocal use of the ancient name Cosimopoli, so called after Cosimo, one of the Grand Dukes of Tuscany.

Count Stahremberg informed me that Murat keeps up the most active military preparations, and that he has certainly increased his army by more than 15,000 men since his return to Naples. He has several persons employed to induce the Austrians to desert, but although the fact is certain, the proof is not yet sufficient to detect these agents. A non-commissioned officer and fifteen privates, Austrians, lately deserted to him from Rome. Officers non-commissioned, and soldiers from France, Piedmont, and Italy, as well as other adventurers, are constantly passing through this place to join his army.

The public spirit in this part of Italy is not tranquil; for, notwithstanding there was an universal and violent dislike to the government of Bonaparte, the people view it now, when past, with less horror. In these States there was always an exemption from conscription; and besides, in consequence of ecclesiastical power having returned with the new order of things, many other impediments to the equal exercise of talent and privilege have been raised up. The civil governor of Tuscany is Prince Rospigliosi, a man of respectable talents and excellent private character, who was formerly chamberlain to the Grand Duke Ferdinand, but without experience in government and a bigot, a slave to religious ceremonies, and surrounded by priests. His system is to establish every regulation and institution which existed in the time of the Grand Duke, upsetting at the same time all changes which were introduced by the Queen of Etruria as well as by the Princess Eliza.[66] No provision is made for those who are removed from their situations. The Museum of Natural History, which was a private collection in the time of Ferdinand, received under the Queen of Etruria four professors to give lectures and instruction. These have received their dismissal, and no successors are to be appointed.

Priests and ecclesiastics of all descriptions have flocked here to resume their ancient customs, and claim their property. There are religious processions, church festivals and illuminations, three or four times a week, during which no labour is performed. One church contained 7,000 waxcandles of eighteen inches each in length. All orders and ages are mixed together in the crowds which throng the streets, the greater part of whom, however, attend for purposes of curiosity and intrigue. The works of Machiavelli and of several other writers, which were formerly considered improper for circulation, are again subjected to the same restrictions, and forbidden to be sold. Masonic meetings are prohibited. The masters of the different eating–houses are directed to register the names of all such inhabitants as eat articles of food forbidden on certain days by the Roman Catholic religion. All this is criticised and disliked by the greater part of the people, who remark at the same time that the

---

66 The kingdom of Etruria was carved by Napoleon, after the Treaty of Luneville, February 1801, out of the Grand Duchy of Tuscany, and bestowed upon Don Louis, eldest son of the Duke of Parma, who had married the Infanta Maria Louisa, daughter of Charles IV of Spain. In 1807, Don Louis having died in the meantime, the Queen of Etruria and her son were expelled by order of Napoleon, and the restored Grand Duchy of Tuscany was given by him to his eldest sister, the Princess Eliza, wife of General Bacchiochi, in addition to those of Lucca and Piombino.

imposts are not diminished, notwithstanding the peace and the general expectations thereby excited.

The Austrians do not appear to be well liked by the Italians, and reports are constantly set afloat with regard to the neighbouring kingdom of Naples, as well as other parts of the country, which tend to prevent confidence and tranquillity. Thus it is said, that Napoleon is to possess Sardinia as a sovereignty; that the Allied Sovereigns have agreed to restore to the Princess Eliza and the Bacchiochi family all their palaces and places of residence at Lucca; that large bodies of Austrian troops are marching in this direction from the northward, supposed to be directed against Murat; that the British and the Sicilians are immediately to unite with them in an attack upon Naples.

I propose to mention these matters in my next despatch to Lord Castlereagh, for although they are foreign to my mission, yet as there is no person accredited by His Majesty's Government in this part of Europe, I think it my duty to state to his lordship all information connected with public affairs which comes within my own knowledge. To obtain this, with the opportunity also of escaping from quarantine, was one of my motives for absenting myself for a short time from Elba, and will, I trust, appear justifiable in his lordship's eyes. The period of quarantine to be performed by vessels from Elba to Leghorn is now reduced to fifteen days.

I am also in daily hopes of receiving instructions from Lord Castlereagh, containing his pleasure as to my remaining at Elba agreeably to Napoleon's wish.

July 1.

Today I met, at the Countess of Albany's, with Lucchesini, formerly friend of Frederick the Great of Prussia, and afterwards minister to the present King. He retired to Lucca after the campaign of Jena, whether of his own accord, or driven away by the King for insincerity, I know not. He then became the chief director of the household of the Princess Eliza. The Swedish Consul proposed to introduce him to me, but I declined.

Countess Albany is the widow of the Pretender, and resides here entirely. She is a charming, clever old lady, and receives the best company for conversation every evening.

July 2-10.

Again met, at Countess Albany's, Marquis Lucchesini and his wife. He placed himself close to me, and then entered into conversation about Napoleon. He did not express any kindness towards him; observed that he was great in a battle, and, wherever he went with his troops, that point would be carried, but that in other ways there were many men more capable.

He related to me the circumstances respecting the exile of General Grouchy from Paris. One day at court he represented to the Duke de Berri the hardship of depriving himself and the other colonels of the different arms of their appointments. The Duke told him, that although the titles of colonel were given to himself and the other Princes of the Blood, yet he (Grouchy) and the other inspectors-general would be the executive persons, and enjoy all the patronage and direction. During this conversation Marshal Marmont happened to approach, and joined in the remarks made by the Duke de Berri. General Grouchy told him pointedly, that he did not address himself to him. Marmont, however, continued in the same strain; on which General Grouchy repeated his observations, adding, 'I have told you already, it is not to you I am addressing myself – you that have the contempt of the whole army.' An officer was thereupon sent from the King to inform General Grouchy, that he must know that, after the conversation which had passed, it was impossible for him to appear again at court, and therefore that he ought to quit Paris. He told the officer that this was not necessary in order to prevent a meeting between himself and Marmont: 'It is not with *him*, with such as the Marshal Marmont, that one can have a meeting.'

Lucchesini appears about fifty, a thin man, about five feet nine inches in height, with a remarkably keen eye and acute physiognomy. His wife, a Prussian, is a very majestic, fine-looking woman, apparently striving to show her dignity from fear that circumstances may have diminished it. Lucchesini told a friend of mine that it gave him great pleasure to hear that the conduct of the Prussian army was so extolled by me.

Count Stahremberg had a parade of the troops, with a *Te Deum*. After the parade they were formed into a square, and he desired one of the Hungarian officers to address them with regard to their services and conduct. On the conclusion of this harangue, he gave out a cheer for the Emperor of Austria, and then, by way of compliment, one for England.

In the evening there was a ball, in the course of which Count Stahremberg received a despatch by courier from Vienna, acquainting him that the Emperor had ordered away the Princess Eliza when close to that city, and that she was gone to Gratz in Styria.

The Swedish Consul here told me that he had seen a letter written by Prince Metternich from Paris to the Princess Eliza in the strongest terms of kindness, and assuring her of the Emperor of Austria's protection. The contents were studiously propagated by her friends.

General Boulaschov, of the Russian service, has arrived here from Naples on his way to Milan. Count Stahremberg told me he was going there in hopes to obtain from Marshal Bellegarde certain information, where a despatch would reach the Emperor Alexander. He was with Murat during the last campaign, and was directed to sign the treaty on the part of the Emperor of Russia, as soon as he should be convinced of his sincerity. He had hitherto evaded it, not being satisfied with the part which Murat had acted; and being now pressed by Murat's Ministers, he had found therein an additional reason for quitting Naples. He has left a General Tully to see what goes on. General Stahremberg himself is convinced of Murat's treachery; for, as soon as the Allies were unsuccessful in February last, he would not advance, and frequently sent officers privately to the Viceroy.

Prince Corsini has been sent for by the Grand Duke, and is ordered to proceed to Vienna immediately. He is a man much looked up to by his countrymen for his talents, and was formerly *Conseiller d'État* at Paris. Prince Molliterno Pignatelli, who accompanied the Queen of Sicily when she left that island, arrived here some days ago, and has since gone to Rome.

I met a gentleman in society here, who told me he was secretary to the Mayor of – (I could not catch the name), a small town near Florence, from whence the family of Bonaparte originated. Some years ago he occupied himself in forming a genealogical tree of them. He found that they were sprung from an ancient and noble family, but which was afterwards subdivided into several branches, and became much reduced in circumstances. One of Napoleon's ancestors transferred himself to Corsica. This gentleman had reference made to the registers there, in order to complete the tree, and he found Napoleon's name inserted as Nicholas-Charles-Baptiste Napoleon. He presented this tree to the Princess Eliza, but received no remuneration.

Two of Captain Usher's officers came here, and called upon the Commandant, desiring to know where the Empress Marie Louise was. They stated that the *Undaunted* had arrived at Leghorn for the purpose of conveying her from the coast to Elba. The same information was conveyed by the officers on board to Count Stahremberg, who wrote to me to express his surprise, as he knew nothing of it, and at the same time his chagrin, that such reports should be thereby propagated through Italy. I questioned the Admiral, who was at this time at Florence, about the matter. He appeared to have given permission to Captain Usher to receive the Empress on board if she came, but he was himself without any orders or information on the subject. After their return to Leghorn, Captain Coghlan wrote to me that the *Alcmène* would, he believed, be appointed to that duty, as Captain Fisher was going home; and he requested me to notify this to Count Bertrand.

July 11.

Arrived at Rome. Pursuing my intentions of seeing the different persons employed by His Majesty's Government in the vicinity of Elba, for the purpose of establishing secure and confidential communication with them, I came here to meet Mr. Fagan, who is employed by Lord William Bentinck. Previously to this I was afraid of entertaining unfair suspicions, and of ascribing more importance to Napoleon's restless activity than it might deserve. As his schemes begin to connect themselves so openly with the neighbouring continent, and my information from Elba is so very detailed and correct, I think the spirit of my duties will for the present be better fulfilled by not shutting myself up in quarantine. Lord Exmouth, the Admiral commanding in the Mediterranean, has, for the purposes of my mission, been pleased to attach to the Elba station His Majesty's brig *Swallow*, which enables me to communicate with all parts, and I propose to proceed to Sicily for a few days, to give Lord William Bentinck all the information in my power, and to benefit by his counsel as to my future proceedings.

Lucien Bonaparte, the brother of Napoleon, resides in this city, and Cardinal Fesch is now at his palace in company with his sister, Madame Mère. The cardinal, I understand, is not out of favour, but performs all his ecclesiastical functions.

Cardinal Mauri was refused an audience of the Pope, notwithstanding repeated applications; and then, after remaining here a short time, went off without leave or any kind of notification to His Holiness.

July 12.

Found here General Montresor, who had arrived some days before. He was brought from Corsica to Civita Vecchia by Captain Tower, of HMS *Curaçoa*, having touched at Elba and remained there one day. Captain Tower carried despatches from Napoleon to Madame Letitia, with a request that she should go in the *Curaçoa* to Elba. He then proceeded by land to Naples, where he rejoined his ship, which had gone round from Civita Vecchia. Captain Tower visited the court of Murat, and was at an evening party. He is expected daily at Rome, in order to accompany Madame Letitia to Civita Vecchia, and from thence convey her in his frigate to Elba.

July 13.

Went to Civita Vecchia, forty-nine miles distant from Rome, for the purpose of seeing Captain James, of His Majesty's brig *Swallow*.

July 14.

Returned to Rome at 5 p.m.

Captain James informs me that the sergeant-major of Napoleon's Guards had deserted from Elba to the Continent, carrying with him 3,000 francs, the chest of the corps; that M. Fayade had gone to sea lately, in the direction of Pia Nosa, when a firing was heard near that, and it was said that he had been taken by the Algerians; that, soon after the French troops arrived from Toulon in Corsica, a party of them carried off two vessels by stealth, and deserted to Elba.

Upon one occasion of Captain James's return to Elba from the Continent, General Bertrand asked for 'Colonel Campbell'. When told that I was travelling in Italy, but would be back soon, he immediately began to inform Captain James that he had had a great dispute (*bataille*) with the Emperor, and shut the door, but he was interrupted.

July 15.

Went to the palace of the Quirinal in company with Mr. Fagan. We were first led into a waiting-room, where were collected a few ecclesiastics. The door of the adjoining room was opened, upon which two of these gentlemen desired us to walk in, and accompanied us. The Pope[67] rose from his chair. We approached bowing, and he too advanced; then held out his hand, but with great modesty, while we bent down as if to kiss it. He has a very placid kindly countenance, but is apparently very feeble. He was dressed in a long white dress, like a *robe de chambre*, tied round the waist. He expressed (in Italian) great pleasure at seeing us, and then, after a few questions as to where we were from, and where we were going, went on to express great uneasiness at Bonaparte being so near Italy. We took our leave bowing low, and he escorted us a few paces.

July 16.

The King, Charles IV, and Queen of Spain, the Queen of Etruria, and the Prince of Peace, are in this city, where they have resided for some time. I sent my card to the Grand Chamberlain.

---

67 Detained a prisoner at Fontainebleau ever since 1809, Pius VII had been released in January 1813, but it was not until after Napoleon's abdication that be was actually restored to his own dominions.

July 17 and 18.

The variety of interests in Italy, the weakness of the Government in the Roman States, the unsettled condition of the kingdom of Naples, the vicinity of Elba to the Continent, which forms the residence of several members of Bonaparte's family – all these various circumstances keep up a ferment, and occasion a concourse of Bonaparte's partisans and other adventurers to this part of the world. This increases every day, and all possible means are taken to disseminate the idea of Bonaparte's future return to influence and power, so that the impression becomes only too general. Various parties of recruits have been sent over to Elba from Italy, and a whole family have been arrested in Leghorn, who had in their possession two lists of men ready to serve Napoleon, to the number of 300 on each.

Having received much confidential and useful information from Count Stahremberg, I have, with a reciprocal view, given him the names of the Italian officers who have passed over to Elba.

Mr. Fagan informs me that the Neapolitan troops still occupy the marches of Ancona, notwithstanding various representations for their removal have been made by the Pope, and commit the greatest possible excesses. They lately marched from 15,000 to 20,000 men to another point of the frontier of the Roman States, but suddenly halted without transgressing the line.

July 19.

Visited Cardinal Fesch, and told him that, as I was returning to Elba, I should be happy to convey to Napoleon any letters from himself or Madame Mère. He told me that his sister had arranged her journey by land to the coast of Italy at a point nearest Elba, when Captain Tower arrived, and of himself offered to carry herself, her suite, and all her baggage, adding that he would give her two days' notice. The Cardinal said he had recommended her to accept the offer. I told him I was persuaded Captain Tower had acted with good intentions, but without reflection; for there were regulations in the Navy, that no foreigners could be conveyed in His Majesty's ships without regular applications and permission from those of superior authority. Besides, the brig attached to the Elba station had left orders for him to proceed immediately to join the Admiral, and then proceed to England.

July 20.

Waited upon the Pope, for the purpose of presenting Captain James of His Majesty's ship *Swallow*. He received us in bed, sitting up with a pillow behind his back, although he had sent to all the Ministers to notify that his indisposition would prevent him from seeing anyone. He spoke with uneasiness of Bonaparte being so near the coast of Italy, but expressed great admiration of England for the steady and consistent policy she had pursued. Notwithstanding his apprehensions of Napoleon and Murat, he placed all his confidence in our Government. He asked whether I had heard any news from Paris respecting Talleyrand. When I replied in the negative, he said he was disgraced, and that he was very sorry to hear it. I found afterwards that he had received a despatch from Cardinal Consalvi at Paris in seven days.

Two days ago a courier passed through here on his way from Paris to Murat. He called himself secretary of the Queen.

July 21.

There have arrived here the Duke of Filangieri, going to Paris on a mission from Murat, and the Duke of—, who gives out that he is deputed to attend the Congress at Vienna. The former belongs to the household, and is a general of brigade. The latter is a general of division, who was out of favour with Joseph on account of his attachment to Ferdinand, but afterwards entered into Murat's service, and went to Russia, where he lost several of his toes and fingers by frost.

Lucien Bonaparte has applied to the Pope for the title of Prince of Canino. He pays evening visits, and leaves cards simply as 'Luciano Bonaparte.' Louis Bonaparte is expected here about August 10, and intends likewise to settle at Rome.

July 22.

Went from Rome to Civita Vecchia.

July 23.

Sailed in His Majesty's brig *Swallow*.

July 25.

Touched at Elba, and saw General Bertrand, who asked me to remain for twenty-four hours; but I could not land on account of the quarantine.

A person called Ludovico Ennis showed me a passport from Lord William Bentinck, to enable him to go to Genoa. In the body of the passport he is called Vice-consul at the island of Elba. He had announced himself as such at Porto Ferrajo. I recommended him to proceed to his destination, unless he had powers to show in addition to his passport!

A Polish officer stated to M. Ricci at Longono, some days ago, that, after he was released from prison in Austria, he went to see the Empress Marie Louise, having a secret rendezvous with her. He then received letters from her, the Empress of Austria, and the young King of Rome for Napoleon, and also a nut from the Archduke Charles containing a ribbon. Couriers were sent after him to Milan, where he was apprehended and searched, but he had hidden the letters in his boot, and the nut was covered like a ball of silk. He says he is to be sent away from Elba soon with despatches. The Pole must vaunt these falsehoods to give himself consequence. The Empress of Austria and Marie Louise, as is well known, are not on terms, and therefore could not be together.

About two weeks ago the curates in the different churches notified that the contributions which were demanded some time ago ought to be paid before the first of August. This created great disturbances, even in the churches, and a great number of persons have in consequence been apprehended. The *Grand Vicaire* is a near relation of Napoleon's.

July 26-28.

Landed at Leghorn, and remained there to await the expected arrival of Madame Mère.

July 29.

Arrived Madame Mère and suite in two carriages, with six horses to each. She came from Rome, and travelled under the name of Madame Dupont, accompanied by M. Colonna, lately *Préfet* at Naples, which office, however, as a Frenchman, he was obliged to resign when that Government declared war against France.

July 30.

Received a visit from M. Colonna and M. Bartolucci, an Italian, resident in Leghorn, and formerly member of the Municipality under the French. They requested a passage for Madame in a man-of-war. Among the reasons alleged for this appeal were, the disappointment of a passage in another of His Majesty's ships, Napoleon's corvette being absent at Genoa, and these seas being infested with Algerian pirates. I promised to speak to the captain of the corvette attached to my mission, who accordingly acquiesced.

M. Colonna paid me a complimentary call to thank me on the part of Madame, and to say that a visit would be very acceptable. Promised to attend in the evening.

July 31.

Visited Madame, in company with Captain Battersby, of HMS *Grasshopper*. She got up, as if with difficulty, some seconds after our approach, and made us sit down upon chairs close to her. M. Colonna, her agent M. Bartolucci, and two ladies, entered and sat down soon afterwards. I addressed her as 'Madame' and 'Altesse'. She was very pleasant and unaffected. The old lady is very handsome, of middle size, with a good figure and fresh colour.

She spoke much of the Empress Marie Louise, of her being at the baths of Aix, and of her bad health, with many sighs and expressions of great regard, as if her separation from Napoleon was not voluntary on her part. Madame Bartolucci, she said, had received a letter from the Austrian General who commands at Parma, saying that Marie Louise had advised him of her intention to be there early in September.

I mentioned to Madame, in the course of conversation, that the papers stated that the Duchess of Montebello had returned to France. She said it was so; and that there was now only one of all her French attendants who remained with her. After remaining for half an hour, we bowed and went off. Madame will sail tomorrow or next day, and I intend to accompany her.

The quarantine is from today taken off the island of Elba, and unlimited intercourse is now open, as no infection has been communicated by the vessels from Malta, which had been captured and carried into Porto Ferrajo in April last.

I have this day received the following despatch from Lord Castlereagh:

London: Foreign Office, July 15, 1814.
Sir,
Your despatches to No. 21 inclusive, of the 13th ult., have been received, and laid before the Prince Regent.

I am to desire that you will continue to consider yourself as British resident in Elba, without assuming any further official character than that in which you are already received, and that you would pursue the same line of conduct and communication with this department, which, I am happy to acquaint you, have already received His Royal Highness's approbation. I am, etc.,

(Signed) CASTLEREAGH

August 1.
Visited by the Commandant of the place, who gave me the whole history of the persons apprehended for enrolling recruits for Napoleon.

An officer of the late Regiment *d'Étrangers* of Elba, a native of Lucca, called Quedlicci, employed a Corsican of the name of Imbricco, resident in Leghorn, to enrol Tuscan non-commissioned officers and privates for a battalion to be formed in Elba. The lists were found, and the soldiers engaged deposed to the facts.

Letters have also been intercepted from Guasco, *chef de bataillon* at Longono, entering into details as to the application of money for this object, and mentioning that only seven recruits had arrived from Tuscany.

Captain Dumont, a Piedmontese, arrived from Elba, stating that he was going home, and had quitted Napoleon's service. Having burnt a quantity of papers in the lazaretto he was detained, with his papers and baggage, after coming out of quarantine. Thereupon he claimed his liberty as an officer of Napoleon's army. Nothing more criminal could be proved against him, but it is evident he was going to Piedmont on a like service, as he wished to dissemble it at first, and to pretend that he had quitted Napoleon's service.

It is known that there are other agents on the same service at Florence, and dispersed through the different parts of Italy. These are watched, until sufficient proofs can be obtained of their employment.

Received from General Count Stahremberg, commanding in Tuscany and Lucca, the following letter:

Lucca: July 30, 1814.

Dear Colonel,

I have received your letter from Rome and from Leghorn with the most lively pleasure. I cannot sufficiently thank you for the interesting news which you have had the goodness to communicate to me. I should have answered your letter to Rome if you had not informed me of your immediate departure from thence.

As business prevents my coming at present to Leghorn, to have the pleasure of conversing with you upon affairs of high importance, I must now do it by writing. You must know that a certain Imbricco and Captain Dumont have been arrested at Leghorn, convicted of having enrolled for the island of Elba. They had already engaged many Tuscan subjects, by giving them 100 francs for enlistment. I have discovered that there was a whole band of these rascals all along the coast, even as far as Piedmont, to corrupt the subjects for the service of Napoleon. I take all possible trouble to discover all this rabble. There have also been three arrested at Massa and Carrara, convicted of having enlisted, and I have named a military commission at Leghorn to try these individuals with the greatest severity. I have thought it my duty to make a very strong representation to His Excellency Marshal Count Bellegarde upon a subject of such high importance, showing him that all these manoeuvres of Napoleon prove that he will never remain quiet, and that his presence in the island of Elba (from his connection with Naples, and with all these adventurers, who, as you very justly remark, "serve him in the hope that he will yet recover his former greatness") will always be very dangerous for the tranquillity of Italy. Every possible means must be employed in order to be constantly well informed of all that goes on in the island of Elba, and you will exceedingly oblige me by communicating to me whatever you know. You inform me that you have had discussions with the captains of the Navy respecting the voyage of Madame Letitia to the island of Elba. I have just received notice that yesterday, at seven in the evening, she passed through Pisa on her way to Leghorn. At Pisa an escort of four hussars was given to her, of which I disapproved very much. I request of you, dear Campbell, to acquaint me whether it is by your authority, or by that of Lebzethern,[68] that she has come to Leghorn, and whether you will convey her to Elba, in order that I may adopt my measures. It is not possible that I can permit her to remain long, above all with her suite. It is much too near and too dangerous.

I receive endless pressing representations from the coast, from Piombino to Leghorn, of the uneasiness which the inhabitants experience by the appearance of the Barbary pirates. I do believe that it is equally a trick of Napoleon to disturb this country. I beg of you to be so good as to engage the captains of the British men-of-war as our allies to protect these coasts to their utmost. If it is possible, I will come and see you – perhaps on Tuesday, before my return to Florence.

Accept my assurances of the utmost consideration, and of the most sincere attachment.

Count STAHREMBERG

August 2.

Embarked in His Majesty's brig *Grasshopper*, Captain Battersby, with Madame Letitia, M. Colonna, and two ladies in waiting, and landed at Elba the same evening.

In leaving the inn at Leghorn to walk to the boat, M. Colonna took the arm of Madame with his hat off all the way. Captain Battersby and myself took the arms of the two ladies with our hats on. Crowds followed us, and, on quitting the shore, a number of persons hooted, and whistled, and hissed.

Captain Battersby and two of his officers, M. Saveira a passenger, and myself, all dined with Madame upon deck. A couch was arranged for her, from which she never stirred during the whole voyage, except once to look out for Napoleon's house, when she mounted upon the top of a gun with great activity.

She told me that Napoleon was first intended for the navy, and studied for it at Brienne with a certain proportion of the other pupils. She went to see him

---

68 The Austrian Minister at Rome.

there, and found that they all slept in hammocks; upon which she prevented his pursuing that line, and said all she could to dissuade him from it. 'My son, in the navy you have to contend with fire and water.'[69] He was then fourteen or fifteen years of age.

She had had a great desire, she said, to visit England for many years. She had formed a particular friendship with one English family at Montpellier, whose address she had kept, but now lost, and forgotten the name. She had opportunities likewise of seeing several others, and particularly Mrs. Cosing (?), the wife of a painter. Her son Lucien spoke very favourably of England. At first he was treated with suspicion, and laid under restrictions, which was unpleasant; but afterwards he found himself quite happy, and formed very agreeable friendships. he has written a poem about the Saracens in Corsica, and another entitled *Charlemagne*.

Louis seems to be a great favourite of hers. His picture is on her snuff-box. She said he had written several romances, which she admired, and was sure they would be generally esteemed, such as would be fit for young ladies to read. Spoke of his fortune as being small, although he did not spend money either on games or women! Her eldest son she called 'le roi Joseph.'

She mentioned that she had been very ill-treated by the Minister of the Interior in France, who wished to take her house in Paris for 600,000 in the place of 800,000 francs. She only wished for what it had cost her. The Minister told her agent, that if she would not take that sum, she would repent of it. She wrote him, 'that she would never give up her rights and property, nor bend to the caprice of an individual.' If the Minister took it by force, she would enter a protestation formally, and then take her chance of justice. She hinted at the treaty, and the guarantee of all the Allied Powers. M. Colonna said her agent should give in a representation to the English Ambassador.

On anchoring in the harbour, a valet of Napoleon, the master of the port, and others came off. They said that Napoleon had been expecting his mother the whole of the preceding day, and had that morning early gone to a mountain at some distance. The ship's boat being manned, and no one coming off to say where Madame would be received, I proposed to M. Colonna to send a boat with a message to General Bertrand, or Drouot, to

69 In a report, 1783, from the masters of the school at Brienne recommending 'M. de Bonaparte [Napoleon], born August 15, 1769,' to the Royal Militaly School at Paris, occur these words: 'Would make an excellent sea-officer.' See Lockhart's, *Life of Napoleon*, vol. i. p. 6, note.

announce her arrival. When he asked her approbation to that, she seemed greatly agitated and mortified at no one coming to her on their part, and gave her assent with great violence, turning round quite pale and huffed. At length Generals Bertrand and Drouot arrived. The Captain and myself disembarked with her. All the officers of the Imperial Guard, the Mayor, etc., received her at the wharf, and from that to Napoleon's house the streets were lined. She went up in a carriage, with her ladies; we in another, with six horses to each.

The contributions were to be paid by August 1, or enforced by military execution. This was notified by criers in every village ten days before, and subsequently to that a similar announcement was made in the churches. Very few persons, however, have paid, and great disturbances have been created.

Napoleon has purchased a considerable tract of land in the richest valley, in the name of Monsieur Lapis; that is, he values the spots belonging to many small proprietors, and orders the act to be drawn out. They have represented the impossibility of removing their families, cattle, goats, etc., to other situations; since which Napoleon has told them they may remain.

A priest of the island went to M. Ricci, and asked whether England would not interfere to prevent the exactions of Napoleon, and whether the inhabitants might not send him a memorial to that effect, to be given to me!

CHAPTER V

INTERVIEW WITH NAPOLEON IN COMPANY WITH CAPTAIN BATTERSBY –
GOES TO LEGHORN TO MEET ADMIRAL HALLOWELL – ARREST OF EMISSARIES –
LETTER FROM COUNT STAHREMBERG – DESPATCH FROM LORD CASTLEREAGH –
DECLARATION OF WAR BY DEY OF ALGIERS – INTERVIEW WITH GENERAL AND
MADAME BERTRAND – CONVERSATION, OF SEPTEMBER 16, OF THREE HOURS
WITH NAPOLEON – ARRIVAL OF POLISH LADY AND CHILD AT ELBA –
HABITS OF NAPOLEON – GOES TO FLORENCE, AND IS PRESENTED
TO THE GRAND DUKE

August 3.

This morning General Bertrand informed me that at 9 p.m. the Emperor
would receive Captain Battersby, M. Saveira, and myself.

On arriving at the palace, the sentry stopped us until the officer on duty
with the guard came out. On telling him we were there by appointment,
he showed us into an antechamber, and called the aide-de-camp on duty,
who said he could not announce us at that moment, as the Emperor was
playing at a game with his mother and the Grand Maréchal. He requested
us to sit down; but when I repeated that we came by appointment, that it
was of no consequence, but he could inform the Grand Maréchal we had
been there; he became very uneasy for fear of my going away, begged me
to have the goodness to stay one moment, said that the Emperor would see
us directly, how much regard he had for me! How much he esteemed the
British nation! etc. etc. We remained about ten minutes more, and then I
said I would go to call on General Drouot, whose house was very near, and
would return again. Just as we were going out, which appeared to cause
them the utmost anxiety, another officer came running out to the door to
say the Emperor wished to see us. We were accordingly ushered into a
room, when Napoleon immediately appeared from an adjoining one. He
bowed to us, and came up tripping and smiling. Asked me how I did? said
I had got fatter. Was I quite well? Where had I been. 'What news? You are
come, then, to stay some days with us?'

I told him I had made a short tour in Italy, and had been at the baths of Lucca. 'Did you take a shower-bath?' 'No, I had applied the water in a stream through a pipe.'

Had I been at Rome? Had I seen the Pope? He was a good man. A good monk, old and feeble. Had he been sick? I said he had a swelling in his legs, and that the last time I saw him he was sitting up in bed. He laughed, and made a joke about the cause of the Pope's indisposition. Then he went on: 'They are very miserable in those States. It is the interest of England to form a kingdom of Italy. Is it not so? That ought to be. Eh?' I told him that whatever might be the interest of England, any interference of us Protestants with the head of the Roman Catholic Church would be peculiarly obnoxious: 'Ah, you can do as you like. Have you not any news?' I told him Sicily was given up entirely to the King, and that all the Ministers had been changed immediately. He asked where the Queen was? Whether she had returned? Where Lord William Bentinck was? Whether he had gone home, or was to remain at Genoa? Who was to succeed him as Minister at the Court of Palermo? Whether it was intended to withdraw the whole of the British troops? 'The possession of that country would not suit you. The small islands are better for England.'

He remarked that the English were not popular in Sicily. Our religion was always in our way with respect to these Catholics. I felt inclined to ask him if he had found it so in the case of Spain and Portugal, but in regard to Sicily I admitted that our measures there had not been received with that popularity, or met with that success, which had been expected: 'Is there nothing new from England? The marriage of the young Princess will not take place, then? Ah! So far as appears to me, you have the prospect of a fine Queen.' He seemed to exult, and said, 'The Regent was inclined to scold her with respect to her marriage.' 'I have not heard that stated, Sire.' I replied. 'Yes it is in my newspapers which I have received from Genoa. She threw herself into a hackney coach.[70] She is hot-headed and of a warm temperament. They must find a husband for her.' I said, Yes; but I did not think the union with the Prince of Orange was a matter of importance either to England or Holland. We must find another husband for her. He asked, 'Why does she not marry one of her cousins?

70 July 13, 1814. All London were startled by hearing that the Princess Charlotte had, on the previous evening, left Warwick House unobserved and gone off in a hackney-coach to the Princess of Wales, in Connaught Place.' – *Reminiscences of a Septagenarian,* pp. 112, 113.

Has the Duke of York no sons?' I told him, No. Her only cousin among our own Princes was the Duke of Gloucester, and it was said she never liked him. If she did not marry, I hoped she would prove a second Catherine of Russia. He said he did not believe the Prince of Orange had ever liked her; that some time ago he intercepted several of his letters to his father, wherein he expressed himself that 'He was not willing to be the husband of a Queen without being king.' I said that I did not believe any objections to the marriage had arisen on his part.

He asked me to get some English papers for him. I replied that I would order him one weekly from Leghorn. He told me he saw, by extracts from them, the Regent's approval of my wearing my Russian orders.

On presenting Captain Battersby, I added that he was very happy to have had the honour of conveying Madame. Napoleon thanked him, and spoke of the very pleasant passage she had had. I remarked I was particularly glad to hear that, as she had experienced so much delay from the expectations Captain Tower had held out to her; but that there were orders in search of him during three weeks to go home, and that it was necessary for him to return immediately.

He spoke of the disappointment and inconvenience she experienced at present from the want of her effects, which had been detained at the mouth of the Tiber by a corsair preventing the vessel from sailing. I told him that the Tuscan and Roman Governments, and all the people along the coast, were alarmed on account of these corsairs, but that they often fancied other vessels tacking in towards the shore belonged to them. He asked Captain Battersby whether he had seen any. He said 'No; but there certainly were some about.'

Seeing the conversation flagging, I told Napoleon that I had lately received despatches in reply to mine, informing Government that he had requested me to remain after the departure of the other Commissioners, and that I was happy to say HRH the Prince Regent approved of my continuing at the island of Elba. He only nodded and said, 'Ah, ah!'

On parting he nodded, and, smiling, said to me, 'To the pleasure of seeing you again soon!' then turned round and went to the adjoining room.

In talking to the officer of the guard, while waiting for the interview with Napoleon, I asked him whether the officers and men enjoyed good health, or whether they suffered from the air of the salt-ponds? He said, No, for that they were all acclimatised. They had campaigned in such a variety of countries – in Austria, Prussia, Spain, Portugal, Poland, Italy, and Russia,

'In all countries except yours'. I said, 'Aye, but I should think the cold of Russia was a bad preparation for the heat of Italy'. 'Ah that is true; those are the extremes'. I had him there, I thought, but it did not excite any awkwardness, for he followed it up with compliments to myself and the British nation.

In going out this evening after dinner, on our way to Napoleon's house, we saw a small display of fireworks in the streets, distributed probably by him to celebrate the arrival of his mother.

There is a theatre of very small size here, and there were in it tonight about fifty or sixty persons.

August 4.

As the man-of-war was to return today to Leghorn, where Admiral Hallowell was expected, I determined to go over to see him. Besides that, I understood that the discontent excited among the inhabitants against the contributions was very great, and I considered it better to absent myself for a time. A priest had proposed to give me a representation to be transmitted to the British Government, praying for their interference. Very few of the inhabitants have yet paid, notwithstanding the threats of military execution which are held out.

August 5.

Disembarked at Leghorn.

August 6.

Admiral Hallowell has not arrived, but is daily expected.

August 7-12.

There is a Count Guicchardi here. I met him first at dinner at the Governor's, and afterwards frequently in society. He was French minister of police at Milan, and one of the deputies who went to Paris to propose that the kingdom of Italy should be governed by the Duke of Modena, the cousin of the Emperor of Austria, as an independent sovereign, or by some other Prince connected with the Allies. This proposition, however, was not made until *after* Bonaparte's abdication, when of course the Italians could not help themselves. Count Guicchardi has probably come here until the popular fury at Milan against the former French authorities has subsided. He wishes, I can see, to flatter me greatly, and asks whether England will not do something for the Italians, by restoring to them a kingdom, and rescuing them from the intolerable oppression of the Austrians. I told him they had been too late with their propositions, which ought to have been made *before* the Allies entered Paris. He and other Italians say that many wished to rid themselves of Bonaparte, and the connection with the French last year, and particularly after Murat declared himself, it was proposed to act in concert with him; but there was no proper head, nor sufficient energy. Everyone spoke and thought the same, but they did not act.

The Consul of the late kingdom of Italy, who was resident at Leghorn, is still here, and speaks the same sentiments. He is a Venetian named Alberti, a clever man, but violent against the Austrians and the partition of Venice made under the Treaty of Campo Formio.

The Marquis Prie, belonging to one of the first families at Turin, tells me that until after Eugene's return from the Russian campaign he was adored by the people. After that period he showed a want of confidence in the Italians, their troops were not trusted in the garrisons. French officers were placed in all the chief commands. This created disunion, and there were daily quarrels between the French and Italian officers, and at length the Viceroy came to be considered no longer as their sovereign, but as a French general placed over them forcibly to preserve their connection with France.

The Italians speak universally against the Austrians, and complain of their rough manners; the hardships of a people who are polished and descendants of the ancient Romans being under Germans. The people of Tuscany and Lucca again declaim against the excessive contributions, and the unfairness of being obliged to support these Austrians, when they can take care of themselves. But I cannot hear, on *good* authority at least, of any malversation on the part of the latter. I know the Austrian military and interior arrangements to be very precise, and I observe the utmost regularity and quiet among both officers and men in the streets. The officers are certainly never admitted into society, and complain, I am told, of the incivility of the inhabitants. The fact is, such different materials as the Italians and the Austrians, with reciprocal prejudices, cannot easily associate; the one devoted wholly to pleasure, the other to military duties.

It is said that the secretary of General Count Stahremberg, M. Rosetti, a Piedmontese, is extremely venal; but if the case be so, I do not think it is known to the General. A proclamation appeared lately, ordering all plate belonging to palaces or public establishments, which had been carried away, to be restored. A few days before this – so the story runs – he came in a carriage by night from Lucca to Leghorn with a box, which was carried into his room. A Jew came to him for a private conference, and carried away the chest, but one of the waiters in the room had taken up a position which enabled him to spy the contents of the box and overhear the bargain!

August 12-18.

Upon the night of August 12, a Saturday, a company of Austrian infantry was under arms all night, and a few hussars patrolled about the streets. It seems that a captain of the Hungarian infantry heard a peasant in the streets talking of a revolt; and although the commanding officer, to whom he reported this with great earnestness and signs of fear, reprobated his conduct, as certainly arising from a misunderstanding and false impression on his part, and put him under arrest, yet it was thought prudent to keep a force under arms.

M. Marescalci, governor of Parma, has written to say that the Archduchess Marie Louise will be there about the 1st of September. He, with others, is to resign his situation on account of the number of persons whom she wishes to put into their places.

It is reported that Murat counts much upon the support of the Austrians through the interest which his Queen has with Metternich, whose *chere amie* she formerly was!

August 19.

A M. Colombini has arrived here from Florence. He is the person who assisted the French guard in scaling the window of the Pope. He comes of a good family and has property. On the Pope's return to Rome he was thrown into prison, but has now received permission to go where he pleases. He relates all sorts of stories as to the discontent existing against the Pope's government and his foolish proceedings. M. Alberti, formerly Consul of the kingdom of Italy, introduced him at the theatre the night before.

The Commandant has given me the names of the following persons as having gone over to the island of Elba, and being much suspected – Locatelli and Dr. Guidotti. The wife of the latter remains here, and is under surveillance.

A person came to me to be engaged as a servant, calling himself first a nephew, and afterwards only a relation of M. Ricci. He told me he was going to Pisa, in case I did not hire him, on account of a wound in the head, received while serving in the French army. He said he had been a soldier for many years, and had a passport signed by the Mayor of Porto Ferrajo. I think he has been sent to me as a spy!

Prince Borghese has arrived at Florence. The King of Spain refuses to restore to him his house at Rome, and the Pope will not interfere.

A small vessel has arrived from Bastia in Corsica. I am informed that when she came away, there was a tumult between the citizens and the military, in consequence of the latter wishing to prevent a religious procession.

August 20.

Arrived Admiral Hallowell in the *Malta*, from Genoa.

August 21.

The Admiral disapproves most strongly of several instances of voluntary court and unnecessary visits paid by naval officers at Porto Ferrajo, and I am persuaded nothing of the kind will recur in future. He continues the arrangements of Lord Exmouth in placing a man-of-war upon this station, in case of any extraordinary event to communicate.

August 22.

Admiral Hallowell sailed for Palermo.

August 23.

A few days ago Napoleon went on board his corvette, and remained for two hours. Fifty of his Guards were embarked at the same time. It is given out that they are sent to receive the Empress Marie Louise; but it is more probable that this measure has arisen from fear of the Algerians, although Napoleon would hardly wish to raise an alarm among the inhabitants on account of so trifling a foe! Since then the corvette has been sent over to Genoa for fireworks, clothing and household stores.

Porto Ferrajo continues to be the resort of a number of officers from Italy, who dislike the service both of the King of Sardinia and of the Emperor of Austria: in the former case, on account of the harsh expressions made use of to those who had been wounded, or obtained distinction under the French; in the latter, on account of the system of corporal punishment and the difference of language. Their expectations of employment are kept up by constant reports propagated purposely to produce that effect. Still many have returned to their homes, sorely disappointed in their prospects, and displeased at the reception they met with from Napoleon, whose manner is very seldom conciliatory.

August 24.

A letter from General Drouot, governor of Elba, to General Spannochi, governor of Leghorn, requests of him to send under an escort to Piombino an officer who had been arrested, and assures him that if the man has committed any crime, he shall be tried by a military commission and punished. The reply from General Spannochi refers him to General Stahremberg, commanding in Tuscany.

August 25.

Arrived from Palermo the Prince of Villa Franca, lately Minister of Foreign Affairs while Sicily was under British dominion, with Lord William Bentinck as governor, the Duke of Ventimiglia, and two other Sicilian noblemen, who found it prudent to withdraw upon the assumption of the government by the King.

August 26.

Received a despatch from Count Stahremberg, with a packet of letters from the Princess Pauline and from various members of the Court of Naples to Napoleon, forwarded by Count Meyer, the Austrian Minister there. They had been left open, he states, and he had accordingly read them; but they contained nothing but felicitations on Napoleon's birthday! 'These are,' he adds, 'artifices easily seen through. They send us letters open to be forwarded to the island, while they have frequent opportunities of sending others of importance direct from Naples to the island.'

He also tells me, that although General Drouot had written twice to General Spannochi on the subject of the persons arrested for recruiting at Leghorn, he had sent no reply; nor should he do so, until the process was more advanced, and something more was known of their proceedings. They were being tried by a military commission, and the details would be forwarded to Vienna. At the same time he promises to inform me of the issue of this affair.

Prince Esterhazy has arrived at Florence, on his way to Rome, upon an extraordinary mission. The Pope has issued a bull, directing the re-establishment of the Jesuits throughout Europe.

Dr. Milner, a Roman Catholic bishop, and a deputation from England, were at Rome in the beginning of last month.

August 27.

Went towards Elba in HMS *Grasshopper*, but returned, as I did not wish to be present at the formal celebration of Napoleon's birthday. This was first ordered for the 15th, but was afterwards postponed to the 27th instant, which is the anniversary of the birthday of the Empress Marie Louise.

It is stated that twenty of the Guards have deserted since the quarantine was taken off, and that all are tired of the place. Some sixty men of the *Bataillon Etranger* and thirty-five of the Line remained in the service of Napoleon. They have been augmented to 350, Italians and Corsicans, but principally the latter. Of these recruits, however, sixty have deserted at various times.

The last order for payment of the contributions fixes the 24th of this

CHAPTER V

month, under pain of military execution.

August 28.

The Commandant showed me a despatch from General Stahremberg, stating that Jerome Bonaparte had left Gratz, and was at Padua on the 22nd. Search was being made, and there were orders to apprehend him.

August 29.

Received a despatch from Lord Castlereagh as follows:

Foreign Office: August 6, 1814.

Sir,

I have the honour to acquaint you that I have received the commands of His Royal Highness the Prince Regent to set out shortly for the Continent, to assist, as His Majesty's principal Secretary of State for Foreign Affairs, at the approaching Congress of Vienna.

It is His Royal Highness's pleasure that you still continue, as on the former occasion, to address your despatches to me at the Foreign Office, sending duplicates of such as you may be of opinion ought to be made known to me without delay at Vienna.

You will transmit your correspondence to me at Vienna by the most favourable opportunities which may offer; but you will avoid any unnecessary expense by sending messengers on occasions which do not appear to you to require immediate despatch.

I am, with great truth and regard, etc. etc.,

(Signed) CASTLEREAGH

August 30.

Went today from Leghorn to Florence, in expectation of the arrival there of the Grand Duke.

Informed that a courier had been arrested at Bologna, with despatches from Joseph Bonaparte to Napoleon. They were taken from him, being supposed to be of importance.

August 31-September 8.

Florence and baths of Lucca.

While at Florence, General Stahremberg showed me a letter from Prince Esterhazy, written from Rome, applying for escorts for Charles IV, late King of Spain, the Queen, the Prince of Peace, and their suites. They propose to come to Florence as private individuals, and they have named Schneider's Hotel for their residence.

September 9.

Returned to Leghorn.

I am informed, that on the celebration of Murat's birthday, August 20, at Naples, the troops were reviewed by him. While a *feu de joie* was being fired, a musket-ball from one of the men's pieces hit an aide-de-camp, and wounded him mortally. Murat turned pale, but soon recovering himself said gaily, 'That wasn't well loaded.' Examinations were made, and several soldiers arrested in consequence of balls being found in their pieces.

September 10.

Received copy of a letter from Admiral Hallowell, stating that the Algerians have declared war against Naples, Genoa, and Elba.

It is addressed to Mr. Felton, the British Consul at Leghorn, and runs as follows:

Palermo Bay: August 31, 1814.

Sir,

I lose no time in acquainting you that I have received a letter from M. Oglander, the British Consul at Tunis, informing me of the Dey's determination not to respect either the British flag, or passports which may be granted to the subjects of Genoa and other Italian States, and that he was fitting out several corsairs for the express purpose of cruising against the vessels of these Powers.

In the same letter he informs me that cruisers from Algiers and Tripoli are at sea with similar orders, and that he had been informed by the Bey of Tunis that some Genoese vessels, having Mr. Fitzgerald's pass, had been captured by the Algerian cruisers. I have therefore to request, that you will warn any vessel belonging to the subjects of Genoa and other States (lying at Leghorn), who may be furnished with such passports, of the danger to which they will be exposed, by navigating any longer under the faith of such protection.

I have received a letter from Mr. MacDonnell, the British Consul at Algiers, wherein he informs me that the Dey has instructed his cruisers to seize all Neapolitan vessels, and those sailing under the flag of Elba, wherever they may be met with, *and the person of the Sovereign of that island also, should any opportunity happily offer of getting hold of him.*

I have the honour to be, etc. etc.,

(Signed) BEN. HALLOWELL

N.B. The last part, marked in italics, was not sent by me to General Bertrand, as being personally offensive against Napoleon.

September 11-12.

One of the persons arrested for enrolling recruits in Tuscany for Napoleon has made an acknowledgment of the circumstances. His name is Quedlicci. He deposes that he was originally commissioned to purchase clothing for the troops; and that when attending at the Governor's residence, for the purpose of receiving his final instructions, at the very moment when the necessary papers were being signed, some one opened the door of the room in which he was, and Napoleon himself appeared; that after looking at him attentively, he inquired whether he was one of the officers charged to enrol recruits; that on his replying that such was not his immediate commission, but that, nevertheless, he had instructions to that effect, Napoleon bid him apprise his comrades that he wished for men, healthy, robust, and capable of executing a *coup de main* of some sort. He also gave him a commission to procure fifteen or sixteen men as musicians to make up a band.

Quedlicci has further given up the names of eight other officers, destined for recruiting in these various localities: Rome, Naples, Bastia and Ajaccio in Corsica, Piedmont, Massa, Carrara, Genoa.

I shall acquaint Colonel Sir John Dalrymple, who commands at Genoa, for the information of the Government of that State, with the name of the officer employed there by Napoleon.

A decree has been issued at Naples, signed by the Duke of Laurenzana, Minister of Police. It states that the Government there have heard with surprise, by means of letters from Civita Vecchia and Leghorn, that several persons, calling themselves officers in the service of the King of Naples, and decorated with his Royal Order, have presented themselves at those ports, professing to be sent from the Court of Naples to the island of Elba. And although no one could be deceived by so miserable a stratagem, yet the said Minister of Police thinks it necessary to declare that such intriguers do not belong to the kingdom of Naples, that they are not even known, and that they are still less charged with any mission to the island of Elba. All local authorities are invited to cause the arrest of any such individual.

September 13.

Sailed from Leghorn.

September 14.

Landed at Porto Ferrajo, and had an interview with General Bertrand, to whom I presented a letter notifying the declaration of war by the Algerians. Some persons were present in the room. General Bertrand went out for some time, and on his return seemed much agitated. When we found ourselves alone, he told me he would send the letter to the Emperor at Longono. I asked whether Napoleon had no communication with the Government of France respecting the treaty with the Algerians. He laughed ironically, and said, 'No. The matter rests with the Allied Powers, if they mean to act in good faith.' I reminded him of the reply of Admiral Sir Edward Pellew some time before, to the effect that he could not interfere, and that the question did not rest with His Majesty's Government. At the same time, if Napoleon wished to make any representation, I should forward it to Lord Castlereagh. To this General Bertrand made no particular answer.

Madame Bertrand, whom I saw on this occasion, told me in the course of conversation, that Napoleon asked Caulaincourt to accompany him to Elba, but he declined. She is persuaded that he had no connection whatever with the apprehension or death of the Duke d'Enghien. The Emperor Alexander was so certain of this, that he asked Louis XVIII to send him as ambassador to St. Petersburg; and, when that was refused, he offered him the place of *Grand Ecuyer* with himself. Savary ordered a lantern to be tied to the Duke d'Enghien's breast, in consequence of his requesting that the soldiers would not fail in their shots. Napoleon had been very unwell for some days before, and advantage was taken of it by Murat and others about him to hasten on the death of the Duke. In another hour it would have been countermanded. This is probably said in reliance upon the success of Josephine's application; but I was told at Fontainebleau that Napoleon kicked her from his knees.

Before Madame Bertrand left Paris she asked Berthier if he would not come to Elba. He told her, 'Yes, he would come to see the Emperor very soon, and that he would pass three months with him every year; that he would have gone with him in the first instance but for his wife and children.'

September 15.

Napoleon came over for a few hours from Longono, in order to press on the repairs of his house, but returned in the afternoon. I did not see him.

September 16.

Had an audience of Napoleon for the first time since my last visit to Leghorn and the baths of Lucca, which are prescribed for my wounds. It was courted by himself, in sending to inform me that one of his carriages was at my disposal to convey me from Porto Ferrajo to Longono, where he has been for the last two weeks. This audience lasted for three hours by the watch, during which time there was no interruption. He constantly walked from one extremity of the room to the other, asked questions without number, and descanted upon a great variety of subjects, generally with temper and good nature, except when the matter bore upon the absence of his wife and child, or the defection of Marshal Marmont.

He began by questions as to Genoa. Understood Lord William Bentinck was to return there very soon. Was there not a British regiment at Nice? Spoke of the state of Piedmont, Lombardy, Venice, and Tuscany; said that the rude manners and different language of the Austrians rendered it impossible for them to become popular with the Italians, who had previously been flattered by the formation of the kingdom of Italy; that it should be the policy of Great Britain to retain this kingdom, as an ally against France and Austria; that it should be equally her object to keep Naples separate from Sicily. The latter, as an island, would be entirely under the influence of England. He inquired where the Queen of Sicily was? Whether I knew the intentions of the Allies towards Murat? Whether the late King of Spain was to remain at Rome? When I told him it was reported that Ferdinand VII had invited his father and mother to return to Spain, provided the Prince of Peace did not accompany them, he inveighed against the latter, and said that his own countenance and support given to him had been very prejudicial to his cause in Spain.

He presumed that England would keep Corfu, and said he had done a great deal there for us. I observed that the proclamation of the British General, on taking possession of the island as commissioner, stated it was 'on behalf of His Britannic Majesty and his Allies,' and that it was generally supposed Austria and Russia would also have claims. He derided this idea, and said that Russia particularly could have no just pretensions.

He then asked whether I had lately received any communication from Lord Castlereagh. I told him not since that which conveyed the Prince Regent's approbation to my prolonging my residence.

He next adverted to the threats of the Algerians, but cursorily, and did not seem apprehensive; said that if it was intended to adhere to the treaty entered into with him at Fontainebleau, he would not be molested by them. I reminded him of the application upon this subject some time before, which I had transmitted to Lord Exmouth, who replied that he could not interfere, and that even according to the treaty quoted by himself; it rested with the Court of France. I also pointed out to him, that while the British troops occupied Sicily and Portugal, and were in the most intimate relations with their Governments, the latter made their own treaties and arrangements with the Barbary Powers without any interference. Besides, I referred to the fate of the Genoese vessels, which had hoisted the British flag, and received licences from the English Consul at Genoa. He expressed his belief that the Algerians were well inclined towards him, and related with good humour that they had ridiculed the crews of two vessels belonging to Louis XVIII near Elba, calling to them with reproaches, 'You have deserted your Emperor!' He added that all the subjects of the Grand Seignior were well inclined towards him as the enemy of Russia, and considered him the destroyer of Moscow.

He asked me if I knew what was intended by the Austrians respecting his wife and son, animadverting with warmth, and in strong language, upon the interdiction to their joining him, which he stated to exist, and said that it excited universal indignation even at Vienna; that no such instance of barbarity and injustice, unconnected with any state policy, could be pointed out in modern times; that he was persuaded England was too just and liberal to approve of it. The Empress had written to him, and he knew her wishes. She was now absolutely a prisoner, for there was an Austrian officer (whom he named and described) who accompanied her, in order to prevent her from escaping to Elba. Before she left Orleans it was promised to her that she should receive passports to enable her to follow him: 'The Emperor of Austria is led by Metternich, but he is led himself; for although he has some talent, he is of a frivolous disposition.'

He then asked me to write to Lord Castlereagh, to inquire whether it was intended to prevent his wife and child, or either of them, from joining him. I told him I had no correspondence with his lordship but what was official. He replied, 'But you can touch upon that matter lightly, or write to some one about him.' I bowed, and told him that I should be happy to do anything that was agreeable to him, and at the same time consistent with my duty. He seemed to receive this as an assent to his wishes. 'Yes, you will do it; you can do that quite well.'

After giving vent to his feelings upon this subject, he next mentioned how very inimical and personal the conduct of General Stahremberg, who commanded in Tuscany, had been towards him. These observations afforded me an opportunity of noticing the apprehensions which were entertained by the General in consequence of persons enrolling and entering in his name some subjects of Tuscany. He admitted the fact, but treated it with ridicule; said he had only 500 or 600 of his Old Guard, who were not sufficiently numerous to guard all the villages and fortifications; that the situation of the island did not admit of his recruiting upon it his battalion of Chasseurs, and therefore the Corsican officers, who remained at Elba, instead of going to France with the rest of the garrison, endeavoured to obtain recruits in Italy and Corsica. Could General Stahremberg be so weak as to be alarmed at this? He was very happy that I remained on, 'to dispel the illusion. I think of nothing outside my little island. I could have kept up the war during twenty years if I had wanted that. I exist no longer for the world. I am a dead man. I only occupy myself with my family and my retreat, my cows and my mules.'

He expressed regret at some difficulties which a few English travellers had experienced some days before from the Commandant and the police at Porto Ferrajo. He reprobated the conduct of the latter, and paid many compliments to the British nation. It was his wish, he said, that every traveller should meet with attention and facility. The mistake arose from advices being received that a person of another nation had come to Elba as an assassin.

(It is probably on account of this information that Napoleon has resided for the last two weeks at Longono within the fortress, and orders are given there that no stranger may be admitted without a written permission from the Commandant. However, he makes frequent excursions in his carriage.)

After continuing to expatiate on the British character, and remarking that, notwithstanding all the abuse directed against it in his name, his sentiments were well known by those near his person, he requested me to obtain for him an English Grammar the first time I went to the Continent.

Conversing with respect to the affairs of America, he repeated his conjectures made some time ago, that the expedition from England was destined for Louisiana, in order to limit definitively the United States to the southward.

He inquired with great eagerness as to the real state of France. I told him that private letters, English travellers, and every source of information, concurred in ascribing great wisdom and moderation to the Sovereign and Government, but that there were many, such as those who had lost good appointments, the prisoners who had returned from abroad, and a portion of the army, who were attached to him. He appeared to admit the stability of the Sovereign, supported as his Government is by all the Marshals, Berthier being captain of the Guards; but said that the attempt to copy Great Britain with respect to the

Constitution was absurd – a mere caricature! It was impossible to imitate the Houses of Parliament, for ancient and respectable families, like those composing the aristocracy in England, did not now exist in France.

After continuing in this strain for a long time, with comparisons highly complimentary to England, he spoke with some warmth of the cessions made by France since his abdication; said it was not wise, on the part of the Allies, to require so much, particularly as regarded Luxembourg and the Netherlands; that she had no defence whatever on that frontier. While Prussia, Holland, Austria, and Russia were aggrandised beyond all proportion on the Continent, and England in the East and West Indies, France had lost all, even to the pitiful island of St. Lucia. He spoke as a spectator, without any future hopes or present interest, for he had neither, again insisting on his own nonentity; but it showed utter ignorance of the French character and temper of the present time. Their chief failings were pride and the love of glory, and it was impossible for them to look forward with satisfaction and feelings of tranquillity, as was stated to be the sincere wish of all the Allies, under such sacrifices. They were conquered only by a great superiority of numbers but not humiliated. The population of France had not suffered to the extent that might be supposed, for he always spared their lives, and exposed the Italians and other foreigners.

These observations gradually led him to speak of his own feats in war and the last campaign. He entered into the details of many operations, in which he had repulsed the enemy and gained advantages with numbers inferior beyond comparison, and then went on to abuse Marshal Marmont, to whose defection alone he ascribed his being obliged to give up the contest.

He alleges that the gratitude which the Royal Family of France feel towards England is viewed with jealousy and contempt by the people of France, as producing a sacrifice of their interests. The King is called 'The English Viceroy!'

In talking of St. Domingo, I remarked that the superfluous portion of discontented military could be employed there. He said it would be bad policy to attempt to re-establish that colony. Better to blockade it, and force the negroes to transport the whole of their produce to France only. This would have been his own plan in case of a peace.

He asked whether I had heard that Parma, etc., were not to be given up to Marie Louise, but to the Queen of Etruria, and that an indemnity in Germany was to be offered to the former. I admitted that this was one among other reports prevalent in Italy.

He expressed his own desire and expectation of being on a good footing with the Grand Duke of Tuscany; presumed that if I returned to the baths of Lucca, I should pay my respects to His Imperial Highness; in which case I should be able to ascertain his sentiments towards himself, and if they were favourable, as he expected (in consequence of favours received from him formerly, when the Grand Duke was on bad terms with his brother the Emperor of Austria), he would send over an officer to compliment him upon his arrival in Tuscany.

He inquired about the Countess of Albany, and asked whether she still received a pension from England. He abused M. Mariotti, the French Consul at Leghorn.

This man was chief of Bacchiochi's staff, and got his place through the interest of Madame Brignolli, who is now with Marie Louise. Napoleon called him a Corsican adventurer. I suspect, however, that he is useful in forwarding communications, and that this abuse was purposely to deceive me!

In the course of conversation Napoleon told me that the Archbishop of Malines,[71] who had been his own chaplain, was extremely addicted to descanting on military subjects, which is very disgusting to military men. He was the person whom he sent for at Warsaw, on his retreat from Russia. Lately, at the table of Talleyrand, this man cast many reflections upon him; said he was no general; was a fool, etc. At length a Frenchman present remarked in a very moderate tone: 'But the Emperor Napoleon has had some successes in his campaigns in Italy.' Lord Wellington had remained silent during the whole of this conversation, but when the same gentleman referred to him for his opinion, he replied that the success which the Emperor had obtained in the last campaign, between the Seine and the Marne, was equally great.

Napoleon appeared to be highly flattered by the praise thus accorded to him by the Duke of Wellington, and asked me whether he was not generally reserved in conversation. I replied that he certainly was not talkative!

Enlarging for some time upon the influence which he possessed over the minds of French soldiers in the field, he said that under him they performed what no other chief could obtain from them. This he ascribed to his manner of talking to them on particular occasions. With soldiers it is not so much the speech itself as the mode of delivering it. Here he raised himself on his toes, looked up to the ceiling, and, lifting one of his hands to its utmost

---

71 Better known as the Abbé de Pradt.

extent, called out, 'Unfurl the eagles! Unfurl the eagles!' He then related to me, that when the battle of Marengo was almost lost, he redeemed it by calling out to the men, who were then in perfect rout. He had then with himself only about forty horsemen; but by putting himself at the head of the retiring troops, and speaking to them in a certain tone and manner, they rallied immediately, crying out 'Come on! Forwards!' It is like music, which either speaks to the soul, or, on the contrary, gives out sounds without harmony.

It strikes me there was something *wild* in his air throughout this last visit, and in many of his observations, the above among others.

September 17.

Madame Letitia, upon her first arrival, proposed to remain only one month, but she has now taken up her permanent residence in the island, and has sent for the rest of her baggage.

Part of the effects belonging to the Princess Pauline have arrived, and vessels have been sent to Naples for the remainder. This looks as if Murat was averse to any public communication with Elba. The Princess herself is expected to arrive from Naples in two or three weeks.

September 18.

About three weeks ago, a lady with a child, apparently five or six years of age, arrived here from Leghorn. She was received by Napoleon with great attention, but a certain degree of concealment, and accompanied him immediately to a very retired small house in the most remote part of the island. After remaining two days she re-embarked, and is said to have gone to Naples. Everyone in Elba believes that this individual is Marie Louise with her son. It is even said that a servant of Napoleon's was put in confinement for propagating the report, as if it was a circumstance intended to be concealed. The Mayor of Marchiana, on her passing through that village on her way to the mountain retreat, ordered preparations for illuminating to be made. For this he was rebuked by Napoleon, and the order was countermanded. The same idea is very generally credited on the opposite coast, but my information leads me to believe that it is a Polish lady from Warsaw, who bore a child to Napoleon a few years ago.[72] It is probable that the concealment used, and her speedy departure to the Continent, proceed from delicacy towards Marie Louise, and the fear of this connection becoming known to her.

---

72 This was Marie Walewska, Napoleon's mistress, and her son Alexander. Alexander, Napoleon's illegitimate child, later became a French politician.

Marie Walewska (courtesy of Anne Brown
Military Collection).

Marie Louise.

The remote house at which Napoleon entertained Marie Walewska.

September 19.

The Intendant tells me that Napoleon's revenue, even with the impositions, does not exceed 300,000 francs; whereas his expenses, including troops, marine, and household, have been at the rate of 1,000,000. A great part of the ten months' provisions, which were left in store here by the French troops, have been nearly all sold by Napoleon, and are supposed to have produced about

500,000 francs. This sum, with the specie brought with him from France (the amount of which, however, is unknown) enables him to continue his extraordinary expenses. The salt has failed this season, and the iron ore does not meet with sale, in consequence of the quantity of guns and old iron sold at Genoa by the British, and at Leghorn by the Neapolitans.

The inhabitants of Capolini have not paid any contributions, nor any of the poorest of the population generally; but the threats of military execution have not been carried out, and the tax will not be levied from them at present. The Mayor of Marchiana is released.

Napoleon is never now saluted with cries of 'Vive L'Empereur!'

There are still many discontented officers from the army of Italy here, and it is said that they are to form a Garde de Corps. Four officers from France have entered the Imperial Guard as private soldiers. A General Lebelle and his family have lately arrived here from France, but he is not employed.

September 20.

Napoleon seems to have lost all habits of study and sedentary application. He has four places of residence in different parts of the island, and the improvements and changes of these form his sole occupation. But as they lose their interest to his unsettled mind, and the novelty wears off, he occasionally falls into a state of inactivity never known before, and has of late retired to his bedroom for repose during several hours of the day. If he takes exercise, it is in a carriage, and not on horseback as before. His health, however, is excellent, and his spirits appear not at all depressed. I begin to think he is quite resigned to his retreat, and that he is tolerably happy, excepting when the recollections of his former power are freshened by sentiments of vanity or revenge, or his passions become influenced by want of money, and his wife and child being kept from him.

Today he went to Pia Nosa, accompanied by several ladies and others belonging to his household. He was to have proceeded there some days ago, but on receiving my information, with respect to the Algerians having declared war against Elba, he sent his corvette there to reconnoitre. She returned yesterday.

This island, as I have before said, is situated a few miles south of Elba, and is about three miles long and one broad.

Being very capable of yielding grain, the acquisition of it is desirable to Napoleon; and it is probable that he has no other view in sending there a detachment of soldiers and some inhabitants. But at the same time it affords him opportunities of receiving persons from the Continent, and particularly Naples and Corsica, without any possible means of detecting it. I have therefore thought it my duty to draw Lord Castlereagh's attention to the circumstance.

September 21.

Embarked for Leghorn.

September 22.

Landed from the *Grasshopper* this morning, and arrived at Florence the same evening.

September 23.

Had an interview with M. Fossombroni, the Prime Minister of Tuscany, and was informed by him that fifty-five Polish Lancers of Napoleon's Guard, who had been at Parma, will arrive at Leghorn by a march-route on October 2, to embark for the island of Elba. There were no explanations about the transports to convey them. General Stahremberg had received this communication from Marshal Bellegarde, and General Stafinini, commanding at Parma, was ordered to communicate with General Bertrand.

September 24.

Florence.

September 25.

Presented to the Grand Duke of Tuscany in the forenoon, and afterwards went by invitation to his box, to see the horse-racing. In the evening attended the drawing-room, and played cards with the two Grand Duchesses.

In the course of my audience, the Grand Duke asked some questions of curiosity about Napoleon; and when I took occasion to speak of the favourable sentiments he had expressed towards His Imperial Highness, he said he had never done him any pointed violence; adding, however, his want of confidence in him, and taking no more direct notice of Napoleon's proposal to send an officer to compliment him.

I made the Grand Duke, as well as his Minister, perfectly aware that I did not charge myself with any mission from Napoleon; but, as circumstances had led me there, and there was no British Minister at that Court, I thought it right to mention the proposal, as I should, in like manner, to Napoleon the substance of his reply.

September 26-28.

I have written to General Bertrand in such terms as may induce both him and Napoleon to believe that there was no encouragement on the part of the Grand Duke to any person being sent to compliment him.

CHAPTER VI

Arrival of Polish Lancers – Tunisian Corsairs – Edict of Napoleon –
Hints thrown out by General Bertrand – Conversation with
Napoleon, October 31 – Arrival of Pauline – Pecuniary
Embarrassments of Napoleon – Writes to Lord Castlereagh on subject
– Resistance to Contributions – Visit to Florence – Interview with M.
Hyde de Neuville – Old Guns sent from Porto Ferrajo – Conversation
with Napoleon, December 4, of three hours and a half – Presents
Captain Adye – List of Napoleon's Vessels – Report of conversation
between Napoleon and M. Litta – Interview with Napoleon, December
21 – Discharge of Soldiers – Gradual Estrangement of Napoleon

October.

Upon the 2nd ult., a detachment of fifty or sixty Polish Lancers, mounted, arrived at Leghorn from Parma with their horses, and were sent over here on the 5th, at the expense of the Commandant of Leghorn. A person came with them, who presented an account of the sum paid for hire of transports. This it was promised to repay; but on settling the account with Napoleon's treasurer, he only paid one-half, without assigning any reason for withholding the rest.

I have been assured, from good authority, that his present funds are nearly exhausted, in consequence of which there is a great diminution in the expenses, but not in the extent, of his household and establishment.

It may be necessary to explain, that the Polish Lancers just mentioned formed part of the volunteers from France; but when the others were embarked for Elba at Savona, in the month of May last, they were sent to Parma by order of Napoleon, to act as a cavalry-guard to Marie Louise.

It is reported that upon the 29th ult., a boat coming to this island from Corsica, with two officers and fourteen soldiers for Napoleon's levy, was overtaken by another despatch from the governor and carried back. Those who have already arrived here are extremely dissatisfied, and would all return to Corsica if they could escape.

132

The checks placed upon his recruiting men from Corsica, by the activity of the new governor, Brulart, have annoyed him extremely.

The troops here are constantly exercised with mortars and guns, throwing shells and firing red-hot shot. This practice increases the surprise of the inhabitants on the opposite coast, and augments the many reports which are in circulation.

Colonel Lebelle (whom I before described as General) is now employed by Napoleon. There is no other Frenchman above the rank of captain who has joined Napoleon since his first arrival.

Sir John Dalrymple writes me from Genoa, that, upon the 4th inst., a French general of the name of Bouriguy, or Persigny, arrived there, stating that he had left Paris ten days before, and intended to travel in Italy. It was discovered that he had hired a vessel to convey him to Elba. Upon being prevented in that design, he went to Milan. He had no passport excepting one from Lord Castlereagh, by means of which he had formerly gone to Corfu as commissioner, to surrender that island to the Allies. I cannot learn that he has yet arrived here. I have written to General Campbell at Corfu, to inform him of the circumstance.

It is stated that a detachment of French troops, from Corsica, lately disembarked at the island of Capraja (which lies to the northward of Corsica, and north-west of Elba), took on board all the military stores, and then returned. It is conjectured that this measure arises from the intention of restoring it to Genoa, to which republic it belonged previously to the year 1792.

October 22.

Napoleon's corvette is still absent at Civita Vecchia, or at Naples, either to receive on board the Princess Pauline, or to accompany the ship which will convey her. Many of her effects have arrived here lately. It has been supposed in Naples and Sicily that they belonged to Murat, and that they were embarked clandestinely in case of his losing his present crown.

Murat's squadron is frequently to the southward of this island, cruising between it and the Bay of Naples, in order to protect their trade against the Barbary Powers, but I do not learn that they hold any communication with this place. The fleet consists in all of two sail of the line, three frigates, and some small vessels.

October 23.

I have heard nothing more on the subject of an officer being sent by Napoleon to compliment the Grand Duke of Tuscany, excepting that M.

Colonna went from this to Leghorn and Florence a few days ago, and it is surmised that such is the object of his journey. He accompanied Napoleon's mother from Rome to Elba, and has remained with her ever since.

It has been reported in Tuscany for some time past, and generally believed, that medals and coins have been struck here on Napoleon's order. Persons lately arrived from Paris have asserted that they have seen them there, describing them to bear the same motto as was reported in Italy – i.e. *Ubicunque felix*. I do not believe that any were ever made in this island, and I presume that these must have had their origin in Paris.

October 24-28.

A small ship, a corsair belonging to Tunis, anchored here on the 24th, and saluted with five guns, which were returned. This State has not declared war against Napoleon. It is only the Algerians who have done so.

Two Genoese vessels carrying English colours anchored here subsequently, in consequence of contrary winds, and put to sea on the morning of the 27th. The corsair wished to pursue them, but was prevented by order from Napoleon, who directed her to be kept at anchor until the others were out of reach.

Napoleon's corvette is stated to be at Baiæ, near Naples, anchored at some distance from the shore, and prevented from landing any of her crew.

October 29.

A few days ago some fifty of the Guards sent separate petitions to Napoleon to quit his service. No answer has been yet given, but the inhabitant who was employed by them to write them out has been sent away from the island.

From the following decree, affixed in various parts of the island, it may be inferred that Napoleon foresees the probability of the officers of the Guard likewise leaving him, and therefore wishes to prepare some of the young men of the island for filling their situations.

[Translated from Italian]
His Majesty the Emperor, has, by an order of the day, decreed as follows:
Porto-Ferrajo, October 13 1814.
Ten military pupils shall be admitted into the artillery of the Guard. They shall be instructed in the necessary artillery movements and infantry drill. An officer of the Grenadiers of the Guard is charged with everything concerning the instruction of infantry drill, discipline and military

regulations. The pupils shall also be instructed in mathematics, fortification and in draughtsmanship.

The pupils shall wear a black hat with red piping, blue trousers, boots, a sword with white sword belt and epaulettes as worn by a second-lieutenant.

The pupils shall be selected from amongst young men of good education and they shall receive from their families pay totalling 360 francs a year. In addition, they shall be paid 180 francs a year by the government and be issued with a soldier's rations. Expenses shall be met by the family concerned.

Governor of Elba, Count DROUOT

October 30.

For the last two months I have perceived that, upon my return from the Continent to Elba, hints were thrown out by General Bertrand as if my visits to the island were expected to be only of short duration. But I cannot say whether this was in order to ascertain the footing upon which my stay was prolonged, or merely in the way of accidental observation from my making frequent excursions to the mainland, without any other meaning. As my reception was always marked with attention and kindness, although I saw less of Napoleon, and as in my interview at Longono he expressed his satisfaction at my being there, as he said, 'to shatter the illusion' I did not feel myself called upon to enter into explanations further than to state (in accordance with Lord Castlereagh's directions) that my residence would continue until after the affairs of Europe were settled by the Congress. After that, I presumed that His Majesty's Government would enable me to exhibit the powers of a permanent and ostensible appointment.

Today General Drouot told me that Napoleon asked why I did not go to visit him, as he had not seen me since my return; and he requested me to come to him for an interview the following day, at an hour which he appointed.

October 31.

His reception was as kind as usual, and after polite questions as to my health, he continued for an hour to make his remarks upon the politics of Europe, occasionally questioning me as to what I had observed in Italy, or heard from other quarters.

In the course of his remarks as to the discontent of the Italians, I observed to him that the situation of Italy would be greatly tranquillised if Murat's position was assured, and adverted to a report of the question being decided favourably for him. He did not seem to derive any satisfaction from this report, and by no means coincided in the idea of its having that effect throughout Italy. He traced the evils which existed in Italy to the influence of the clergy, and attributed the discontent which was increasing daily, among other causes, more particularly to the national pride in losing the name of a kingdom. These evils were too extensive and radical to be influenced by Naples alone, or by Murat. He praised the Italians, and ridiculed the Germans. He would engage always to beat 30,000 Germans with 20,000 Italians. The former were stupid, slow, and without pride, contented with their pipes, cows, and farms, whereas the latter were quick and proud, and had now become military. He had quite changed their habits, and abolished much of their degeneracy. All the young men were attached to the French, from having served with them in the army, and their minds were bent upon the formation of Italy into a kingdom. The Government of France had only been nominal. That part of Italy which had been incorporated with French departments was only to have remained so until certain of his projects were fully realised, and the people knew this. They held their places, and felt themselves as one people and one kingdom, from Piedmont to Naples. After this it was impossible for them to be reconciled to the changes which were now being made, through the Austrians, with different language and names, the disgusting measures of the King of Sardinia, and those of the Pope and his priestcraft.

He inquired whether Lord William Bentinck had yet returned to Genoa, if our troops were still there, and whether the Republic was to be reinstated?

He asked as to the probable duration of the Congress of Vienna, adverted to the reports which are in circulation in Tuscany, of its lasting a considerable time, and that the sovereigns would separate before it was closed. He had thought that all arrangements had been made and thoroughly understood before their arrival at Vienna, and that their confirmation only was wanting, which would have been affixed immediately. How could so many sovereigns remain together for any length of time? Their separation without a final settlement of Europe, and a publication of the terms, would have a dreadful effect, particularly in Poland, Italy, and France. He enlarged upon this at different times, as if he dreaded the consequences, and pretended even to express his wish that the Congress should conclude speedily and amicably.

With regard to Poland, he said that if Russia could attach the minds of the Poles to her as one people, she would be the first Power in Europe. But this was the difficulty. It was a problem yet to solve, and one which he thought not at all likely to be solved. If the Emperor Alexander sent a viceroy, with all the appointments and the government in the hands of Russians, the Poles would never become attached to them, nor contribute to the strength of Russia. The nobles were numerous, high-spirited, well-educated, and not to be deceived, and therefore would not be satisfied by a mere show of independence and with the name of a kingdom without the reality. The rest of the nation were in a manner slaves without instruction, but they would follow their own nobles with confidence and with perseverance in any cause they espoused. But, on the other hand, if the Russians succeeded in uniting the Poles heartily in a common interest, the whole of Europe ought to dread them. It would be impossible to foresee or to limit the consequences. Hordes of Cossacks and barbarians, who had once seen the riches of more civilised countries, would be eager to return. They would overrun Europe, and some great change would probably result from it, as had been the case in former times from the incursions of barbarians. His own opinion, however, was, that the Poles and Russians would never be united in one cause; there were so many difficulties in the way.

He afterwards changed the subject to the state of France, principally in respect of Belgium, and his favourite topic, Antwerp. He gradually became warmed, and was frequently much agitated. The state of humiliation to which France is now reduced by her cessions and the aggrandisement, so unequal, of the other leading Powers!

'England with all her riches, her foreign possessions, and her maritime strength! Austria with the whole of Italy. Prussia with Mayence, and as far as Luxembourg! The French at Danzig were not so extraordinary as the Prussians at Luxembourg. What a humiliation for France after so many years of superiority acquired by her glory! Holland with Belgium!' It was a great object for England to have Antwerp in possession of her former ally Holland, and taken from France. But if this was to be effected, what prospect was there of a lengthened state of tranquillity in France? He certainly thought none. He might be wrong, but time would show. There could not be quiet in Europe, if the French were humiliated, and reduced out of proportion with the other leading Powers. He was of opinion that the Ministers of England were as much persuaded of this as himself, and

137

considered the present frontiers of France were quite unreasonable; but it would be impossible for them to convince the people of England of that, and therefore he presumed they acted contrary to their own opinions. He was perfectly ready to have made peace at Chatillon, if Antwerp had been left to France.[73] It was England, therefore, that prevented the peace. The whole of France knew that, and approved of his determination never to cede it, but to stake everything upon it as he did. Metternich was bribed by England at that time. He knew the particulars of every sum that he received, and even the debts which he owed in Paris, and which were all paid for him. At present Holland and Prussia, and probably Russia also, would be the constant allies of England, and this would throw France and Austria together.

He again descanted upon the feelings and qualities of the French people, pointing out that there would be a violent reaction of the whole nation before five years were over, similar to what took place at the Revolution, in consequence of their humiliation and so great a diminution of frontier. The Rhine was the natural boundary. Every man in France considered it so, and this opinion would never alter. There was no want of male population in France, and all martial beyond any other nation, by nature as well as in consequence of the Revolution and their ideas of glory. Louis XIV's memory, notwithstanding their sufferings under him, was still beloved by the French, because he had flattered these feelings. It was the battle of Rosbach[74] which produced the Revolution in France, more than any other of the causes to which it was ascribed. In many instances Louis XVIII and his supporters showed good sense, in others a total ignorance of the French character. It was Peltier who wrote the newspapers in France; and nothing could be more calculated to disgust the mass of the population. Their spirit, if once roused, cannot be opposed; it is like a torrent. Neither ministers nor marshals, nor anyone else, can either direct it differently or stem it. It is otherwise in England. The nation is directed by parties and by reasoning. Perhaps the King of France might send a part of his army to St. Domingo, but that would be seen through. He himself had made a melancholy attempt to conquer that island with 30,000 men, which had proved the inutility of such an expedition.

---

73 The conference at Chatillon took place in February 1814. The Allies insisted that France be reduced to her 1790 borders; Napoleon refused and continued fighting.

74 'In 1757, between 22,000 Prussians under Frederick the Great, and 55,000 French and Imperialists under the Prince de Soubise, a favourite of Madame de Pompadour. The former had 500 killed and wounded; the latter, 2,800.' – Hozier's *Seven Weeks' War*, vol. i. p 342.

The appointment of the Duke of Wellington as ambassador at Paris was an open insult and injury to the feelings of the French people. He, who had been one of the most successful instruments against them, could not be considered in any other light. He knew, by persons from France, that there was a universal disgust there at their present humiliation, and that the Bourbons had very few partisans in the army, and among the bulk of the population.

He was then at pains to show that he had no personal motives or expectations.

'I am a dead man. I was born a soldier. I have mounted the throne, and I have descended. I am ready for everything. They can transport me. They can assassinate me. I would stretch out my breast to receive the dagger. As General Bonaparte, I had possessions that I had gained, but they have taken all.'

He asked me whether I had lately received any letters from Lord Castlereagh, and whether I had written to his lordship, to report the sentiments he had expressed respecting the detention of the Empress and his son? I said I had, but as yet had received no answer.

Napoleon's sister Pauline arrived here today on board of his corvette, escorted as far as the channel of Piombino by a Neapolitan frigate, which then returned to Naples without any communication with Elba.

November 1-12.

I have ascertained from undoubted authority, that M. Colonna has gone to Florence, charged with a letter from Napoleon to the Grand Duke of Tuscany.

After the Tunisian corsair left this harbour, she gave chase to some coasting vessels near Piombino, and blockaded them there. It appears certain that Napoleon has established himself on an amicable footing with this Power, or that he has bribed the captain of the ship with the advantage of taking shelter in his ports, so as to be able perhaps to communicate with France. For it is said that she came direct from Toulon in four days. I shall pursue this investigation, as the circumstance appears remarkable.

MEMORANDUM OF INFORMATION WHICH IT IS DESIRABLE TO OBTAIN AS SOON AS POSSIBLE, OR ANY OTHER CIRCUMSTANCES CONNECTED THEREWITH

1. Whether the amicable understanding between Elba and the Tunisian corsair is with it only, or whether it extends to all vessels of the Bey of Tunis?

2. The extent of these relations in detail?

3. By what means and channel they have been effected?

4. Whether by way of Genoa or by way of Naples, and how far Murat or his Government has been concerned in establishing this communication?

5. Whether the corsair came from Toulon, or from whence, when she arrived at Porto Ferrajo upon October 24?

6. Whether she has conveyed persons or letters to or from Napoleon, by way of France or Corsica, Naples, or other parts of Italy?

7. If not from Napoleon or to him, whether she has conveyed letters to or from other persons in Elba? The nature and extent of this communication, as much in detail as possible.

Napoleon appears to be agitated by the want of money, and to be impressed with a fear that there is no intention of fulfilling the treaty made at Paris, in respect of the sums stipulated for himself and his family. In writing to Lord Castlereagh, I have set down the only expressions which have fallen from himself, but those about his person cannot dissemble their belief in the reports which are circulated in Italy, to the effect that it is intended to remove him to St. Helena or St. Lucia.[75] The wife of General Bertrand lately said that he has scarcely a shilling, not even a ring to present to any one, and that his situation is frightful.

I have expressed myself to Lord Castlereagh as follows:

[Despatch No. 34.]
If pecuniary difficulties press upon him much longer, so as to prevent his vanity from being satisfied by the ridiculous establishment of a court which he has hitherto supported in Elba, and if his doubts are not removed, I think he is capable of crossing over to Piombino with his troops, or of any other eccentricity. But if his residence in Elba and his income are secured to him, I think he will pass the rest of his life there in tranquillity.

---

75 In September 1814 French Foreign Ministry officials were debating whether Napoleon should be sent to America or South America. Consideration was also given to transporting him to a Pacific island or St. Helena. In October French diplomats were discussing with the Portuguese whether Napoleon could be sent to the Azores and were willing to pay 2,000,000 francs for one of the islands. By February 1815 Joseph de Maistre, French Minister in St. Petersburg, was suggesting to his allies that Napoleon should be despatched to Botany Bay.

November 13-18.

The last party of recruits who arrived from Corsica upon October 25 have been sent back, and it is given out that Napoleon does not wish to receive any more. It is difficult to say whether this is on account of the expense, the general discontent of these recruits, or that Napoleon's views and hopes are more extensive than they were upon his first arrival at Elba.

Upon the 15th instant a party of gendarmes were sent to the village of Capolini to enforce the arrears of contributions, but the inhabitants resisted. In consequence, Poles and Corsicans, amounting to nearly 400, were sent there upon the 17th during the night, and are to remain until the tax is paid, receiving each one pound of meat and an allowance of wine from the inhabitants of this small village, who do not probably exceed 400 or 500. Two priests and three others of the principal inhabitants were arrested at the same time, and conveyed to Porto Ferrajo.

November 19-30.

Florence. I have come to this place for the purpose of comparing my intelligence respecting the Tunisian corsair with that in possession of the Grand Duke's minister. I also requested Captain Adye, commanding His Majesty's ship *Partridge* on the Elba station, to assist me in these inquiries, in case of his falling in with the Tunisian in the course of any of his cruises. He returned to Leghorn on November 20, and as he could not obtain any information respecting the corsair, he is of opinion that she has returned to Tunis.

Previously to my application to Captain Adye, the Tunisian had anchored a second time at Elba, but in the Port of Longono, where she remained from October 31 until November 10. She was in quarantine during the whole time, and I cannot ascertain that there was any underhand communication. The captain stated that he had sailed from Tunis for the express purpose of cruising on the Roman coast, but that the winds and bad weather had forced him to put into Toulon, where he had remained eighteen days in quarantine; that the same causes had induced him to put into Elba, and that he had no orders to seize the vessels of that island.

I have likewise been anxious to ascertain the result of the examination of a spy – one Ettori – who went from Elba to Leghorn, and was arrested there. The man is now here under the inspection of the police, but the information obtained respecting him has been far less important and conclusive than had been expected. In fact he appears to have been equally in the confidence of Marshal Bellegarde and Napoleon!

M. Ricci, who acts as vice-consul at Elba, and obtains private information for me there, has just transmitted to me a report respecting the embarkation of guns and shot. This is certainly a matter calculated to excite alarm, and deserves the utmost and most immediate attention. But I am persuaded it will prove to be old iron shipped for sale to the Continent, as a cargo of old guns, broken shells, etc., had been already sent by Napoleon to Civita Vecchia.

There has been a further reduction of servants and other expenses of Napoleon's household for the sake of economy. This reduction is estimated at 35,000 francs per month.

Four of the officers of Napoleon's corvette received decorations from Murat, but have been expressly forbidden to wear them. I do not yet know the grounds upon which this interdiction has been given.

Having supplied all the information in my power to Lord Burghersh (who has arrived here as His Majesty's Minister to the Court of Florence) with respect to my mission, and the objects connected therewith, I propose returning at once to Elba.

I have received the following despatch in reference to his lordship's appointment:

Foreign Office: October 13, 1814.
Sir,
His Royal Highness the Prince Regent, having been pleased to appoint Lord Burghersh to be His Majesty's Envoy Extraordinary and Minister Plenipotentiary to the Grand Duke of Tuscany, and it being desirable that his lordship should be kept constantly informed of the state of affairs at Elba, I have to signify to you His Royal Highness the Prince Regent's commands, that you send your official correspondence with this office under flying seal through Lord Burghersh at Florence. You will at the same time omit no opportunity of sending duplicates of your despatches by sea.

I am, etc. etc.,

Colonel Campbell, etc. etc.,
(Signed) BATHURST

While I was at Florence, M. Hyde de Neuville[76] arrived there. From his distinguished zeal and ability in the Bourbon cause, this gentleman was sent to Italy by the King of France's confidential friends, to collect information respecting Napoleon's situation and conduct at Elba. The mission conveys in itself an evident proof of the apprehensions they entertain, that the internal state of France and Bonaparte's situation were incompatible with the tranquillity of the nation. The French Consul in Tuscany, Monsieur Mariotti, informed me of M. H. de Neuville's arrival. The real object of his mission was imparted to me by M. Mariotti, as well as by M. Fossombroni, the Minister of the Grand Duke of Tuscany, although the ostensible object was said to be some arrangements respecting the Barbary Powers. The information of these gentlemen was sufficient to induce me to lay aside every reserve with M. H. de Neuville, although possessing no previous acquaintance with him, nor any other introduction. Perceiving that he was greatly in error upon many points, I showed him Lord Castlereagh's instructions, and gave him every information connected with my own duties, Napoleon's situation, and his

---

76 Memorandum respecting M. Hyde de Neuville, given to M. Planta, Secretary to Lord Viscount Castlereagh.
London: April 7, 1815.
This gentleman came to Italy in November last, upon a pretext of arrangements between France and the Barbary Powers, but in fact (as he afterwards confessed to me, and as M. Fossombroni, the Minister of the Grand Duke of Tuscany, told me) to see what Bonaparte was doing in Elba. This was previous to the arrival of Lord Burghersh.
Being assured, from undoubted sources, of his attachment to the Bourbons, of his intimacy with Sir Sidney Smith (with whom he had served on the coast of France, and with whom he was then in correspondence), I gave him the fullest information respecting Bonaparte's conduct and situation, and even respecting my own situation in Elba, his restlessness, the emissaries he had sent abroad to recruit for men, the extraordinary circumstance of his harbour being frequented by a Tunisian ship, which ship had last come from Toulon, that it was impossible to say what project might be masked under that connection. This vessel might pass in the Mediterranean from one port to another with less suspicion than his own, and his appearance in France might only be known after he was in possession of Toulon and the fleet.
I expressed my great surprise that the King of France had not yet sent any confidential person to Italy, to remain there for the particular purpose of watching Bonaparte, who would discover his emissaries and plots among the various States of Italy, which would be done more effectually by one person employed for that object; also some ships to guard him.
He was very thankful for the information, acquiesced in all my remarks, and set off immediately for Paris to report upon these subjects; and, very soon thereafter, several ships of war belonging to Louis XVIII came to cruise near Elba. But I did not hear more of M. Hyde de Neuville, or any other agent of France.
M. Hyde de Neuville, known to be a firm adherent to the King, must of course have given all that information to his Ministers, pointing out to them how very little check against any sudden aggression of Bonaparte there was by my residence, and how necessary it was to watch him.

dispositions, desiring to call his attention to the unlimited freedom of person and communication with the Continent which Napoleon possessed. I then distinctly pronounced to him my opinion that Napoleon was not sufficiently watched; that I had no means of preventing him from escaping; that he was still of a most restless disposition; that discontented persons of an adventurous spirit, from France and Italy, frequented Elba; that it was a very suspicious circumstance, the communication held with the Tunisian ship; that I had traced her having come to Elba. I even supposed it possible to him, that a conspiracy might be formed in Napoleon's favour at Toulon; he could be conveyed in that ship, and that the first intelligence might be his being in possession of that important place and the fleet.

M. Hyde de Neuville took memoranda in writing, in my presence, of this information, and departed the following day in post haste to Paris.[77]

December 1-2.

Leghorn. Since my arrival here, upon my way to Elba, I have ascertained that the guns, etc., which were embarked there, were (as I supposed) old iron to be sent to the Continent for sale. So persuaded was I of this, that I would not have transmitted the report to Lord Castlereagh, had I not been certain that it would reach Vienna through the Tuscan Government, and in more alarming terms.

---

77 Two French frigates were soon afterwards sent from Toulon to cruise round the island of Elba; but the evil could not be averted by them, and they were of no use whatever, as will be seen hereafter.

M. de Neuville was afterwards Minister to the United States of America. When referred to for minutes of the above conversation he wrote as follows (*Translation of the above by Sir Neil Campbell*):

'I have not forgotten any of the circumstances mentioned in it, and indeed I am of the opinion that it would not be possible for any sovereign to find anyone more zealous in his cause than yourself. Not only do I well recollect our conversation, but, had I my papers with me at present, I could cite the most minute details of it, as that interesting conversation is preserved in my journal.

The circumstances which you call to my recollection, Colonel, are stated by your letter with most scrupulous correctness. It is a fact that, being at Florenee upon a mission with which the King my master had honoured me to several Courts in Italy, and having the good fortune to meet you there, you expressed to me the utmost satisfaction at having at length been able to communicate with one of the subjects of Louis XVIII, who had ever been faithful to his cause. You stated to me that at length you could speak without reserve, which you did with the greatest frankness and kindness. You certainly did avow to me, Colonel, that Bonaparte was not sufficiently watched, that you did not possess any means for preventing his evasion, and that you were not without uneasiness upon the subject, in consequence of many circumstances which you then disclosed to me. This communication, and others which were made to me, caused my return to Paris with greater haste.'

December 3.

Porto Ferrajo, Elba. I am now able to report on the above subject from personal observation. About three months ago Napoleon directed the old guns and part of the military stores to be removed from Longono (which is a considerable fortification on the Italian side of Elba) to this place, and part of them were afterwards sold at Civita Vecchia as old iron. The brig *Inconstant* is now receiving an additional quantity for the same purpose.

I have seen the correspondence which has passed between General Drouot and two merchants – one here and another at Naples – as to the terms of sale. The principal reasons alleged are the want of money, and the fact that, as the fortification is of no use to Napoleon, it only occasions an unnecessary expense. He therefore proposes to dismantle it entirely by degrees, in proportion as his means enable him to remove the stores.

In order to raise money, he has, within the last few days, sold a large public building in this town, formerly occupied as a soldiers' barrack, for 1,500 francs.

The agent sent to Florence, M. Colonna, was for the purpose of promoting a correspondence with Marie Louise; in the first instance openly, by an amicable intercourse with the Grand Duke of Tuscany, afterwards clandestinely; but both of these have failed.

December 4.

Had a conversation with Napoleon, which lasted three hours and a half.

After some general inquiries as to my health and last visit to the Continent, he said that Talleyrand was 'a villain, a renegade priest, a revolutionist'; in fact, everything that was bad. He knew that he was inimical to him long ago, and would betray him if an opportunity offered. He therefore told Cambacérès, who was charged to remain at Paris with the Empress Marie Louise, and who accompanied her to Orleans, not to leave Talleyrand alone at Paris; but he weakly yielded to *his* application to remain there, so pitifully supplicated for at the very moment of his quitting it.

I asked him whether the letter which had appeared in some of the newspapers as if written by Talleyrand, dissuading him from the war in Spain, was true. He said it was not – not one word of it; no such letter was ever written. It was Talleyrand who first proposed to him the invasion of Spain. After being turned out of office by him, in consequence of representations from the Kings of Bavaria and Württemberg that he demanded sums of money for himself on several occasions, he nevertheless continued for a long time to frequent his evening parties along with Fouché,[78] who was in office at that time. It was in hopes of reviving his credit with him (Napoleon) that Talleyrand advised him to profit by the dissensions which existed in Spain, between Charles IV and his son Ferdinand, and to put one of his own family upon the throne. He presented to him a memoir written to that effect by a friend of his own in Spain, who was intimate with the Prince of Peace. In fact he declared that Talleyrand was a Jacobin of the vilest heart; that he very often urged on him to get rid of the Bourbons by assassinating them; or, if he would not accede to that, to let them be carried off from England by a party of smugglers, who were in the constant habit of coming over. He always rejected the proposal, so long as they kept out of France. It was different with the Duke d'Enghien, who came to the frontier of France, even to the gates of Strasbourg, in order to foment conspiracies. But his death also was an act of Talleyrand's, it was proposed by him; and but for him too the Duke's life would have been saved, even after he was arrested. It was told him (Napoleon) that the Duke d'Enghien requested to speak to him. 'That touched me. I wished to see the young man, but it was already too late. He had taken measures to prevent it. It was he, Talleyrand, who was the cause.'

[In this relation Napoleon showed much enmity towards Talleyrand, but very little emotion or regret at the circumstance itself.]

He asked me whether I had heard of the divorce which it was proposed to institute between himself and the Empress. I told him I had, but only through the foreign papers, and there were so many untruths in the newspapers on the Continent, that I only read the English papers and the *Gazette* of Florence. He said the story had been inserted in the journals of Genoa and Milan. I told him I was persuaded, that although Genoa was occupied by British troops, the officer who commanded there did not interfere with nor influence the press, but confined himself to his military duties. I then mentioned an anecdote which had been related, that Marie Louise had been greatly chagrined at mistaking the Princess of Wales' courier for one of Napoleon's; and, when complimented by the Princess on her proficiency in music, she said she had 'studied it particularly in order to please Napoleon, for that to her he always was and would be perfect!'

---

78 Fouché was the arch-intriguer of the Napoleonic wars and was Napoleon's Minister of Police for much of the First Empire.

Here he showed considerable emotion; spoke of the weakness and inhumanity of the Emperor of Austria, in keeping away his wife and child. She had promised to write to him every day upon her return from Switzerland to Vienna, but he had never since received one letter from her. His child was taken from him like the children taken by conquerors in ancient times to grace their triumphs. The Emperor ought to recollect how differently he had acted towards him when he was entirely at his mercy, and no ties of marriage existed. He had twice entered Vienna as a conqueror, but never exercised towards the Emperor such ungenerous conduct. It was not he who solicited the marriage; it was Metternich who proposed it to Narbonne. 'I have been very happy with my wife, but the marriage has proved very disastrous for me. I should have done better to marry a Russian Princess.' His Council deliberated upon the proposition. Had it not been for the difference of religion, he would have married a Russian Princess. A Greek chapel would not have answered in Paris. To have seen him going to one church, and his wife to a Greek chapel, would not have looked well, and therefore this other marriage was decided upon. As to settlements, he told them to copy the contract of marriage between Louis XVI and Marie-Antoinette: in half an hour it was signed by Schwartzenberg.

He again spoke of the weakness and ingratitude of the Emperor of Austria, who had once come to his camp to supplicate for forbearance. So weak was he as to tell Marie Louise lately that Metternich was Napoleon's friend, and had assured him that he would attend to Napoleon's interests.

In answer to a question, I said that if he gave me a letter for the Empress, I would send it to Lord Burghersh, who had desired me to announce his arrival at Florence, and to offer his services in any way consistent with his duty. He said this might be prejudicial to Lord Burghersh and myself. I replied that I did not apprehend so. The letter would be forwarded to Lord Castlereagh, who would either openly deliver it, or return it honourably.

He was prepared, he said, for every act of personal hostility and oppression, even to the taking his life. Was it not evident that there was some such intention against him in the choice made of the governor of Corsica – Brulart – a man who was employed for many years by the Bourbons while in England in plots and conspiracies with Georges and others? Brulart had even changed his residence from Ajaccio to Bastia, so as to be at the point nearest Elba. Since then he had never gone out to take exercise except with four armed soldiers to accompany him. Brulart could not have been selected with any other view, for he had no connection whatever with Corsica; so far otherwise, that one of the regiments now there had been employed against him in La Vendée.

They spoke of removing him to England. There he would have society, and enjoy an opportunity of explaining the circumstances of his life, and doing away with many prejudices, such as was not possible in the island of Elba. In England he could even see and communicate with his partisans better than at Elba; four-fifths of the French people were in his favour.

He pointed out, as he had frequently done before, the misguided policy of humiliating France; that the trouble there would break out one day or other, and the Sovereigns of Europe would then perhaps, for their own interest and repose, find it necessary to call him in to tranquillise the country.

At present nothing could be wiser than the conduct of the King of France, but the Government acted differently. They openly ordered the restoration of property to the *émigrés* and ancient families. Even he himself dared not do so. Whenever he brought them forward, he felt that 'The reins trembled in my hands.' Much might be done for them in the way of restitution without proclaiming it to all France, and thus affecting the security of so much property.

He had been abused in numerous publications; the epithets of Nero, Brutus, etc., had been applied to him. It had been said that he had received lessons for attitude from Talma, and similar circumstances were stated which had no foundation whatever, while others were exaggerated or perverted. These things proved the adage, 'It is the *truth* alone that can wound,' and therefore he had not been affected by them.

The French knew what he had done for them; how many millions he had brought into the country, and expended in works of public utility. Many of these, which were entirely executed by him, were now ascribed to his predecessors. Before him there was not a sewer in all the streets of Paris; water was scarce. The quays were entirely formed by him. Posterity would do him justice.

I told him he ought to fulfil the pledge given at Fontainebleau by writing his *Memoirs*; that I had received letters from booksellers in London, totally unknown to me, expressing great anxiety on the subject. One in particular, who had published his brother Lucien's poem of *Charlemagne*, wished to propose terms. 'Yes,' he said; 'I shall publish my *Memoirs*, but they will not be very long.'

The Bourbons ought to pursue towards him the same forbearance he had shown with regard to them after he ascended the throne. He would not allow either praise or invective, either good or evil, to be published respecting them.

He had been called coward. 'I say nothing of my life as a soldier. Is it no proof of my courage to live here, shut up in this *cell* of a house, separated from the world, with no interesting occupation, no *savants* with me, nor any variety in my society, excepting when I have occasionally the pleasure of conversing with yourself – even without money?'

Here he stated the sum he had brought with him from France. 'So small were his means,' he said, 'that he had been under the necessity of obtaining an addition, sent to him from Orleans by the Empress, before he could even leave Fontainebleau!'

There had been abuse against him even in the *exposé* of the French budget. It was a false statement, for there was no notice of four hundred millions of *domaines privés* taken by the Royal Family. It was at one time his intention to have replied to this paper, but he afterwards thought it better not to do so.

He inquired about the Congress. I told him the most perfect secrecy was preserved, but it was generally understood that the greatest harmony prevailed.

It appeared extraordinary to him that Murat's fate was not known. He had ordered a levy of 25,000 infantry and 6,000 cavalry, which betrayed a want of confidence on his part towards the Allies. Murat, however, I might depend upon it, did nothing but in concert with Austria. When his sister, Princess Pauline, left Naples, the Austrian Minister was king there! He ridiculed the idea of Murat resisting any terms the Allies might choose to impose upon him. All he could do, was to seek his own death; to fall with arms in his hands, rather than yield to their demands.

He was surprised at the bad policy of England in wishing to restore the family of Ferdinand to the throne of the Two Sicilies. How much more her interest to separate the island of Sicily!

With what hope could the sovereigns of Europe look forward to the enjoyment of tranquillity, with discontent boiling in France and Italy, countries which formed so great a portion of the Continent? Even in Germany it appeared that many of the petty princes were not satisfied. Prince Fürstenberg and many others had presented an address to the Emperor of Austria, at which he had shed tears. Bavaria and Württemberg could not but view that with uneasiness.

He ridiculed the nomination of the Sovereigns of Russia and Prussia to be colonels of Austrian regiments, and their asking leave of absence as such from the Emperor of Austria. What childishness! 'The Emperor Alexander is an actor, and very false; a complete Greek.' Frederick the Great of Prussia having put on the uniform of the Austrian levies when he paid a visit to the Emperor of Austria was not a similar case. Nor did the meeting between Francis I and Henry VIII bear any resemblance to the meeting of the Allied Sovereigns. It might be very well to give the use of a regiment to that Ostrogoth the Grand Duke Constantine, wherewith to amuse himself. During the preparation for the Peace of Amiens, Lord Cornwallis asked him for a regiment of cavalry, the exercise of which he constantly attended, but that was very different too.

In talking of the entry of the Allies into Paris, and the operations at that period, he said that his Guards were only one march from Fontainebleau with the design of attacking them; that, in that case, Schwartzenberg would have abandoned Paris, and taken a defensive position on the other side. General Koller had told him so, and Funti said the same.

Here he stopped himself, and seemed embarrassed at having mentioned the name of the latter. He has always asked me, on my return from any of my late visits to the Continent, whether I had seen Funti, who was formerly a senator at Paris and now lives at Florence.

I told him he had a more favourable opportunity for attacking Schwartzenberg at Arcis, when Blücher's army was separated. He said that might be so – perhaps he was wrong; but his views at that time were to have attacked the Allies in detail from the rear; and that had he not been disconcerted by Marmont's disobedience of orders (who did not push on to Chalons, as directed), he would have destroyed the one army, and then turned back upon Blücher.

Here he related the view of affairs which had induced him to abdicate. He could have supported the war in France for years, and perhaps have carried it out of the kingdom. But although the people would have flocked to his standard, and the army would have stood firm, this would have been the ruin of France. With the armies of Blücher and Schwartzenberg in Paris, Wellington pressing forward from Toulouse, Augereau beaten at Lyons (for he did not then know that he was indisposed to exert himself at all), a faction in Paris against him, and the senate weak enough to assemble by the orders of their enemy, he had no hesitation in descending from the throne, as it appeared to be the only way of saving France. But he would never have done so had not Marmont deserted him – except, indeed, on the regency of the Empress and her son being secured. In his own person he could not even consent to any peace except according to such a treaty as that proposed at Frankfurt. France could not submit to any other line than that of the Rhine, and he had himself openly said that, if he made peace at Chatillon, he should not be able to keep it three months. The people generally might be tired of the wars into which his conquests had led them (*entraînés*), but they would never be satisfied to remain at peace on the terms now imposed. In France there are 800,000 men who have carried arms. He had now no regret in his abdication, nor yet in his refusal of the last propositions for peace. He would do the same over again. Lord Castlereagh prevented the peace at Frankfurt. The other Allies were perfectly willing to consent to it, but England wished to diminish France. I reminded him that Lord Castlereagh did not arrive until after the Allies had crossed the Rhine.

On his asking what were the observations of English travellers who had come lately from Paris, I told him that the people in France, particularly the military, did not show so much good-will towards the English as at first. Many of the French officers, I believed, felt sore at having been put on board the prison-ships; but this arose from many of them, of all ranks, breaking their paroles and deserting.[79] He said we had done the same. I told him that no officer who deserted would be received either by the Commander-in-chief or by his own corps. He said he had published a list of them in the *Moniteur*. I assured him that these were civilians, some of whom might be in the yeomanry or militia, but not in the regular army or navy. He said they were, in his view, equally prisoners of war. As we, immediately on declaring war, had seized all French subjects and their property on the sea, although not belonging to the military service, he in like manner detained all British subjects whom he could lay hold of on the Continent.

I related to him the anecdote of the Princess of Wales' wig and crown tumbling down at the feet of Lucien Bonaparte, adding that she was frequently at his house in Rome. But this did not produce any observation from him respecting his brother, excepting that he supposed they had met in England. I told him, certainly not.

---

79 One of the most notable instances was that of General Lefèbvre-Desnouettes, who had been taken prisoner at Benevente, while pressing Sir John Moore's retreat. He broke his parole in England the following year, and escaped to France. Napoleon at once reinstated him in the command of the mounted Chasseurs of the Guard, and ever afterwards treated him with marked favour.

He said England had not acted generously in prosecuting the war against America, but showed a spirit of inveterate revenge. It weakened her voice at present at the Congress, so great a portion of her force being absent from Europe. She had not occupied Louisiana, nor acquired any great or permanent object. The Americans would gradually improve, and we should have to be satisfied to make peace without having gained any accession of strength or power. Our character, after standing lately so high in the eyes of all Europe, would diminish by the sort of warfare in which we indulged against private property, trading vessels, storehouses, etc. I told him the Americans had no right to expect generosity from us after their ungenerous provocation in forcing us into war when the whole of Europe was arrayed against us. The first excesses were practised by them in burning towns and villages in Upper Canada, even after threats of retaliation were held out to them.

I asked him whether it was true that he had proposed to the British Government, during the Peace of Amiens, to unite in an expedition against the Barbary Powers. He said he had; that the present state of things was a disgrace to all the civilised Powers; but that it depends only on England to put an end to it; and as we had been the means of abolishing the slave trade, or nearly so, so we ought in like manner to make this a national object. I told him that societies had lately been formed with this view, and that they were daily increasing.

He then related at great length his own history, from the beginning of the Revolution, and with more fire and precision than usual.

In the commencement of the Revolution he marched with his company of artillery to Douai, where he witnessed some scenes of violence without taking any part in them. By chance the routine of service sent him to Toulon, where the operations had been very badly conducted under the *Représentants du Peuple*. He had been conspicuous among his schoolfellows and comrades for his knowledge of mathematics, and had been selected by them to compile a Memoir, according to custom, against the Engineer department. From the character thus acquired, he was desired to draw up a Memoir with his plan of operations against Toulon. He did so, and was then allowed to take a detached work, which he had pointed out as the key of the place. On this he immediately received the command of the artillery, and the direction of the operations, according to his own plan, which proved successful. This gave him confidence in himself. He was appointed general of brigade, and came to Paris. There he was named to a command in La Vendée as a general of infantry, but not liking that war, nor to be employed out of his own line in a subordinate situation, he declined it, saying he was an officer of artillery.

Soon afterwards Menou, who commanded the Army of the Interior, was beaten by the Parisians, who likewise threatened the Convention. He himself was at the theatre, in perfect obscurity, and going out, by chance he heard the boys bawling out a decree of the Convention, in which his own name was vociferated. He listened; and as it could be no other but himself, he gave two *sous* for one of the papers, went to one side, and there read the decree of the Convention, by which he was named General of the Interior. He proceeded towards the Committee of Public Safety, and in the course of his walk there again heard his name vociferated about the streets. On entering the Hall, he found the members despatching persons to find him out, if possible, in his obscure residence. 'General Bonaparte, the little general of artillery' was resounded everywhere upon his being perceived. He was ushered into another room by some of the members, where he found Menou in arrest. 'What do you want with me, citizen?' he demanded of one of the Convention. 'Citizen, you are nominated to the command of the Interior!'. 'I said that, before I accepted the offer, I must ask some information of General Menou. Very well. I asked the General where was his artillery? At (I could not catch the word). How many pieces? Forty. Guarded by what force? About forty or fifty cavalry. I immediately called Murat, who was standing by us in the uniform of a captain of cavalry. What number of cavalry have you at your immediate command? Two hundred. Mount instantly, and bring here all that artillery. Sabre all that oppose you. He executed my order. I placed the artillery so as to sweep the streets that day – it was the 13th Vendemiaire – and secured certain other parts with barricades and palisades – forced the Parisians to remain quiet, and restored the power of the Convention.' He remained in this command during three months, after which he was named general of artillery to the Army of Italy, and afterwards to the chief command.

After his successful campaigns as General Bonaparte, commanding the Army of Italy, he returned to Paris, where he remained some time in a small house in perfect retirement, wearing only a *froque*, or covering himself up in his cloak, in order to go to the Institute, of which he was a member. This was in consequence of the military calling out, 'We wish to have General Bonaparte, our little general, for our chief.' Others said, 'He ought to be king. We must make him king.' This gave him great uneasiness, for he was a

Republican in opinion, and had no wish to avail himself of the desire of the army and Parisians. If he had not preserved the most cautious conduct, it would have led to his destruction, either by causing his assassination, or getting him put out of the way upon false charges.

Notwithstanding his determination not to profit by the feeling in his favour, nor to give any pretext for suspicion, the Directory became jealous of him. Talleyrand was therefore sent with a proposal, that he should carry an army to Egypt. He was as much overjoyed, and entered as ardently into the project, as if it had originated with himself. He resolved to give his whole heart to the expedition, looking forward to it as his only object, in order that he might either march on to India, or to Constantinople, according as circumstances might arise in the course of time.

By one of the arrivals from France, while in Egypt, he received a decree of the Directory, which was to be inserted as an *ordre du jour*, according to the practice at that time. This decree related to the electors, and it so disgusted him that, from that moment, he was no longer a Republican. He said to himself, 'I will put an end to all that.' For a long time afterwards he received no intelligence from France, but one day Sir Sidney Smith (who was always eager to send flags of truce, and keep up communication with him by these means) forwarded some newspapers of a recent date. In these he read of the reverses of Italy, the taking of Mantua, etc. Now is my time, he exclaimed to himself, and immediately took his measures, and returned to France.

'You will perceive', he continued, 'that I have engaged but little in the disorders of the Revolution. I was born in an island, half Italian, half French, but I am a Frenchman in soul (*en âme*). I left Corsica at an early age, was educated in France, and have passed my life there.'

I told him that many persons in England asserted that, upon his quitting Egypt, it was his intention to have restored order for the Bourbons. He turned round quickly towards me, and looking with an air of agitation, replied, 'It is not true, never; that would have been treason towards the French. That would not have been to consult their happiness and their interests.' 'After the battle of Marengo the Abbé Montesquieu', he said, 'gave me a letter from Louis XVIII, wherein he asked my assistance to restore him to the throne. Without me he had no hope! Without him I could have no security! I replied, with all the respect that was due to him, that I could not accede to his proposals; but that I should always be happy to contribute, as far as I could, towards the welfare of himself and his family in other respects.'

December 5.

Today I presented, at an interview with Napoleon, Captain Adye, commanding HMS *Partridge* on the Elba station.

Captain Adye having informed Napoleon that he had served on board of Lord Nelson's ship at the battle of Aboukir, he at once entered minutely into the details of that action. As I have perceived in many similar conversations upon naval matters, Napoleon has no idea of the hazard incident to movements upon a coast, nor of the difficulties occasioned by winds and tides, but judges of changes of position in the case of ships as he would with regard to troops upon land. He said that Admiral Brueys expected Lord Nelson's attack would have been on his left, but he ought to have made sail instead of waiting for it at anchor. In a book of Regulations and Instructions for the French Navy there is a plan of a fleet at anchor, with another attacking in the same way as Nelson. It was singular enough that at L'Orient, while he was on board Admiral Brueys' ship, the latter showed him this very plan, and pointed out the disadvantages a fleet would labour under, in waiting for an attack in such a position, instead of getting under weigh. Captain Adye said that Admiral Brueys could not well expect that Lord Nelson's attack should have taken place before the following morning, and that, as far as he recollected, the wind would not allow of his getting under weigh when the attack was about to begin.

Napoleon spoke of Sir Robert Calder's action, and blamed Villeneuve for not attacking the British on the second day. Instead of losing time by putting his vessels into order and arranging their numbers, he ought to have borne down to the attack in any order. I remarked that if the French lost two ships on the preceding day, while the British had only one out of action, the former of course were comparatively less able to engage on the next day. He said those two ships were taken by manœuvre and accident, not by force. If the British Admiral had confidence in his own strength, why did he not attack on the second day, and prevent the French from going into Vigo? I replied that the British Admiral was to leeward, and it depended upon the French to attack: this they made a show of doing, but never came down. The Admiral had another object in view, and could not follow the French fleet to the coast, where he would also have had to encounter the fleet then in Ferrol. He said that was only an excuse, advanced from national pride, for the Admiral ran away during the night of the 23rd (July, 1805).

He lamented deeply the conduct of Villeneuve in disobeying his orders in various ways during the cruise, so as to occasion an improper and unnecessary loss of time in the West Indies, and in going to Cadiz instead of up the Channel, where he was anxiously awaiting him, in order that he might cross over with his flotilla. He explained his plan of deceiving us, by mounting guns on the transports, as if he intended to force his passage across. He would have landed either in Kent or, if possible, on the right bank of the Thames, so as to turn all the defences of towers, canal, etc., made by Mr. Pitt. This danger must always hang over England. An invasion is perfectly practicable whenever France can assemble a larger army than England, and at the same time obtain, for a week or ten days, the command of the Channel with her fleet. On this account the formation of the port of Cherbourg is a serious consideration for England. Our possessions are so extensive, that we must have fleets to guard each of them, and to watch the movements which may be directed against them. While engaged in this, it is easy to mislead so great a proportion of the British navy, that the French must infallibly obtain that superiority in the Channel which is required for a time, in order to effect the invasion. However, he himself foresaw that, if his preparations were not put into execution, it would have the effect of making England a military as well as a naval Power, by rousing the spirit and energies of the whole people, and causing them to form both armed associations and a great army. In the event it had proved so, for it was this which gave both the impulse and the materials for the British army, as particularly shown in Spain.

I told him it was often doubted in England whether he intended to accompany the first body of troops who were to attempt the invasion, and hoped he would excuse my asking him the question. He told me, certainly, he meant to command it in person. The whole would have left Boulogne together, and disembarked as quickly and as much in company as they could. But if the wind admitted of it, he should prefer landing in or near the Thames – so as to turn all the defences constructed by Mr. Pitt – rather than on the coast of Kent. No British force could be collected in sufficient numbers to oppose him. His subsequent measures, in case of success, must depend upon circumstances, but he should certainly have separated Ireland from Great Britain, and success he considered certain.

At first there was a brig placed by Admiral Lord Exmouth upon the Elba station, to act in concert with me. But, upon his departure, Admiral

Hallowell directed this vessel never to remain longer than twenty-four hours at Elba, for fear of causing jealousy to other Powers. On my making a representation to the latter, a partial relaxation of the order was allowed, in case of a positive necessity and direct application on my part.

For some time past the *Partridge* has been under orders to be in readiness to accompany a Sicilian frigate from Leghorn to Sicily, as soon as the Prince Leopold of Sicily should arrive there from Vienna. As this would leave me without means of communication, I have this day written to Rear-Admiral Penrose, now commanding in the Mediterranean, as follows:

Porto Ferrajo, Isle of Elba: December 5, 1814.

Sir,

I avail myself of the first opportunity to acknowledge the receipt of your letter dated November 21, and to express my thanks for your offers of assistance to the objects of my mission.

I beg leave to assure you, that every circumstance connected with the isle of Elba, and which appears to me in the smallest degree interesting to you as Commander-in-Chief of His Majesty's fleet in the Mediterranean, shall be regularly transmitted.

I presume you are in possession of my correspondence with Lord Exmouth and Rear-Admiral Hallowell, by which you will perceive that I submitted to the latter the inconvenience which might arise to the interests of His Majesty's Government from the restrictions which he had placed upon the man-of-war employed here, subsequently to the departure of Lord Exmouth, and the intention of withdrawing her entirely to accompany the Sicilian frigate, neither of which circumstances can have entered into the calculation of His Majesty's Government according to my instructions.

I beg leave to submit to your consideration my representations to that effect, and am supported in the same opinion by that of His Majesty's Minister at the Court of Florence – particularly until the proceedings of the Congress and the affairs of Italy are finally settled, and especially those of Naples.

Notwithstanding these surmises, I hope I shall not excite your apprehensions; but it is necessary to be prepared for possibilities. A thousand reports and conjectures are afloat as to an understanding between Napoleon and Murat. I have no reason myself, however, to believe that the enmity which existed between them has yet been removed, and the alarming apprehensions circulated respecting Napoleon arise from old guns, shot, and shells having been sent from the dismantled fort of Longono to sell at Civita Vecchia.

It is impossible for me to advert further to all the reports which have been circulated, even by persons in public situations in Italy. The correspondence which I have had with Captain Adye, and which I presume he has transmitted to you, arose more from these prevailing rumours than from any belief of my own in the circumstances to which I requested his attention, by means of a memorandum to that effect:

It is with great satisfaction that I avail myself of this occasion to express to you that cordial and zealous cooperation which I received from Captain Adye in the execution of our united duties.

(Signed) NEIL CAMPBELL

December 6.

In a despatch under this date [No. 38], I have written to Lord Castlereagh thus:

I beg leave to repeat my opinion that, if the means of subsistence which he was led to expect on coming to Elba are given to him, he will remain here in perfect tranquillity, unless some great opening should present itself in Italy or France. He does not dissemble his opinion as to the latter, in regard to the present temper of the people, and what may be expected hereafter.

I keep a strict look-out upon all vessels belonging to this island, a list of which I do myself the honour of enclosing for your Lordship's information. I have also given the same to Admiral Penrose, commanding His Majesty's fleet in the Mediterranean, and to the naval officer on this station.

LIST OF VESSELS BELONGING TO NAPOLEON BONAPARTE IN THE ISLAND OF ELBA.

1. One brig, *L'Inconstant,* 16 guns, commanded by M. Talliade, formerly of the French Imperial Navy.

This corvette was given to Napoleon, at the time of his abdication, by the Provisional Government, and has lately returned from Naples with Napoleon's sister, Pauline. At present she is taking old guns, shot, and shells at Longono, to carry to Italy for sale.

2. One bombard, *L'Étoile,* with two masts – Captain Richon – unarmed, 90 tons.

3. One felucca, *La Caroline* – two four-pounders, 26 tons.

4. One felucca, *La Pastorella* – M. Cornevali—5 tons, unarmed.

Remarks. The bombard is generally employed in bringing grain and flour from Civita Vecchia; the two feluccas in carrying provisions to Pia Nosa, and in watching the coast near Rio, to prevent the inhabitants from sending away ore from the mines on their own account.

Besides these vessels, which are the private property of Napoleon, there are seventeen belonging to the inhabitants of Rio, which are employed in carrying the iron ore to the coast of Italy and Genoa for sale. They are from 50 to 100 tons each, consisting of 10 pinques, 2 brigs, 5 xebecs, and 1 brigantine.

December 7-10.

I really believe that Napoleon's reason for preventing the officers of his brig from wearing the decoration of Naples is on account of his enmity towards Murat.

The inhabitants of Capolini paid their contributions, upon which the troops were withdrawn. The priests are confined to the town of Porto Ferrajo, and suspended from their functions by the *Grand Vicaire*, at Napoleon's desire.

The *Intendant-Général* of the island of Elba informs me that Napoleon's troops and vessels cost him one million of francs per year, while all his sources of revenue, including the contributions, will not net four hundred thousand this year. In addition to the discharging a number of servants lately, he has reduced to one-half the salary of his surgeon, treasurer, and some others who hold civil appointments in his household, and who accompanied him from Fontainebleau.

December 11-19.

Leghorn. M. Mariotti, the French Consul here, read to me the substance of a conversation which Napoleon had with a M. Litta, who came to Elba about six weeks ago from Milan. He has been described to me as a native of that city, well connected, possessing ability and enterprise, much attached to Napoleon, and inveterate against the Austrians.

M. Mariotti did not inform me by what means he obtained a knowledge of this conversation. It is not probable that any person could have overheard it, or that M. Litta would divulge it; and I believe that persons who are employed by different governments to watch over Bonaparte's actions sometimes exaggerate, falsify, or invent stories, in order to appear the more zealous in their duties. However, I shall enclose a copy of the conversation to Lord Castlereagh, as near as I can recollect it.

Napoleon. 'What do you want?'

Litta. 'I come to pay homage to your majesty and to assure him of my fidelity.'

N. 'Is General Bellegarde in Milan?'

L. 'Yes, Sire.'

N. 'Is he liked?'

L. 'No, Sire.'

N. 'And the Duke of Modena, is he liked?'

L. 'He tries to be, Sire, but as all his subjects are so disgusted by being made so small, it is impossible.'

N. 'I want to do much for the Italians.'

[Firstly, Napoleon asked about the spirit of the Piedmontese, the Tuscans and other Italians].

Litta told him that one sentiment reigned supreme except for amongst a few men who were older than sixty.

N. 'But are they reliable?'

L. Your majesty can count on them; and had Your Majesty been with us circumstances would have been much different from how they are now.'

N. 'Did Prince Eugène command you well?'

L. 'We regret his loss, Sire.'

N. 'And what does Caprara do?'

L. 'He suffers much, Sire.'

N. 'How many Italians have taken service with the Austrians? '

L. 'Around 6,000 as well as General Palombini.'

N. 'And my Guards, how many of them have taken Austrian service?'

L. 'None, Sire, most of them have gone to Naples.'

N. 'How many troops do the Austrians have in Italy?'

L. 'They say 60,000 but many will return to Austria.'

N. 'Are you here alone?'

L. 'I am accompanied by a young man who has also seen service beneath your eagles.'

N. 'And where are you going?'

L. 'To Naples.'

N. 'Naples?' (he seemed pensive). 'Then I shall see you before you depart.'

I have since learnt that M. Mariotti had this conversation from a person in particular intimacy with M. Litta, to whom he confided it.

December 20.

Returned to Elba.

December 21.

Had a conversation with General Bertrand concerning the statements which appeared in some of the continental journals that General Koller (the Austrian officer who accompanied Bonaparte from Fontainebleau) was now on his way from Vienna to this place.

Soon afterwards I received a message from Napoleon, requesting to see me the same evening at 8 p.m. I have no doubt it arose from his anxiety upon the same subject; for, very soon after saluting me, he asked as to the foundation of the report, and again introduced it several times during a conversation of two hours which I had with him upon various other subjects. He inquired if I had read the report? If I knew it from any other source? What did I suppose to be the object of the journey? Was it respecting Marie Louise? Of course I could only express my entire ignorance, excepting having read the report in a French newspaper, under the head of a letter from Vienna. He seemed to me to view the report more with feelings of hope and eager curiosity than of apprehension.

He discussed the proceedings of Congress at Vienna, and asked me whether it was expected there would be a renewal of war. He knew there were serious differences of opinion, and he did not think they would be easily adjusted. The Congress might be continued for five years, during which time Prussia would keep possession of Saxony, England and Holland of Belgium, and Russia of Poland.

I asked him what he thought of Marshal Soult being appointed Minister of War in France. He did not appear to relish the news, but admitted that the King of France could not have made a wiser choice. 'He will be faithful to the Bourbons,' Napoleon added, 'so long as there is no weight in the other scale; but if ever a patriotic party (as he called it) arises, they need not confide in him! He cannot forget twenty years of service for the glory of France.'

In talking of France, he said that many of his Guards had letters from their comrades and relations, who described the discontent to be very general, and congratulated them on having accompanied him to Elba; that he had no correspondents there himself, but he received many anonymous communications, which described the same state of affairs, and expressed great fears of another revolution and the reign of terror.

'The present Government is too feeble. The Bourbons should make war as soon as possible, in order to establish themselves upon the throne. With such an army as they could assemble, it would not be difficult to recover Belgium. It is only for the British there that the French army has the smallest awe.'

He inquired whether it was true that the French established in Leghorn were ordered to quit it. I told him I had not heard so.

The other parts of his conversation were not remarkable, and, as usual, contained much repetition.

December 22-27.

It is reported in this island, and at Leghorn, that proposals have been made by Napoleon to the Grand Duke of Tuscany for the sale of his brass guns.

I was misinformed in stating lately to Lord Castlereagh that some of the Corsican recruits had been sent back. So far from it, that they still continue to come over here in small parties, clandestinely; eight arrived here on the 10th ult.

Napoleon has lately sold some provisions which were in store in the fort of Longono.

December 28.

Although General Drouot informed me that the *Inconstant* brig had gone to Civita Vecchia for grain, yet, as it was currently reported and generally believed in the island that Bonaparte had sent her to the Levant, supplied with three months' provisions, I was induced to request Captain Adye, commanding HMS *Partridge*, to look in at the former port.

He returned here this morning, and informs me that the *Inconstant* and another of Napoleon's smaller vessels are in the harbour of Civita Vecchia, but that the Pope has refused them permission to export any more grain to Elba from his States. This will prove a considerable annoyance to Napoleon, as there is no other State from whence he can so economically draw this indispensable article for the supply of his troops, workmen, and household.

December 29-31.

Napoleon's spirits seem of late rather to rise than to yield in the smallest degree to the pressure of pecuniary difficulties; although his mother, and some of the principal persons who have followed his fortune, are constantly absorbed in grief and effusions of discontent. They place their last hope for amelioration in the Congress, the members of which, they expect, will fix the regular payment of Napoleon's annuity, according to treaty. They appear also to entertain sanguine hopes that Marie Louise will reside at Parma as sovereign, and even that she will come to Elba after the Congress is dissolved; from all which they draw favourable conclusions.

Of late Napoleon does not oppose the return to France of officers or soldiers who urge it; but most of them prolong their service with him only to await the issue of the Congress.

Fourteen non-commissioned officers and privates received their discharges last week, and have taken their passages in vessels for Genoa. I have seen several of these discharges; they are regularly stamped upon parchment, with the title, 'Leave Granted, Garde Impériale, Bataillon Napoléon'. The services and descriptions of the men are recited, and the motive assigned for the discharge is, 'the present needs of their families for them'. They are signed by Count Drouot, *Général de Division*, Governor of Elba, and by several other officers, precisely according to the previous forms under the government of Napoleon. They are stamped at the top with a seal, upon which there is an eagle.

It is universally supposed in Italy, and publicly stated, that Great Britain is responsible to the other Powers for the detention of Napoleon's person, and that I am the executive agent for this purpose. Napoleon believes this. He has gradually estranged himself from me, and various means are taken to show me that my presence is disagreeable. Of this, however, I could not be certain for a long time, as it was done by hints which could not well be noticed.

I think his inviting Lord Ebrington[80] to dine with him, without me, was intended as a marked slight, for the purpose of inducing me to quit Elba entirely. But, always expecting the Congress to be brought to an end, I have resolved to make the sacrifice of my own feelings until that event, occasionally going to Leghorn, Florence, and the baths of Lucca for my health and for amusement, as well as to compare my observations here with the information of the authorities on the Continent and the French Consul at Leghorn. My return always gives me an opportunity of asking for an interview with Napoleon, to pay my respects. Of late he has evidently wished to surround himself with great forms of court, as well to preserve his own consequence in the eyes of the Italians as to keep me at a distance; for I could not transgress on these without the probability of an insult, or the proffer of servile adulation inconsistent with my sentiments.

---

80 December 8, 1814. Lord Ebrington (afterwards Earl Fortescue) published a record of his conversation on this as well as a previous occasions under the title of *Memorandum of Two Conversations between the Emperor Napoleon and Viscount Ebrington at Porto Ferrajo, on December 6 and 8, 1814.*

CHAPTER VII

Goes to Genoa – Interview with Napoleon on Return – M. Ricci Vice-Consul – Suspicious Persons at Porto Ferrajo – Warm Argument with General Bertrand – Visit to Continent – Meets Mr. Cooke, Under-Secretary – Suspicious Circumstances – Embarks in *Partridge* for Elba – Landing and Discovery of Napoleon's Escape – Interviews with Mr. Grattan, Madame Bertrand, M. Lapis, and Pauline – Pursuit of Napoleon – Return to England

January 1815.

Early in this month I went to Genoa, in hopes of affording to the Austrian General, Koller, the means of coming here with the man-of-war belonging to this station, and being desirous also of conversing with him previously to his arrival in this island. Receiving no instructions of any sort from Vienna, I was anxious to let General Koller know my uneasiness respecting Napoleon, and my suspicions of his holding communications of an improper nature with Murat. As, however, he did not arrive here within the period calculated upon, I returned to Elba.

During my absence, accounts had been received at Porto Ferrajo that many Italian officers, including some generals, had been arrested at Milan, and that General Koller had gone there from Vienna.

In the first interview I had with Napoleon after my return (January 14), he asked many questions as to the nature of the charge against those officers. I told him that I had no knowledge beyond the public reports at Genoa, which ascribed their arrest to the discovery of a plot against the Austrian Government; and it was more over stated that the information as to their plans had been given by Murat. He said repeatedly, 'They will not find anything against me. At least, they will not find that I am at all compromised.' These expressions, as well as the whole tone of his conversation upon the subject, bore evident marks of anxiety. He did not believe, he added, that these persons were guilty of any crime, but that it was merely a pretext of the Austrian Government, in order to confine them, and then remove them out of Italy.

He then spoke of the statements which had appeared in some of the newspapers respecting his removal to St. Helena or St. Lucia, in a way which showed his belief in them, said he would not consent to being transported from Elba, but would resist the attempt by force to the last. 'Before that, they will have to make a breach in my fortifications. We shall see!' I told him I did not believe these stories, which had no foundation beyond vague report.[81]

(He has lately placed detachments of his Guards in two advanced works of considerable strength, which were erected a few years ago to retard the approach to the fortifications of Porto Ferrajo in case of a siege.)

He asked me, with a kind of suspicious curiosity, whether I had met with any of the ships of war belonging to Louis XVIII, which have lately cruised off Corsica and Elba.[82] He repeated his invectives against the present governor of Corsica,[83] asserting that an assassin, sent by him, was lately landed in Elba from one of these same French men-of-war; that the gendarmes were in search of him, and he would undoubtedly be apprehended; that the crews of these ships were attached to himself, and gave him intelligence of everything which passed in the squadron. He appeared much agitated, and impressed with a belief in the truth of what he stated. In reply, I assured him that I did not believe for a moment that the Bourbons were capable of sending emissaries to make attacks upon his life, and that if I became aware of any circumstance which could induce me to suspect anything of the kind, I would lose no time in acquainting him with it.

His brig returned here from Civita Vecchia last night, having touched by the way at Naples and Corsica. She failed in procuring any grain. This morning (January 16) she was driven on shore by a violent gale of wind, but

---

81 'I asked if he thought that it had been the intention of the Allies to have sent him to St. Helena?' 'Why,' replied the Emperor, 'it was much spoken of. However, Colonel Campbell denied it.' – O'Meara, *A Voice from St. Helena*, vol. i. p. 460.

82 Two French frigates were sent from Toulon to cruise round the island of Elba, soon after my interview with M. Hyde de Neuville.' – *Note by Sir N. C.*

83 'Bonaparte had particular reason to dread Brulart. This Chouan chief had been one of the numbers who had laid down their arms on Napoleon assuming the Consulate; and who had been permitted to reside at Paris. A friend of Brulart, still more obnoxious than himself, was desirous of being permitted to return from England, to which he had emigrated. He applied to Napoleon through Brulart, who was directed by the Emperor to encourage his friend to come over. Immediately on his landing in France he was seized and executed. Brulart fled to England in grief and rage, at being made the means of decoying his friend to death. In the height of his resentment, he wrote to Napoleon, threatening him with death by his hand. The recollection of this menace alarmed Bonaparte, when he found Brulart so near him as Corsica.'– Scott's *Life of Napoleon*, ch. lxxxii., *note*.

by taking out her guns and stores she will be got off again without any material injury.

A sloop of war belonging to Murat anchored here yesterday, having on board a Princess of Saxe-Gotha. This ship left Genoa ten days ago, bound for Naples, and it is said that she will proceed from this to Leghorn, to repair some damages. I can only consider this as a pretext to cover some other intention, as the wind is now favourable for Naples, and the distance to the latter place so little beyond that to Leghorn.

February.

In my interview with Napoleon (February 2) he was unusually dull and reserved; but from that manner wearing off by degrees, it afterwards appeared to me as if it had been studied.

He goes less abroad than before, and appears much more tenacious of his dignity in exterior show and form. He never takes exercise, excepting in a carriage drawn by four horses, and accompanied by Generals Bertrand or Drouot, who sit uncovered, whatever may be the state of the weather, while passing through the town and fortifications.

For some time past Napoleon has suspended his improvements as regards roads and the finishing of his country residence. This is, I think, on account of the expense. Some of the roads, as well as a bridge built entirely for his own use, and unconnected with the public, have yet, by his order, been paid for entirely by the inhabitants.

Council of State was lately held at Porto Ferrajo, to determine whether the town-hall (*hôtel de ville*) can be sold for his private emolument; but as the opinions were divided, the project has not yet been carried into execution.

Some time since, I recommended to Lord Castlereagh M. Ricci, who was formerly British Vice-consul at Longono, whilst that port belonged to the King of Naples, as a person very fit for the appointment of vice-consul in this island. As it was very desirable that some one should in the interim represent this character, in order to send out pilots, and afford other assistance to British men-of-war or trading vessels which might touch here, I took it upon myself to give M. Ricci a letter of recommendation, requesting all captains who might enter to consider him in such a capacity, so long as the appointment might be vacant; to call upon him for every necessary aid and protection, and to pay him the usual trifling fees. I informed General Bertrand of the circumstances of the case, stating that although no exequatur or formal acknowledgment of his appointment could be asked for, or was expected for the present, yet that I requested he might tacitly be accepted in that office. This was agreed to. Soon afterwards, in consequence of his informing me that the priest and some other of the inhabitants of Capolini – who were then in revolt on account of the contributions – had made use of very strong language with reference to Napoleon, and had requested his interference, I cautioned him against any such communications, and furnished him with written instructions for his guidance.

Upon my return here lately from Leghorn, after a short absence, M. Ricci informed me that he had been called upon by the governor to state the nature of his appointment, and was informed that my instructions, of which he gave a copy, were not official, and therefore he could not be considered as consul until he had received his formal commission from London.

When speaking to me on the subject, General Bertrand did not say that M. Ricci would be prevented from acting as consul, but that it was necessary for him to receive a commission as such from the British Government before he could be recognised in any manner. At the same time, he acknowledged that M. Ricci's character was highly respectable, and that he had not committed any act which could justly give offence.

I cannot precisely account for this sudden and apparently useless stir about M. Ricci's powers, unless it were from disappointment at finding that he had not received any commission from the British Government, as had been reported, and in which it is possible that Napoleon expected his own titles might have been inserted. Or it might be to intimidate him from giving me information of what passes in the island, and to authorise, perhaps, a sudden seizure of his papers, after having deprived him by the commandant's letter of that protection which might be understood to attach to his public character, or to resent his interference with regard to vessels which frequent this island under British colours, without being in reality entitled to them. He has also taken up the case of a British vessel which was lately wrecked on the island of Pia Nosa.

If any personal insult be hereafter offered to M. Ricci (which has never yet been the case, but, so far from it, he has always been assisted hitherto in the execution of his duties), such as I have supposed, it will be a proof of the existence of some improper and guilty connection, in regard to which Napoleon is anxious to ascertain how far my knowledge extends. Nothing injurious to M. Ricci could possibly be discovered, as I have invariably directed him, since my first arrival, neither to ask nor speak in any way which could be considered hostile or exceptionable, confining himself entirely to his duties, and to giving me information.

However, I have again told M. Ricci to be very careful to give no cause for suspicion, either by indiscreet language or by holding any communication with the discontented people at Capolini; nor to keep by him any paper which can possibly be made a charge against him as one of Napoleon's subjects. For at present they had deprived him of the inviolability which belonged to his public character, and therefore he must be very circumspect not to put himself in their power, nor to retain any documents which might be suddenly seized, and might compromise him. At the same time he was to be particularly on the alert, to give me constant information; and if anything extraordinary occurred while I was absent, not to consider expense, but to come off instantly himself and report the matter both to me at Leghorn and to the British Minister at Florence.

The letter written to M. Ricci by the Governor was noticed by me in conversation with General Bertrand, in order to make them feel their responsibility in case of any indecorous proceedings towards him, and looking upon it also as a want of delicacy and politeness towards myself. Their chief motive, I suspected, arose from a wish to disgust me, and induce me not to remain in the island. I often reflect whether this is really from some improper projects going on, or merely because Napoleon has appeared to those about him, and to all persons in Italy, to be a sort of prisoner of England under my charge.

Notwithstanding that the licence of Genoese vessels to trade with British colours, formerly granted by Admiral Lord Exmouth and Mr. Fitzgerald, acting consul at Genoa, has been withdrawn for several months, this island is frequented by small feluccas and other boats, which carry British colours but are certainly not British. Some of them possess these licences renewed by a person signing himself R. Waller, British Proconsul at Naples. Others are originally granted by the same person, with every appearance of irregularity, although bearing the British arms and seal. Some, too, are renewed by a person signing himself Joseph Towies, Proconsul, and dated at Castellamare, in the Bay of Naples. Most of these vessels come in here for shelter in the course of their voyages from Naples along the coast, so that it appears to be an expedient of Murat's for giving to the Neapolitan trade the security of the British flag. M. Ricci, who was desirous to obtain further particulars on the subject, has been refused access to the register of the harbour-master.

British trading-vessel of considerable size was lately wrecked upon the island of Pia Nosa, where there is a detachment of Napoleon's troops. The master of the wreck has presented a petition to M. Ricci, setting forth that the commandant demands a daily sum for protection, and also a proportion of the cargo as salvage for Napoleon. This petition has been transmitted to General Drouot as governor of Elba, by M. Ricci, but as yet no answer has been received.

In the channel of Piombino, which is from four to five miles in width between the north-east point of Elba and the nearest part of Italy, there is a small rock called Palmayola, situated about one mile from Elba, and rather more than three miles from the town of Piombino. There is a surface of not many square yards upon its summit. During the late war two guns and a howitzer were placed upon it by the French, to annoy the British men-of-war. These guns were left there. No possession of this rock was given to Napoleon, but he always spoke of it as being an appendage of Elba, no less than Pia Nosa. He has lately sent a few soldiers there. This can only be for one of two motives – either to apprehend any of his men who might desert, and possibly touch there, or to hold secret communication personally or through others with anyone who may come over from Italy. I mentioned this circumstance to General Bertrand as having attracted observation in Italy. He did not attempt to explain the matter in any way, but treated it quite lightly.

Without attaching too much importance to this rock, or the facts in connection with it, it is worthy of remark that there is another island, without any inhabitants, called Monte Christo, south of Elba, and not double the distance of Pia Nosa, to which Napoleon's fancy or projects may also lead him, and others at similar distances again to the southward, approaching the coasts of Rome and Naples. So that his absence from Elba could be less easily known, while any pretext remained for quitting it. He has paid three visits to Pia Nosa since his arrival here, and before the winter set in. His brig has been repaired of the damages sustained by running aground last month, and she is again ready for sea. It is given out that she will proceed to Longono, to convey here the stores of that fort – an operation in which another of his vessels has been employed for some time. The officer who commanded the brig when she was driven on shore has been discharged, on the plea of incapacity and peculation. But some persons say that Napoleon suspects him of a secret understanding with the existing Government of France, and of a wish to destroy the brig. His successor is M. Chauslard, *capitaine de frégate*, who came here from Toulon a few months ago.

The ships of the French squadron are sometimes seen near this island. There is a brig and a schooner under the immediate orders of the Governor of Corsica, and two frigates from Toulon. In my last conversation with Napoleon, when the subject of these ships was mentioned, he did not seem so irritated or apprehensive as at first.

Quarters are provided for twelve men in each of the villages nearest to Corsica; but whether this circumstance is in order to prevent the Corsican soldiers from deserting, (many of them have gone off lately), or as a blind to draw off attention from Porto Ferrajo, it is impossible to say. As usual, this arrangement has been accompanied by a report, purposely circulated to cause a stir, 'that a very great personage is expected to disembark there shortly.'

February 14.

Today there was a review of the Corsican battalion, when it was notified to them, that all who were desirous of quitting Napoleon's service should declare it, and discharges would be given to them. None came forward; so far from it, that the men generally called out, '*Vive Napoléon!*' This probably arose from the fear of being stripped of their uniform, and sent away without any clothing, for there have been frequent desertions of late.

February 15.

M. Litta, whose conversation with Napoleon I have before related, went lately from this to Naples.

Similar mysterious adventurers and disaffected characters continually arrive here from France and Italy, and then proceed on to Naples, giving out that they are disappointed in the hopes of employment by Napoleon, and that they expect to realise them with Murat.

One of the most remarkable of these characters, who lately fell under my observation here, was a M. Theologue, a Greek, said to have come here from Paris. He is much attached to Napoleon, and has been greatly employed by him in the affairs of Turkey and Persia. He left this for Naples about ten days ago.

A person, who calls himself Pietro St. Ernest, has arrived here under the guise of a sailor from the Bay of Spezzia. The *commandant de place*, the commissary of police, and other officials, have been with him, and have ordered him not to be disturbed.

Madame Bertrand gives out that M. Talliade is going at once to Paris. He belonged formerly to the French Marine, and is married to a native of Elba.

M. Kundtzow, a Norwegian gentleman, was presented to Napoleon lately. His first question was, 'Are you a Norwegian?' next, 'What is the population of Norway?' Mr. K. answered, 'Two millions, Sire.' 'One million eight hundred thousand,' said Napoleon immediately. Some of Napoleon's admirers will say in this, as in so many other instances, that it shows wonderful knowledge and minutely correct information – unless indeed he had referred to his library to prepare himself for the interview!

The *Adjudant de place* of Longono – an Italian named Bellucci – has lately returned from Naples, whither he went some months ago. He speaks openly of Murat's preparations for war, and states that the fortress of Gaeta has been provided with stores, as if for a siege.

It is scarcely possible to convey an idea of Porto Ferrajo, which is like the area of a great barrack, being occupied by military, gendarmes, police officers of all descriptions, dependents of the court, servants, and adventurers – all connected with Napoleon, and holding some place of honour or emolument in subservience to him. The harbour is constantly filled with vessels from all parts of Italy, bringing over almost hourly supplies of provisions for this great increase of population, as the island itself furnishes nothing but wine. Vessels, too, of all nations frequently anchor here, from motives of curiosity and speculation, or detained by contrary winds.

I have before alluded to the claim made by the Commandant of Pia Nosa to a part of the wreck of a British vessel cast away there. This he stated to be by Napoleon's order, and I have every reason to believe it was so. This claim, however, has now been withdrawn, or rather is postponed for future reference to the owners at Leghorn, in consequence of the master's petition to M. Ricci and my interference. Napoleon's habits of unprincipled rapacity appear not to have been as yet forgotten.

In a conversation which I had with General Bertrand, I perceived that my mediation in support of these unfortunate persons was not relished by Napoleon, as well as a request which I had made to be permitted to visit Palmayola, in order to ascertain its exact position and extent.

General Bertrand expressed his feelings in very strong terms; said that the Emperor and all of them were under great obligations for all the facilities afforded by me as the British Commissioner, and were very happy at my prolonging my stay; that they wished to show me every attention (*bienséance*); that I must know all the reports about Palmayola were absurd. M. Ricci, he added, could not be considered as British Vice-consul without holding a commission as such. There could be no treason or injury to the British Government in a few small vessels arriving there from Genoa or Naples, although they might perhaps carry the British flag. The Emperor lived quietly in his retreat, and therefore considered all this as meddling (*tracassant*)! I told him this was a strong expression; that to be sure, I was not accredited, and therefore had no right to interfere in these matters, holding no ostensible situation excepting that of Commissioner, which had been prolonged there originally for their advantage and at their request. Now, however, it was my duty to notify to him, that neither Pia Nosa nor Palmayola had been given over to the possession of Napoleon, and that I should report to the British Government what had passed in regard to the points now under discussion. Our conversation was loud and warm; but however disagreeable the prolongation of my stay might be under such circumstances, I resolved to remain, being in daily expectation of the Congress terminating.

On February 16, I quitted Elba in HMS *Partridge* (Napoleon's schooner, *L'Étoile*, commanded by Captain Richon, sailed out of Porto Ferrajo with us, supposed to be bound for Longono), upon a short excursion to the Continent for my health, having agreed to meet Captain Adye at Leghorn, in ten days, in order to return. I was anxious also to consult some medical man at Florence on account of the increasing deafness, supposed to arise from my wounds, with which I have been lately affected. Captain Adye promised to cruise round the island during my absence, as well as to visit Palmayola for my information. His doing so, I thought, would excite less suspicion and attention on Napoleon's part.

My despatch to Lord Castlereagh [No. 43], under date February 15, was delivered by me to Lord Burghersh on my arrival at Florence. It was read by Mr. Cooke, Under-Secretary of State, who had just come from Vienna. He seemed to think my uneasiness with respect to Napoleon quite unnecessary, and at Lord Burghersh's table on the same day said, 'When you return to Elba, you may tell Bonaparte that he is quite forgotten in Europe; no one thinks of him now.'

Before leaving Florence, when I told Mr. Cooke that of course Napoleon would ask me many questions as to the Congress upon my return, and that I should be glad if he could give me any information which

The Vienna Congress: the great and the good meet to settle the fate of Europe.

might be particularly interesting with regard to his money, Marie Louise, Parma, etc., he very sarcastically replied, 'You may tell him that everything is amicably settled at Vienna; that he has no chance; that the Sovereigns will not quarrel. *Nobody thinks of him at all. He is quite forgotten – as much as if he had never existed!'*

I did feel very uneasy at the position of Napoleon and the seeming inconsistencies of his conduct; but, after Mr. Cooke's remarks, I began to fancy that my near view of him and of the state of Elba had induced me to exaggerate circumstances. I had thought it probable that he was preparing to desert to Murat, in case the latter should commence operations against the Allies, and that he was suspicious of an attempt to seize his person before these were fairly begun.

I had written to Captain Adye at Leghorn, to say, that as I knew it was his intention to go over to Elba on February 22, and from thence shortly after to Genoa, to complete his provisions, I feared it would be too long an absence for me from Elba to wait his return, and therefore requested he would land me there previously to his going to Genoa.

In answer to this, Captain Adye wrote to me that he should go to sea on the afternoon of Wednesday the 22nd, and return to Leghorn for me by Sunday the 26th.[84]

I returned from Florence to Leghorn February 25, and on the 26th, while anxiously waiting for Captain Adye, the *Partridge* being becalmed for several hours off the harbour, and after my suspicions had been increased by information which General Spannochi, M. Mariotti, and I myself had obtained, I wrote a despatch (No. 44.) to Lord Castlereagh, and also forwarded by courier to Florence a letter for Lord Burghersh. Another letter, containing a similar outline of information received up to midday, I left with Mr. Falconer, the British Consul at Leghorn, to be sent by post the next day.

---

84 Capt. Adye's report of subsequent events was as follows:

'I anchored in the harbour of Porto Ferrajo about midnight on Thursday the 23rd, and landed there about 9 o'clock a.m. on Friday the 24th. After seeing General Bertrand, and ascertaining that Napoleon Bonaparte was still on the island, I put to sea again about 2 o'clock in the afternoon, with the intention of inspecting the island of Palmayola, agreeably to the wishes of Sir Neil Campbell; but as the wind was light and variable, I did not get near enough before dark to accomplish my wishes, and therefore lay to in the passage of Piombino the whole of the night of Friday the 24th. The next morning, February 25th, I went towards the island, but was refused a landing, in consequence of the order of Bonaparte not to allow any person to visit it, although both Sir Neil Campbell and myself had been assured by General Bertrand that no opposition should ever be made to our landing.

At daylight on Friday morning, the 24th, Bonaparte's brig of war *L'Inconstant*, put to sea, and shaped her course to the northward. The captain of the port, on his coming on board, told us she was bound to Leghorn to repair her damages, in consequence of having been on shore twice. About 9 o'clock a.m. she was perceived to tack, and for about a quarter of an hour her head was towards Porto Ferrajo. She soon afterwaids wore round, and appeared to have little wind, but about noon was lost sight of, close in with the Italian shore.

On my getting into the passage of Piombino about 5 o'clock p.m., I was rather surprised to see the brig with the bombard *L'Etoile* and *La Caroline* (a row-boat which I had seen leave Porto Ferrajo about an hour after noon) coming down from the southward, as if from Longono. I afterwards saw them round Cape Bianco, and haul in to Porto Ferrajo.

On Saturday morning, the 25th as before mentioned, I made the attempt to land at Palmayola. Soon after 1 o'clock p.m. (having light winds from the NE.), I made sail in the direction of Leghorn, and about 6 p.m. plainly saw the brig *L'Inconstant* at anchor in Porto Ferrajo. Shortly after noon on Sunday the 26th, I anchored in Leghorn Roads, and about 2 p.m. saw Sir Neil Campbell, who embarked with me about 8 p.m. that evening. Had there been a breath of wind, I should have instantly sailed, as Sir Neil Campbell from information which he had gained, was most anxious to ascertain the movements of Napoleon. About 4 a.m. on Monday the 27th, a light breeze sprang up from the eastward. I instantly weighed and made sail, but the wind was so light and variable that at the close of the day, we had not got the length of Capraja.

On Tuesday morning the 28th, at daylight, from having had a light breeze during the night, we had advanced to about six or seven miles from Porto Ferrajo. At 8 a.m., having little or no wind, and Sir Neil Campbell being very anxious, he went in one of the ship's boats into the harbour, agreeing with me that if he did not return in two hours, it should be considered as a proof of his being detained, and that I was accordingly to despatch an officer from Piombino to Lord Burghersh at Florence. Sir Neil Campbell returned in about an hour and a half, with the information that Bonaparte had left the island with his generals, and all his French, Polish, and Corsican troops.'

Although mixed up with some other very absurd, contradictory, and confused reports, M. Ricci's letter to me,[85] dated February 18, contained matter of such nature as a to excite the gravest suspicion. And on

---

85 Memorandum of information from Elba received at Leghorn February 26, 1815:

1. Upon the night of the 16th arrived at Longono, from Porto Ferrajo, a Captain Raimondo, accompanied by an orderly dragoon, with a letter from General Drouot to the Commandant, recommending him. He immediately embarked on board a small vessel belonging to Marciana, commanded by one Nanzi (which was supposed, before his arrival, to have been destined for Civita Vecchia), and sailed.

2. Napoleon's vessel, *L'Étoile*, commanded by Richon, went upon the 16th from Porto Ferrajo to Longono, and took on board military stores and salt meat, with which she returned there.

3. Upon the 20th two of the vessels usually employed in conveying iron over from Rio to the Continent, sailed from thence to Porto Ferrajo in ballast only.

4. The *Inconstant* brig, with three other vessels, was in Porto Ferrajo upon the 21st inst., and it was suspected that all of them had on board military stores and salt provisions. It was understood that the voyage of the *Inconstant* was to Naples, and that it would take place in a few days.

5. Upon the 16th, General Bartolozzi inspected the detachment of the Corsicans at Longono, made some promotions of non-commissioned officers, and was busy with his interior organisation.

6. Upon the 17th, M. Colonna arrived at Longono from Porto Ferrajo, and was expected to embark for Naples, to prepare a residence there for Napoleon's mother.

7. A Greek from Cephalonia, named Demetrian Calamalli, was at Elba for ten days, and presented Napoleon with a work of his own composition, after which he left the place.

8. The police has now been more active and suspicious than ever. Detailed instructions are given to the master of the port, health officer, etc., which are said to have been drawn up by Bonaparte.

9. It is reported that the horses of the Polish Lancers are to be brought up from Pia Nosa immediately, and that the saddlers are busily employed. The troops are full of expectation of some great event. Innumerable reports are afoot, so that it is impossible to trace the origin of any. It is said that Napoleon was out in a boat all night; that some days ago his mother had an interview of two hours with Napoleon, during which a very loud discussion took place. She was observed to be much affected on separating from him to return to her own house, and gave orders for immediately packing up part of her effects.

10. Some time ago a contract was made with a M. Rebuffat, of Longono, to supply a considerable quantity of grain, which is ground into flour at Rio, and sent to Porto Ferrajo, where it is put in store.

11. It is said that a Genoese merchant has lately sent part of the brass guns, dismounted at Longono, to the Barbary States, where they were sold.

12. It was reported lately in Elba, that one of Napoleon's officers had employed a person to purchase a vessel of eighty or ninety tons, and that the money was deposited in readiness.

13. I ascertained that, upon the 23rd inst., four or five large cases belonging to the Princess Pauline were disembarked at Leghorn, from Elba. A person of credibility told me that he saw them landed, and the person to whom they were consigned (M. George Bastacchi, a merchant there and a Greek) told him that, about a week before, he had received a letter from M. Sisca, a merchant of Porto Ferrajo, to inform him that these cases were embarked and insured for the sum of 5,000 dollars, that they contained the Princess Pauline's plate, and that they were sent there to be sold, but that the keys and instructions would be sent to him.

14. The same person wns informed upon February 26, by M. Constantin, that he had lately received orders from M. Sisca to freight a British vessel for four months certain, and the option of two more. A contract was made for one of 250 tons about a week ago, but, upon February 25, directions were sent to him not to execute the order.

15. A magistrate and a brigadier of gendarmerie lately left Corsica, and there is reason to know that they have gone over to Elba.

comparing it with information in the possession of M. Mariotti, the French consul, and General Spannochi, the governor of Leghorn, also received from their agents at Elba, it became evident that Napoleon was on the point of embarking a military force with stores and provisions. General Spannochi, indeed, is a feeble old man, who knows little and believes less. But M. Mariotti's reports have always been so superior to those of M. Ricci, that I have constantly had recourse to them as the basis on which to found my personal observations; and now, after being employed together the whole of the morning in tracing the connection of the various suspicious circumstances respecting Napoleon and his adherents at Elba (which we have been in the habit of doing reciprocally, in order to combine and check them), we felt persuaded that he himself was prepared to quit the island immediately with his troops. I have been in habits of very friendly communication with M. Mariotti, and have perfectly coincided in every observation and measure, always looking with anxiety towards Naples on account of its vicinity. My access to Napoleon has for some time past been so much less than at first, as to afford me very little opportunity of personal observation; and besides, the etiquette of a sovereign and court were studiously adhered to. So that during the last few months our intercourse has been continued under different feelings upon both sides, although no expression to that effect was ever pronounced by either of us; and when he did grant me an interview he always received me with the same apparent courtesy as formerly. Sometimes I could only ascribe his reserve to a dislike of his appearing in the eyes of the world as a prisoner, and to my stay being prolonged beyond the period which he perhaps expected, owing to the duration of the Congress. Or possibly he had projects and communications of an improper nature, which he was afraid might be discovered by me, in case of my associating with his mother and sister. The latter, I knew, desired such intimacy, and had taken several steps for that purpose, in which she was counteracted.

Whatever the fact might be – however disagreeable this situation had become for some months past, acting upon mere conjecture and suspicion – with great responsibility in case of Napoleon committing any eccentricity – remaining at Elba as an obnoxious person, upon a kind of sufferance, and gradually slighted by inattentions – I nevertheless considered it my bounden duty not to break off the ties which still existed, in hopes of being useful to my sovereign and his ministers, who

Napoleon quits Elba, a German print of 1815.

had been pleased to honour me with this confidential appointment. Nor was it in my power to quit my post, until the sanction of my employers should be communicated to me. So that I have looked forward for a long time, with impatience and daily anxiety, to the conclusion of the Congress of Vienna, as the period which would produce an order to that effect from Lord Castlereagh and close my mission.

By absenting myself occasionally from the island, I had a pretext for requesting an interview both before my departure and again upon my return, and this became latterly my only opportunity of conversing with Napoleon.

In one of my former despatches to Lord Castlereagh, I observed that 'I did not think Napoleon would ever commit himself, unless some very favourable opportunity occurred in France or Italy; but that if the payments promised to him at the time of abdication were withheld, and the want of money pressed upon him, I considered him capable of any desperate step, even that of crossing over to Piombino and landing there with his Guards'.[86] There is a probability that, about this time, the decision

86 In fact Czar Alexander spoke to Talleyrand on February 13, lambasting the French government for not having paid the funds due to Napoleon. Talleyrand replied that, given the present state of Italy, it would be foolish to provide resources to such a man. After Napoleon's escape, Alexander commented 'Why should we expect him to keep his word with us when we did not do so with him?'.

of the Congress as regards Murat may have become known both to him and to Napoleon. I think it almost certain that Napoleon is prepared to join Murat, in the event of the latter throwing down the gauntlet in defiance of the sovereigns of Europe.

In case of Napoleon quitting Elba, and any of his vessels being discovered with troops on board, military stores, or provisions, I shall request Captain Adye – who has instructions from Admiral Penrose to afford me every facility in the objects of my mission, and who has assisted me very cordially upon every occasion – to intercept, and, in case of their offering the slightest resistance, to destroy them. I am confident that both he and I will be justified by our sovereign, our country, and the world, in proceeding to any extremity upon our own responsibility in a case of so extraordinary a nature. I shall feel that in the execution of my duty, and with the military means which I can procure, the lives of this restless man and his misguided associates and followers are not to be put in competition with the fate of thousands and the tranquillity of the world.

At midday, February 26, the *Partridge* came to an anchor. Immediately after Captain Adye landed at Leghorn in the afternoon, I inquired of him, with abrupt anxiety, whether anything extraordinary had occurred at Elba, and when he left it? He smiled at my anxiety, and replied, 'I neither saw nor heard of anything extraordinary. Upon the 24th I was on shore for some time. In the forenoon Bonaparte was there in good health. I visited General Bertrand. I walked about the town of Porto Ferrajo, and saw the soldiers of the Imperial Guard all busy in carrying earth and in planting trees in front of their barracks. Upon the afternoon of the 24th I again sailed out of Porto Ferrajo. Upon the forenoon of the 25th I was off Palmayola, and went in my boat to the landing-place of that rock, but the guard refused to let me go on shore. Everything was quiet at Elba. Last night at sunset I could see the topmasts of the *Inconstant* within the harbour of Porto Ferrajo!' I then informed Captain Adye of the suspicious information which M. Mariotti and I had obtained; that some chests of plate, belonging to the Princess Pauline, had been secretly sent to Leghorn; that I had succeeded in tracing a proposal lately made from Elba to a person at Leghorn, to hire a British merchant-vessel; that the Polish Lancers had been employed in mending their saddles, etc. I requested Captain Adye to endeavour to recollect whether there was any circumstance which could *now* bear a suspicious construction, although it might not at the time have attracted his notice. He then recollected that at daylight, on the morning of the 24th, the *Inconstant* left Porto Ferrajo, and in the forenoon was seen at a great distance to the northward, off the coast of Italy. It was said on shore that she had sailed for Leghorn or Genoa, to undergo repairs for the damage received when driven on shore at Porto Ferrajo, January 12. In the course of the day the *Inconstant* was observed by some of the officers of the *Partridge* to return southward, keeping close to the coast of Italy. In the afternoon, when the *Partridge* got out of the harbour and turned into the channel of Piombino, she perceived the *Inconstant* with one of Napoleon's smaller armed vessels and one of the island mine-vessels, which passed her and entered the harbour. Captain Adye then recollected that the smaller vessel had been hastily manned, and left the pier while he was on shore at Porto Ferrajo in the forenoon; but he paid no attention to it at the time, nor could he afterwards assign any particular motive for it. It is probable that the latter vessel was sent to communicate with the *Inconstant*, in consequence of the arrival of the *Partridge* occasioning some alarm in the mind of Napoleon that his project of quitting Elba was discovered.

General Bertrand inquired particularly of Captain Adye respecting my movements and probable return, which were frankly communicated to him.

At 8 p.m. went on board the *Partridge*, and at once sat down to write Lord Burghersh hastily the information I had obtained from Captain Adye.

While on shore at Porto Ferrajo upon the forenoon of the 24th, Captain Adye did not see Napoleon. But General Bertrand's wife told him that she had walked with him in the garden on the preceding day, and that he had a bad cold. I think this must be true, so far as relates to his being there on that day; and that Madame Bertrand would neither be made the tool of covering his departure, nor is she capable of dissembling her uneasiness, if any such circumstance had taken place.

If I may venture an opinion upon Napoleon's plans, I think he will leave General Bertrand to defend Porto Ferrajo, as he has a wife and several children with him to whom he is extremely attached, and probably Napoleon will not communicate his intention to him until the last moment. But he will certainly take with him General Cambronne (a desperate, uneducated ruffian, who was a drummer with him in Egypt) and those of his Guards upon whom he can most depend, embarking them on board *L'Inconstant*, *L'Étoile*, and two other vessels, while he himself probably, with General Drouot, will precede them in *La Caroline*. The place of disembarkation will be Gaëta, on the coast of Naples, or Civita Vecchia, if Murat has previously advanced to Rome. For I cannot persuade myself that Napoleon will commit himself openly, until the former has moved forward with his troops; but it is very likely they will endeavour to have an interview immediately at Pia Nosa or Monte Christo. To divert attention from the real point, it is possible that General Bartolozzi may at the same time disembark in Corsica with some of the Corsican battalion.

As there is a line-of-battle ship, a frigate, and a brig at Genoa, I have requested Lord Burghersh to transmit the last accounts immediately to Captain Thomson, RN, the senior officer there, in hopes that he will at once detach one of the ships under his command either to watch or pursue Napoleon, as the case maybe, as well as to be ready to convey information of occurrences. If I find that Napoleon is really as criminal as appears at present, I shall propose to take immediate possession of Palmayola and Pia Nosa, so as to leave him no pretext for quitting Elba, and being absent without its being known where he is.

As the first object is to ascertain whether Napoleon is still there, I shall, in the usual manner, request an interview, after which I shall remain almost entirely on board ship, in order to watch and examine all vessels which approach the island, and as soon as possible to communicate with some of the French men-of-war.

Captain Adye does not intend to anchor in the harbour of Porto Ferrajo, for it is probable that Napoleon would seize the *Partridge* when he puts his plan in execution, as well as my person, in order to prevent intelligence being sent.

At 9 p.m. I went down below, and thought the brig was getting up her anchor. But as it turned out, on account of there being no wind, she did not leave the harbour until early this morning (the 27th). In the course of the day we saw the French brig *Zéphyr*.[87]

February 28.

Being becalmed several miles north of Porto Ferrajo, I went on shore in a boat of Captain Adye's, at 10 a.m., in order to ascertain if Napoleon was still there, and then transmit whatever information I could collect to His Majesty's Minister at Florence, acting afterwards according to

---

87 We must have been nearly in sight of Napoleon's flotilla, as the the *Zéphyr*, it is since known, spoke *Inconstant.* – Note by Sir N. C.

circumstances. We agreed that the ship should not enter the harbour, and that if I did not return in two hours it would be a sure proof of my detention; in which case Captain Adye would immediately despatch an express from Piombino to Lord Burghersh with this information and all he could obtain otherwise of the state of affairs.

Upon entering the harbour I immediately perceived, from the appearance of the National Guards as sentries on the fortifications, that the French Guards were no longer there; and, on proceeding alongside of the health-office, was informed, in answer to my inquiries after General Bertrand, that he had gone to Palmayola.

Expecting to be detained, I thought to push off immediately, but, after a moment's deliberation, considered that this would not be sufficiently satisfactory to others, although it might be so to myself, and therefore resolved upon the risk (or rather sacrifice more probably), as Captain Adye would be able to transmit the information required.

Accordingly I landed, and, proceeding towards General Bertrand's house, was met by Mr. Grattan, an English gentleman, who had been conveyed to the island by Captain Adye on the 24th inst. He informed me that, about 3 p.m. on the 26th, there was a sudden bustle among the troops and inhabitants, and a parade of the Corsican battalion took place. Soon afterwards the gates were shut. His servant, who had a brother a lieutenant in the Corsican battalion, told him that the Emperor and the whole of the troops were about to embark for Italy. Some spoke of Naples and Milan, others of Antibes and France. He applied several times to see General Bertrand, but could not obtain access to him under various pretexts.

At 7 p.m. the troops marched out of the fortifications without music or noise, and embarked at the health-office in feluccas and boats which were alongside, a part of them being transported to the brig which lay in the harbour. At 9 p.m. Napoleon with General Bertrand passed out in the Princess Pauline's small carriage drawn by four horses, embarked at the health-office in a boat, and went on board of the brig *L'Inconstant*. Immediately afterwards the whole flotilla got under weigh with sweeps and boats, the soldiers crying out 'Vive L'Empereur!'

Mr. Grattan says that his curiosity tempted him to hire a boat to go alongside of the brig, as he could scarcely believe his eyes and senses. There he saw Napoleon in his grey coat and round hat pacing the quarter-deck of the brig, which, as well as all the other vessels, was crowded with troops.

Napoleon leaves his island empire for France.

One of his boatmen called out that there was an Englishman on board; upon which he was questioned by an officer from the poop in English, what was his business there, and who he was? He told who he was, and said that he had come merely to see the Emperor; upon which he was ordered to go away. This he immediately complied with, for he expected every moment to be fired at or seized.

Mr. Grattan informed me that, ever since their departure, there had been very little wind. Upon the preceding day, the 27th, they were still in sight till 2 or 3 p.m., a short distance north of the island of Capraja. I proceeded to General Bertrand's house in company with Mr. Grattan. There I found his wife alternately smiling and expressing her anxiety. She told me that her husband had known nothing of Napoleon's intentions until the moment of his departure; that he had only a quarter of an hour given him to prepare his portmanteau; that she was not aware where they were going to, as they had spoken only of Pia Nosa. I thought that by moving her feelings something might be discovered, and therefore told her it was a most desperate step; that the whole of the project was known for some time; and that they must be already taken. She immediately asked me, with great earnestness, where was her husband, and what was become of him? Were they really taken? If so, she, as an Englishwoman, claimed my protection, as well as that of Lord Burghersh, the British Minister at Florence. I told her that I could not exactly say they were taken, but that they were so situated they could not escape, for there were British as well as French men-of-war all round them; that the squadron from Sicily with the Admiral were looking out for them between Elba and Gaëta.[88] On this she became more relieved and quite collected; from which I concluded that her opinion of their destination was north, and not south, as I thought at first.

She told me that Napoleon had left M. Lapis[89] as governor. (This gentleman, a native of Porto Ferrajo, had formerly been mayor before his arrival, and afterwards one of his chamberlains.) I proceeded to his house, but was directed to find him in the citadel, whither I went accordingly with the expectation of being detained. However, to intimidate him from so much responsibility, I told my servant who accompanied me to say that the whole would be *certainly taken*!

A Piedmontese surgeon, whom I had been in the habit of meeting at General Bertrand's, and who accompanied me, confirmed most distinctly all Mr. Grattan's information as to seeing the flotilla in the situation described, adding, further, that Napoleon had given Lapis the rank of general of brigade and the appointment of governor.

M. Lapis received me in his uniform as commandant of the National Guard, his doors being open, and a dozen of persons in the passage. I told him that 'I came to him as one of the Commissioners of the Allied Powers, who had accompanied Napoleon to Elba, in which character I had likewise prolonged my stay there. Therefore I requested to know from him in what position was I to consider him.' He said, 'As governor of the island of Elba.' 'Governor for whom?' I asked. 'For his sovereign.' 'What sovereign?' '*L'Empereur Napoléon*.' I then said that 'I wished to inquire of him whether he would give up possession of the island to the British, or the Grand Duke

---

88 A Neapolitan fortress of considerable strength.

89 The following proclamation, in a strange handwriting, and very badly spelt, occurs among Sir Neil Campbell's papers:

Translation from Italian. General Lapis, to the Inhabitants of the Island, Your august Sovereign, recalled by providence, has had to leave this island. He has commanded me to entrust the government of this island to its must distinguished inhabitants and recommends its defence to your valour. He said that he parted from the island extremely satisfied with the conduct of the inhabitants and that he entrusted the defence of such an important place to their energy. As a sign of his faith in their abilities he was entrusting his mother and sister to their care. The members of the Junta, and all the inhabitants, can count on his especial protection. this is now a fortunate time for you and a memorable one. Your glory and your happiness depend on your conduct. if you wish for either, obey the sage leadership of your Junta. You shall be happy if you defy not to be seduced by the enemies of good order.

of Tuscany, or the Allied Sovereigns?' He smiled and said, 'Certainly not; that he had the means of defending Porto Ferrajo until he received orders from the Emperor.' I told him to recollect that he had taken upon himself the responsibility, and therefore that it only remained for me to notify to him that the island would now be considered in a state of blockade, speaking very audibly, on purpose that what I said might be heard by others.

After bowing to retire I advanced again, and told M. Lapis in a loud voice, that in order to prevent misery to the inhabitants individually throughout the island, it would be proper for him to announce the fact to them, and that they ought to hold no communication with the Continent. I acted in this manner in order to impress M. Lapis with a sense of responsibility, and prevent him from detaining me. I was also in hopes that the inhabitants would, for their own sakes, induce him to hold no more connection with Napoleon or Murat, and surrender the island to the Allies, perhaps even give intelligence of importance, and take some friendly step after my departure, as my time would not allow me to follow up this object.

In passing the house of Madame Mère and the Princess Pauline, I observed sentries of the National Guard at their door, while an officer and a Pole were walking together as if on duty. I told them that if Madame or the Princess had any letters to transmit to Leghorn, or would express any wishes which it might be in my power to execute, it would give me pleasure to serve them. While on my way to the boat, the Princess sent to request me to return. After being detained for a minute or more in the antechamber, I sent in to say that I was under the necessity of departing immediately, as the frigate would otherwise leave without me.

She then came out and made me sit down beside her, drawing her chair gradually still closer, as if she waited for me to make some *private* communication. I merely told her that as perhaps she might have some commands for the Continent, I would willingly receive them. She asked me, with every appearance of anxiety, if I had nothing to say to her, and what I would advise her to do; said she had already written to her husband, Prince Borghese, who was now at Leghorn, and requested me to tell him that she wished to go to Rome immediately. I told her that my advice in the meantime would be to remain at Elba. She then went on to protest her ignorance of Napoleon's intended departure till the very last moment, and of his present destination; laid hold of my hand and pressed it to her heart, that I might feel how much she was agitated. However she did not appear to be so, and there was rather a smile upon her face. She inquired whether the Emperor had been taken? I told her I could not exactly say he was, but that there was every probability of it. During this conversation she dropped a hint of her belief in his destination being for France: upon which I smiled and said, 'Oh no, it's not as far as that, it's Naples'; for I fancied (for the moment) she mentioned France purposely to deceive me.

Two or three minutes afterwards I took my leave, and proceeded to the boat without any opposition, accompanied by Mr. Grattan. He agreed, at my request, to proceed in a boat to Leghorn with my despatches. After going out of the harbour, I forced a fishing-boat to accompany us, in order to have the means of conveyance for him. At 3 p.m. he left the frigate, carrying with him my despatch for Lord Castlereagh, No. 46, which he was to convey immediately from Leghorn to Florence. I also gave him a copy to be forwarded from Leghorn, by a courier, to Colonel Sir John Dalrymple, commanding at Genoa, for his information and that of Captain Thomson, commanding the navy there. Copies were to be forwarded by the former to Paris, to London, and to Vienna.

At the same time M. Ricci, provisional vice-consul at Elba, who came off in a boat, was to go to Piombino, in order to proceed direct from thence, by the horse-road of Sienna to Florence, carrying with him for Lord Burghersh my despatches to Lord Castlereagh, Nos. 45 and 46.

After fully deliberating with Captain Adye upon all the circumstances, and comparing the information of Mr. Grattan and M. Ricci in their own presence, we determined to proceed towards *Antibes* for the following reasons. (In so doing Captain Adye had the goodness to sacrifice his own opinion, which inclined to Naples, to mine.) There was always a probability of overtaking Napoleon and his flotilla, if he had gone in that direction; there was none if he had gone to Naples. The horses and guns, which he was said certainly to have embarked, could be of no use at Naples, but only an encumbrance; although, to be sure, it might be a mask to make one believe that he had not gone there, and he might afterwards have thrown them overboard.

Would he, however, also have encumbered himself with so many civilian followers, and with all the Corsicans, if he was destined for Naples? He could not throw *them* overboard, and they could be of no importance as an additional force.

But, what was still stronger than all, would he lose the whole of the first night, and the following day, in going north instead of south, and so be obliged to retrace his route? Had he gone out during the day, he might do so to deceive until that night, but certainly not for so long a time (nearly twenty-four hours), encumbered with soldiers broiling in the sun, and with a dead calm, and every minute of the utmost consequence.

I think his destination is for the frontier of Piedmont next France, and that he will take possession of some strong place near Nice, or between that and Turin, dispersing his civil followers immediately over North Italy, of which he will proclaim the independence, raising the disaffected there, while Murat does the same in the south.

This plan will be more reconcilable to the national feelings of his officers and men, and they will think it probably less hazardous than raising the standard of rebellion in France, where they would be considered traitors. General Drouot gave in his adhesion to the present dynasty of the Bourbons before quitting France, and I believe General Bertrand did the same.

No part of Napoleon's plan for quitting Elba could have increased my *general* suspicions of his possibly taking that step at some time or another, even had I been there from the 16th to the 26th, nor could have authorised me to report to the British Government any fact which could be considered as a certain proof of that intention. There would have been no positive criminality in any act previous to his embarkation of the troops and his actual departure, a period of six hours, during which time the gates of Porto Ferrajo were shut. He had been for months employed in dismantling the fortress of Longono, situated in the passage of Piombino, and in conveying the arms, ammunition, and provisions from thence to Porto Ferrajo in three of the vessels taken with him. Two of the others are feluccas from his mines at Rio, the arrival of which at Porto Ferrajo could not attract observation. Had His Majesty's ship *Partridge* been in the harbour on Sunday, February 26, she might have been detained. Captain Adye, the first lieutenant, and myself would probably have been invited to General Bertrand's house, where we sometimes dined, and we might have been easily arrested there, and thus made more subservient to the easier execution of his plan.

HMS *Partridge* was at anchor in Porto Ferrajo harbour upon the 24th, and Captain Adye went on shore during the day. He was also off the mouth of the harbour upon Saturday the 25th inst., and ascertained, for his own information and mine, that the *Inconstant* was there at anchor at 6 p.m. Thence he proceeded immediately to Leghorn, to bring me back to Porto Ferrajo, according to previous agreement made some days before.

M. Ricci, the person who gave me private information of a suspicious character, observed on the 25th that he was constantly followed by two gendarmes; but he had knowledge of his being watched for some time before.

When he heard of the gates being shut upon the 26th, he wished to go over to Piombino with the information, but could not obtain a boat for any sum, as they were all under embargo.

For a few weeks previously to his departure, Napoleon employed people in planting trees upon the roads leading to Porto Ferrajo, and in forming an avenue near his house, also in making a garden close to the barracks of his Guards. When Captain Adye was on shore there on the 24th, there were about thirty soldiers busily employed in shaping beds and forming gravel walks in the garden; and they were probably employed all day on Saturday the 25th in finishing the work, in order to deceive the various spies who, he knew well, watched all his proceedings.

As to the immediate execution of Napoleon's project, I do not believe that any person in Elba, except General Drouot, knew of his intentions until the gates were actually shut upon the afternoon of the 26th.

I had long thought Napoleon so restless and unprincipled a person, that he would lose no opportunity of employing himself in war upon the Continent; and, particularly if pressed by want of money, or subjected to any humiliating treatment, that he was capable of any eccentric or desperate act. But all accounts from France, and the apparent tranquillity of the country, have induced me to judge that he has no chance of success there, and that he himself has despaired of every hope in that quarter. Neither did I think that he would commit himself openly in Italy, until Murat had made some progress, and this would give sufficient time to secure his person, if at least it was wished to do so. For many months he has furnished a just pretext for this measure – has given ample cause for such a step, by his violation of the law of nations and breach of good faith, in sending officers clandestinely to Corsica and Italy to recruit soldiers; and therefore I no longer considered this to be an object which was sought for or intended on the part of either the French Government or the Allied Sovereigns.

With the free sovereignty of Elba, four armed vessels of his own, and seventeen belonging to the mines, which sailed in every direction, I knew well that Napoleon had it in his power to avail himself any day of these means of escape, without any chance of my preventing him, dependent as I was on the occasional calls of a man-of-war, which cruised between Civita Vecchia and Genoa, and the frequency of whose visits was subject entirely to the captain. In justice, however, to the four captains successively employed in this service, as well as to Admirals Lord Exmouth and Penrose, I must say that they entered liberally and cordially into my wishes and the objects of my mission.

What I considered as the surest means of security for Napoleon's person were the two frigates and some smaller vessels belonging to Louis XVIII (none of them were to be seen either on the 27th or 28th), which were constantly cruising between Corsica, Capraja, and Leghorn; while I knew also that the French consul at Leghorn and the governor of Corsica had their respective spies over him.

At 7 p.m. spoke the British merchant-ship, *Lady Ann*, Captain Segur, by whom I wrote to Mr. A'Court, minister in Sicily.

Napoleon's flotilla consists of seven sail; i.e. *L'Inconstant*, a brig, 18 guns and about 300 tons; *L'Étoile*, a bombard, 80 tons and a few guns; *La Caroline*, half-decked, 25 tons and 1 gun.

Four feluccas of 40 or 50 tons each.

There is also a French merchant-brig, of between 300 and 400 tons, which had anchored at Porto Ferrajo by accident, a few days before Napoleon's departure. He seized her, and put a guard on board to prevent its being known.

LIST OF PERSONS WHO EMBARKED WITH NAPOLEON IN ELBA, FEBRUARY 26, 1814

General Count Bertrand

General Count Drouot

General Baron Cambronne

Adjutant-General (Colonel) Lebelle

Baron Germanowski, commanding the Poles.

Chevalier Fourreau, *médecin*, Frenchman.

M. Gatte, *pharmacien*, Frenchman; married, a few months ago, a Mdlle. Nenchi, whose father is a merchant at Leghorn.

M. Peyrouse, *trésorier*, Frenchman.

M. Deschamps, M. Baillon *fourriers de palais*, Frenchmen.

M. Pons, *administrateur des mines*, both before and since the arrival of

Napoleon in Elba, formerly *chef de bataillon* under Masséna, who, with Lacépède, the chancellor of the Legion of Honour, are his friends and patrons – a violent, intriguing fellow.

M. Talliade, formerly of the French Navy, and, until lately, commander of Napoleon's brig – married to a woman of Longono.

M. Chauslard, *capitaine de frégate*; lately appointed to command of *L'Inconstant* brig.

M. Richon, of the French Marine, commanding the bombard *L'Étoile*.

Colonel Socoski, a Pole; his wife is with the Princess Pauline.

Captain Roule, *officier d'ordonnance*, confidential officer about Napoleon's person; Frenchman.

M. Perez, M. Vantini *officiers d'ordonnance* of Porto Ferrajo

M. Phillidore, captain of the port at Porto Ferrajo; probably taken away by force, in order to return to Elba or Naples with the flotilla.

Captain Paoli, Corsican.

Captain of gendarmes.

These are all names of principal persons who accompanied Napoleon (excepting a few officers and men who were at Longono, Pia Nosa, and Palmayola, and who were too late to embark); every person, French and Italian, whether in the military or civil service, secretaries, servants, etc., went with him.

His whole force may be estimated as follows:

Old Guard	600
Polish Lancers	100
Corsican Battalion	300
Gendarmes, mostly Italians and Corsicans	50
	1,050
Civilians, including servants	100

General Bartolozzi, formerly commandant de la place, was left behind at Porto Ferrajo.

Wednesday, March 1.

About 2 a.m. a light was discovered. We beat to quarters, as it was reported that there were several sail. We thought our sanguine hopes were accomplished, but upon nearing and hailing, found it was a French frigate. Captain Adye and I went on board of her. It proved to be the *Fleur-de-Lys*,

commanded by Captain Chevalier de Garat, belonging to the station of
Corsica and Elba, and now five leagues north of Cape Corse. He did not
know of Napoleon's escape till we informed him, although his only duty
was to prevent it, and he ought to have been off Elba as a watch, unless he
was accessory to it.

It is fair to state, that on Marshal Masséna hoisting the tricolour flag at
Toulon, in the course of the month of March following, the Chevalier de
Garat was at once dismissed from his ship, but again restored to his rank by
the Bourbons on August 1.

In a formal defence of his conduct, addressed to the Comte d'Iancourt,
minister of Marine, and dated August 28, 1815, he wrote as follows:

> The commander of this frigate shall not describe in detail the difficult voyages
> made in the middle of harsh winter conditions that took place after January 2.
> We examine the situation for 26 February, the day when Bonaparte left Porto
> Ferrajo. On that day Colonel Campbell reported that the Usurper had quit that
> port in a moderate breeze which, however, turned into a calm at around 8 in
> the evening. The *Fleur-de-Lys* spotted the *Melpomène* at around 9 in the
> morning as she was to the south of Capraja; and as we had not been in contact
> with her for ten days we began to make sail towards her when, suddenly, we
> spied a number of sails around Gorgona.
>
> The *Fleur-de-Lys* therefore turned and made ready to pursue these vessels,
> but, having hailed a British brig, from which we learned that these vessels were
> Swedish and British and had set out from Livorno that morning. However our
> pursuit took us into the mouth of the Gulf of St. Florent.
>
> The wind being favourable, the captain took the opportunity of
> returning to our usual station near Capraja and as we did so spied the
> *Melpomène* to the SSW.
>
> On the morning of the 27th, just before noon, the *Fleur-de-Lys* passed Cap
> Corse but by four in the afternoon there was a drop in the wind. We were
> north-west of Capraja, covering the area between Gorgona, Elba and Capraja;
> and still in contact with the *Melpomène*, off to the west; two smaller vessels were
> also spied heading west.
>
> During the night of the 27th and the morning of the 28th, the *Fleur-de-Lys*,
> patrolled the area off Cap Corse, Gorgona and Capraja. The commandant, then
> decided to visit Porto Ferrajo as the weather seemed favourable. Just as we came
> round Capraja, however, the wind dropped and we spent three hours becalmed.
> Bonaparte's brig, which we had seen on a number of occasions in Porto

Ferrajo, as well as another vessel which was recognisable to our officers on account of it having been given by our king to Bonaparte, was not in port. Given the distance of Elba from Italy and the dangerous waters around the isle, it would have been a miracle to stop or catch Bonaparte's brig which could have sheltered off shore quite easily in any case. Lord Castlereagh himself said on April 19 before Parliament that the entire Royal Navy would not have been sufficient to prevent Bonaparte's escape and he was not contradicted by a single person. So what could two isolated, clumsy frigates do in such circumstances?

Early during the forenoon, the Chevalier de Garat came on board the *Partridge*, when it was agreed (in consequence of what he had stated with regard to his being near Capraja on Monday, and yet not having seen Napoleon's flotilla), that it might possibly have gone there or to Gorgona; that Captain Adye should therefore return and examine them more minutely; that Captain de Garat should proceed direct to Antibes, and if he did not find Napoleon there he should despatch an officer immediately to Paris with the news of Napoleon's escape. I gave him a despatch, No 47, for Lord Castlereagh, enclosed to the Duke of Wellington, or British *chargé d'affaires* at Paris, and open for perusal.

I have been induced to change my opinion, in concert with Captain Adye, for various reasons. It seems unnecessary for both ships to proceed in the same direction, and Chevalier de Garat must pursue that of Antibes, in order to despatch an officer to Paris. The conjecture upon which we set out yesterday from Elba is now less likely to prove fortunate, from Chevalier de Garat's statement, and our not having seen Bonaparte. In thinking over every project that Napoleon may have intended, and endeavouring to reconcile Chevalier de Garat's information with that of Mr. Grattan, it appears possible that he may have secreted himself for a few days in Capraja or Gorgona, in order to lead away the *Partridge*, and be able at night to take Leghorn by surprise. This seizure might be effected. He would obtain money, provisions, ammunition, and stores of all kinds, and a ready communication with Murat, who might send a part of his force to meet him at Florence. A portion of Murat's fleet with some troops might replace him at Porto Ferrajo, or even the whole fleet come up there from Naples.

The Chevalier de Garat approved of this change in our plan. He pursued his voyage to Antibes, and the *Partridge* returned towards Capraja, taking on board a midshipman belonging to the *Fleur-de-Lys* M. Fortis, for Corsica, as the captain was anxious to communicate with the Governor, Brulart.

March 2.

Very little wind all day. Standing towards Capraja, which at sunset bore east, thirty miles distant.

March 3.

At 2 a.m., near Capraja, saw a sail; sent on board, and found it to be the French schooner *Antilope*, Captain Fernahaye. I went on board with the midshipman belonging to the *Fleur-de-Lys*.

Went on shore at Capraja in two boats from the *Partridge* and *Antilope*, in hopes of obtaining information. The escape of Napoleon was not known. The commandant and mayor both stated circumstantially and separately that a brig, with six feluccas in company, was off the island the whole of Monday standing NW, and was lost sight of in the evening, having then very little wind. This confirms Mr. Grattan's information, although difficult to reconcile with what the Chevalier de Garat stated, and proves almost to a certainty that our first conjecture was just. Captain Adye, therefore, has again shaped his course for Antibes.

March 4.

At 7 p.m. Captain Croker, of His Majesty's ship *Wizard*, came on board. She left Genoa yesterday, and is bound for Leghorn and Palermo. Sir John Dalrymple, commanding there, had received my despatch on the 2nd instant, and the troops were put in movement to the westward on the 3rd. Wrote by the *Wizard* to Lord Burghersh and Mr. A'Court.

March 5.

At midday spoke to the Sicilian ship with Nautical School bound for Palermo. She had left Genoa yesterday at 3 p.m., at which time it was reported that Napoleon had been refused a landing by the Commandant at Frejus, and had disembarked at Antibes.

Nearly calm all day.

March 6.

Nearly calm. Off Savona spoke to the transport *Lord Wellington*, with Colonel Bourke and the Italian levy bound from Savona to Nice. There were two other transports in company. Informed that Napoleon had landed a few days ago near Antibes, and, upon finding he could not get possession of that place, had marched into the interior.

I am persuaded it will soon be proved that the invasion of France by Napoleon did not originate with himself, and that it has not long been decided upon, although he had the means of preparing and executing his plans without any possibility of detection on my part.

It was the delay in communicating with the *Fleur-de-Lys* which alone prevented the *Partridge* from arriving at Antibes nearly about the same time with Napoleon, and lost us the glorious chance, which was so nearly at our command, of destroying him.

March 7.

At 2 p.m. went on board HMS *Aboukir*, Captain Thomson, from Antibes, bound to Genoa, and learned, certainly to our mortification, that Napoleon had disembarked at midday on March 1, in Juan Bay, between Antibes and Frejus. In a few hours after, he had marched off towards Grenoble without opposition. Five officers and thirty men, who had been sent to Antibes to summon it to surrender, were detained by the commandant. Wrote to Lord Castlereagh, enclosed to Lord William Bentinck and open for perusal.

March 8.

Anchored at Antibes. The *Fleur-de-Lys* and *Légérie*, French men-of-war, were in the offing. The latter came in close to us, and sent a boat on board of the *Partridge*. Captain Adye and I returned the visit. Afterwards went on shore at Antibes, and visited General Corsin, the governor. Informed by him that, upon the 1st inst., about 11 a.m., Napoleon stood in from sea, fired two guns, and hoisted the tricolour flag on board of his brig, which was in company with several other smaller vessels. They made for Juan Bay, west of Antibes, where Napoleon disembarked his force upon the beach.

The general himself happened to be at the island of Marguerite, in the Bay of Juan, with some friends, and had no idea it was Napoleon. He and his party were looking through glasses, and when the brig hoisted the tricolour flag, thought it was an Algerian corsair who had captured some Genoese coasters, and was coming in to water. Early in the afternoon, the general went on to say, he received a note from the officer commanding at Antibes in his absence, requesting him to return immediately, 'for that a most extraordinary circumstance had occurred!' He thought it was merely some scuffle between the soldiers and the inhabitants, and immediately despatched an officer to the place. Later in the afternoon he received a second express, explaining the real cause of the alarm. He at once returned, but being obliged to make a considerable detour, and to scramble over rocks and bushes (the marks of which he showed me on his hands), in order to avoid Napoleon's piquets, did not arrive at Antibes till 2 a.m. on the second. He sent out parties to ascertain Napoleon's forces and intentions, but it appears they neither impeded nor followed him.

Napoleon's march inland was not resisted.

It seems most extraordinary that the disembarkation should have taken place, and the encampment been continued from midday till nearly sunrise the next morning, without attracting more notice, or causing any measures to be taken on the part of the authorities.

However a detachment which Napoleon, after forming his camp, had sent to Antibes, had been taken prisoners without resistance. They were transferred to Toulon under a strong escort, the officers particularly having behaved in the most frantic manner, and attempted to escape during the night. One of them, a Captain Casabianca, leaped over a part of the ramparts and broke his back. They would not give any information whatever.

An officer of the garrison, who is a Corsican, and a cousin of the Bonaparte family, was put into arrest on account of some suspicious circumstances.

All the horses seized near Antibes were paid for liberally.

At Cannes a butcher got his musket with the determination of going to Juan Bay and killing Napoleon; but the inhabitants surrounded him, and begged him to desist, as their village would be burnt down, and they would all be sacrificed.

General Corsin further told me, that by the last account Napoleon was on the mountain-road from Cannes towards Grenoble. Upon the 4th he entered Digne, with only about a hundred men. The rest of his force was scattered along the road, coming up as fast as they could, and pressing mules and horses to assist them. Several desertions had taken place, and neither soldiers nor others had joined Napoleon. So far, however, he had not met with any troops to oppose him; as there were scarcely any nearer than Grenoble, where there is a considerable force of artillery, with between 1,000 and 1,500 infantry.

Marshal Masséna had marched after Napoleon with a force from Toulon, but was supposed to be considerably in his rear.

On the afternoon of the 1st the vessels again sailed out of the bay in a south-easterly direction. Napoleon remained in bivouac till 2 a.m. on March 2, when he marched to Grasse, on the road towards Grenoble, with his whole force and two pieces of cannon. Having behind him the rest of his artillery, sixteen ammunition wagons, and a carriage marked P., belonging to the Princess Pauline. While in camp a great noise and mirth were kept up; people were sent out in all directions to procure horses, and several proclamations in writing were distributed. These proclamations call upon the people of France to rise against their present Sovereign and Government, who have broken their faith and promises, and sacrificed the interest and glory of France to the priests and emigrants! Nothing is said of Italy; so far from it, that Napoleon pledges himself to abandon all thoughts of foreign conquest, and to employ himself only in promoting the internal happiness of France.

The proclamation began thus:

'Napoleon, by the Grace of God and the constitution, Emperor of the French'; and they are countersigned by '*Le Grand Maréchal*, acting as *Major-General de la Grande Armée*, Bertrand.'

There is likewise an address from the officers and soldiers of the Imperial Guard who accompany him to the Generals, officers, and soldiers of the Grand Army.

We found at Antibes the French merchant-vessel which Napoleon had seized at Porto Ferrajo to convey a part of his force.

March 9.

There being no safe anchorage at Antibes, the *Partridge* weighed from there and proceeded to Villa Franca, near Nice. Went over to the latter place, and waited on the Governor, General Osarce. Saw also General Dejeany, commanding the military force sent from Genoa by the King of Sardinia, the French Consul Marquis de Candolle, and the British Consul.

The French Consul confirms all the information received yesterday at Antibes. He read me a letter, received while I was with him, from the prefect of Draguignan, of yesterday's date, wherein he details the marches of the regular troops and National Guards, from Toulon, Marseilles, and other points, directed to Napoleon's rear. He states that no partisans had joined him, nor had there been any symptoms of discontent; and he praises the enthusiastic ardour universally displayed by the population. At the same time he regrets that no opposition had been made in Napoleon's front during his march, nor any steps taken to occupy or destroy the bridge at Sisteron before his arrival there. He takes no notice of Napoleon's movements after reaching that point. It seems strange that the prefect should have had no later information.

From all that I can gather, Napoleon's marches appear to have been as follows:

Wednesday morning, March 2, left his camp, and marched by Cannes to Serenon.

Thursday, March 3, marched to Barème.

Friday, March 4, marched to Digne.

Saturday, March 5 marched to Sisteron.

The French Consul at Nice seems jealous of any circumstance being mentioned which can reflect a doubt upon the exertions and spirit of the French nation as against Napoleon. He admitted, however, that the conduct of the general commanding at Antibes was suspicious, but said his authority did not extend beyond the glacis of the fortress.

It is stated also by other persons, that General Count Gazan, who commanded at Cannes, ran away and hid himself, without taking any steps whatever. (This he admitted afterwards, on my questioning him.)

The Governor of Nice, however, seems to have acted with energy, and being disposed to give little credit to the accounts received there, he has sent confidential officers as far as Digne, but he has no report since the 5th. Although he thinks Napoleon has got as far as Sisteron, he has no confirmation of the fact. He judges that the spirit of France is not so good as might be expected, or else that the event is so very extraordinary and unexpected, that the people are stupefied. One of his officers states, upon the authority of a respectable person who witnessed it, that Napoleon entered Digne with about fifty mounted officers and cavalry and a few infantry, without any opposition. The people called out, 'Vive L'Empereur! Down with the *droits reunis*!' He replied, 'Yes, my children, when I get to Paris I will arrange that. I'll be there soon!' Part of the road by which he has marched is very bad, mountainous and narrow, where an opposing force might arrest very superior numbers; and he has now no guns with him.

The French Consul as well as the Governor say that between twenty and thirty of the garrison of Antibes deserted the third day after Napoleon's disembarkation, when the gates were opened, and it is conjectured that they have followed him. Before being sent away, the prisoners belonging to Napoleon's Guard were treated like friends, and were seen playing bowls with the garrison.

And this is confirmed by an English gentleman, who had observed their treatment during their removal from Antibes to Toulon.

March 10.

It is probable that the test of Napoleon's success will be made at Grenoble, and that he will endeavour to bring it to that issue as soon as possible, before the accumulation of force renders his passage of the Isère more difficult. If he is foiled there, he has no alternative but to retreat to Gap, and there turn off the main road by a mule-path, which leads over Mount Dauphin and Mount Genèvre, by the river Durance, to Turin, passing by Sesana and Exele. This route is scarcely passable for a horse in many places.

As he advances, he propagates reports that he has many partisans among the principal persons in France, and that he will arrive at Paris before March 24.[90]

March 11.

Being very uneasy at not hearing any circumstantial facts, and being also desirous to transmit the best and earliest news to Ministers at home, as well as to Lord William Bentinck at Genoa, and Lord Burghersh at Florence, I resolved to follow Napoleon into France. Accordingly at 3 a.m. I set off towards Antibes, in the hope of obtaining certain information, and being able to judge of the spirit of the people for myself.

At Juan Bay I saw the customs officer and the *commissaire*, who gave me the whole story of Napoleon's disembarkation as they witnessed it. He came on shore about 3 p.m. on the 1st. During the afternoon the band continued to play occasionally. 'Where is better than in the bosom of your family?' He walked about under the trees, sitting down from time to time. He wore a grey great coat. At night he lay down on a mattress with a coverlet turned over his head.

General Bertrand was constantly with him, and always kept off his hat when he approached him, as did all others.

---

90 In fact, he arrived on the evening of the 20th.

General Cambronne went on horseback along the road towards Cannes, three or four miles off. He gave out that 3,000 men were with him, and that a large body in conjunction with the Allies had passed on by sea to Toulon and Marseilles. Detachments were placed about a mile to the right and left, to prevent anyone from passing. They at first said they had come from Corsica; afterwards that they were from Elba, and had been discharged; but when they arrived at Cannes, they gave out that the Emperor was with them, and that 4,000 more of his troops had landed west of Frejus. The mayor was directed to go to Napoleon with the public authorities, but he refused.

Between 2 and 3 a.m. on the 2nd the whole party arrived. The officers supped together at the inn. One officer paid for a horse which he bought, but all others were requisitioned, and left in the road when fatigued, and changed. Napoleon did not enter the town, but remained outside, where the men halted in position. After remaining there an hour or two, they turned to their right off the great road, and took the mountain road to Grasse. It was so bad that they were obliged to leave the guns behind.

At Grasse Napoleon dined on a height above the town. A table was brought out, and he sat upon a soldier's pack. The troops were encamped round him, and employed themselves in cooking and eating.

The courier who travelled with me on the road from Nice to Draguignan told me that Napoleon was certainly taken by this time. A circular letter had been sent by the postmaster of Valence, with the assurance that he was trapped (*cerné*) by the National Guards and garrison from Grenoble, between that city and Gap.

March 12.

Arrived at Draguignan, the chief town of the department of the Var, and visited the prefect, Comte de Bouthillier, a very clever man, and at the same time frank and communicative.

Nothing, as it appears, could have been better than his dispositions. By 6 a.m. on the 2nd, he had sent off messengers to Digne on one side, and Toulon on the other. However the prefect at Digne did not circulate the information for several hours after he received it, and took no steps to assemble the National Guard, or destroy the bridge at Sisteron. His proclamation is only dated the 6th, two days after Napoleon had passed. The mayor of Castellane gave him a dinner. At Digne he obtained a number of blank passports, signed by the present authorities. Still the Comte de Bouthillier was sanguine in the expectation of hearing every moment that Napoleon was taken, as he was surrounded, he said. And the same idea was universal at the Count's house in the evening, where a numerous party was assembled for the prefect's weekly party. All praised the good disposition shown by the National Guards, but it is evident that the troops of the line are not equally trusted.

March 13.

About one in the morning a person with a lantern entered my room very silently, and told me that the prefect requested to see me immediately. In order to avoid all noise and observation, he led me by a back way, and through a stable, into the house. I found the Count in a state of extreme dismay, and occupied with his secretary. I sincerely participated in his feelings on hearing from him the intelligence he had just received from Aix and Valence, viz., that Napoleon had entered Grenoble upon the 7th at 8 a.m., and that General Marchand, with the staff and most of the officers, had retired. It may be inferred from this that the rest and the private soldiers have betrayed their duty.

This state of affairs is so serious, that I determined to go off immediately to Nice, in order to convey the earliest intimation of these melancholy circumstances to Lord William Bentinck at Genoa. I shall also report to him my observation as to the bad disposition of the troops at Antibes, and the little reliance that can be placed upon the regular army, so that he may prepare for the worst.

No actual disposition has been made by the Piedmontese for the passage of the long bridge over the Var, which separates them from Antibes.

Set off from Draguignan at 3 a.m., and arrived at Nice at 5 p.m. At 10 p.m. went on board of HMS *Partridge* at Villa Franca, but it blew so hard that she could not with safety attempt to beat out.

Lord Sunderland[91] has arrived from Marseilles. There it is universally believed that the English had favoured Napoleon's return, and the people are furious against us. The same idea also prevails everywhere in the South of France and in Piedmont. A newspaper of Turin, just arrived at Nice, states positively this to be the case!

March 14.

Sailed out of Villa Franca at 6 a.m., and arrived at Genoa at 8 p.m.

March 15.

Wrote Lord Burghersh with news from Draguignan of the 13th inst., and mentioned a report of Napoleon having entered Lyons.

Madame Mère, as I am informed, states that Napoleon had three deputations from France before he consented to quit Elba.

---

91 Succeeded as fifth Duke of Marlborough, March 5, 1840.

March 18.

HMS *Aboukir* sailed for Leghorn

March 19.

HMS *Partridge* left Genoa for Leghorn and Sicily.

March 20.

Left Genoa. During the night robbed of my watch and between fifty and sixty guineas by brigands near Novi.[92]

March 21.

4 p.m. at Milan.

March 22.

7 a.m. Domo d'Ossola. 7 p.m. Left the Simplon.

March 23.

11 a.m. Sion. Carriage-wheel broke. 8 p.m.Vevay.

March 24.

Midday, Morat. Overtook Mr. Perry, the courier, who had left Genoa the morning before me.

March 25.

11 a.m. Basle. 7 p.m. Fribourg.

March 26.

2 p.m. Rastadt. 5 p.m. Karlsruhe.

March 27.

3 a.m. Manheim. Passed the Rhine.

March 28.

10 a.m. Lisère; crossed the Moselle in a ferry.

4 p.m. Trèves. At midnight, Luxembourg. Stopped four hours to pass through the fortress.

March 29.

4 a.m. Left Luxembourg.

March 30.

6 p.m. Brussels. Remained three hours.

March 31.

6 p.m. Ostend. Sailed at 8 p.m. in HM brig *Rosario*, Captain Peak.

April 1.

9 a.m. Landed at Deal, and at 9 p.m. arrived in London. Next day had interviews with Lord Castlereagh, and with HRH the Prince Regent at Carlton House.

---

92 Ironically, on March 20 Napoleon entered Paris in triumph.

Neil Campbell, 1776-1827

INDEX

Colombini, M.: 116

Colonna, M.: 105, 108, 109, 134, 139, 145, 175

Consalvi, Cardinal: 104

Cornevali, M.: 158

Corsin, General: 193, 194

Corsini, Prince: 100

Crichton, Dr.: 28

Croker, Captain: 192

Cromwell: 48

Dalrymple, Sir John: 121, 133, 185, 192

Davenport, Mr.: 84

Dejeany, General: 195

Drouot, Count: 17, 28, 36, 42, 45, 47, 58,
67, 69, 72, 85, 89, 109, 110, 111, 117,
118, 135, 145, 162, 163, 166, 169, 175,
180, 186, 187, 188

Dumont, Captain: 107

Dupont, General (French Minister of
War): 25, 44

Duval, General: 72

Ebrington, Lord: 163

Eliza, Princess (Napoleon's sister): 23, 95,
96, 97, 98, 99, 100

d'Enghien, Duc (Royalist intriguer): 29,
74, 122, 146

Ennis, Ludovico: 104

Esterhazy, Prince: 118, 119

Eugène, Prince: see Italy, Viceroy of

Exmouth, Lord: 101, 117, 123, 156, 157,
168, 188

Fagan, Mr.: 101, 102, 103

Falconer, Mr.: 174

Fayade, M.: 102

Felton, Mr.: 94, 120

Fernahaye, Captain: 192

Fesch, Cardinal: 38, 101, 103

Filangieri, Duke of: 104

Fisher, Captain: 101

Fitzgerald, Mr.: 120, 168

Flahault, Count: 17

Fossombroni, M.: 131, 143

Fouché (French politician): 146

Fox, Mr.: 49

Francis, Emperor of Austria: 22, 29, 33, 44,
95, 99, 100, 117, 124, 127, 147, 149, 150

Fourreau, M. (French surgeon): 28, 188

Funti: 150

Gabrielli, Lieutenant: 92

Garat, Chevalier de: 190, 191, 192

Gatte, M. (French surgeon): 89, 188

Gazan, General: 196

Gérard, General: 63

Germanowski, Baron: 188

Gordon, Lady: 56

Graham, General: 18

Grant, Mr.: 94

Grattan, Mr.: 181, 182, 183, 185, 191, 192

Grouchy, General: 99

Guicchardi, Count: 114

Hallowell, Admiral: 114, 117, 120, 156

Hardenberg, Baron: 21, 24

Hastings, Thomas: 45, 58

Hood, Lord: 56

Hutchinson, Lord: 18

Italy, Viceroy of: 23, 56, 61, 68, 74, 160

James, Captain: 76, 77, 82, 102, 103

Jerome, King (Napoleon's brother): 23, 119

Joseph, King (Napoleon's brother): 23,
109, 119